BURT FRANKLIN: BIBLIOGRAPHY & REFERENCE SERIES 490

A SHORT SURVEY OF THE LITERATURE
OF RABBINICAL AND MEDIÆVAL JUDAISM

A Short Survey of the Literature of Rabbinical and Mediæval Judaism

BY

W. O. E. OESTERLEY, M.A., D.D.

AND

G. H. BOX, M.A., D.D.

BURT FRANKLIN

New York, N. Y.

Published by LENOX HILL Pub. & Dist. Co. (Burt Franklin)
235 East 44th St., New York, N.Y. 10017
Reprinted: 1973
Printed in the U.S.A.

Burt Franklin: Bibliograph and Reference Series 490

Library of Congress Cataloging in Publication Data

Oesterley, William Oscar Emil, 1866-1950.
    A short survey of the literature of Rabbinical and mediaeval
Judaism.
        Reprint of the 1920 ed. published by Macmillan, New York.
        Includes bibliographies.
        1. Rabbinical literature—History and criticism. 2. Jews. Liturgy and ritual
    —History. 3. Hebrew literature, Medieval—History and criticism. I. Box, George
    Herbert, 1869-1933, joint author. II. Title.
    BM495.5.035 1973   296.1   72-82352
    ISBN 0-8337-2602-1

PREFATORY NOTE

THE object of this volume is to provide *in outline* an introduction to the literature of post-Biblical Judaism. We wish to emphasise the fact that it *is* an outline, and nothing more, that has been attempted. The field is vast, and only a very broad survey has been possible. Many interesting tracts have perforce been passed over in silence, or dismissed with bare mention ; and even when a subject seems to occupy, proportionately, a considerable space, *e.g.* the general Historical Survey, it must be remembered that only the slightest treatment of the theme has been possible. Anything like an adequate exposition would have required several volumes. Our work is essentially an Introduction, in the elementary sense. We have in mind the needs of a very large body of readers to whom the whole field of later Jewish literature is absolutely unknown. We hope that this manual will open to them a new and fascinating field of study. We have more especially tried to bring out, by way of the suggestion of points, the importance of so much of this literature for the study of Christian origins ; this applies more particularly to the earlier phases of Rabbinical literature, when Judaism and Christianity

were more nearly allied to a common original. As
time went on they diverged more and more, though
even in the later phases a certain amount of mutual
influence, conscious and unconscious, must be allowed
for. An interesting instance of how an element which
was original to Judaism, and was afterwards for a
considerable time either suppressed or driven into the
background, only to re-emerge after the lapse of
centuries, is the case of the apocalyptic or mystical
tradition.   Such writings, *e.g.*, as the Book of Enoch,
which has survived in an Oriental version of a Greek
rendering, meet us again to a large extent in a Hebrew
form in the Geonic period, *i.e.* the seventh and eighth
centuries A.D. ; the bearing of such a fact as this on
the study of Christian origins has not hitherto been
adequately recognised.

   In seeking, then, to cover so vast a field within the
compass of a single volume, only a bird's-eye survey
has been possible; but in some respects the readers we
have in view will find this a gain.   If the study of our
book should in any way serve to stimulate others to
delve more deeply into this interesting literature, or
should be the means of sending them to larger works
which specialise upon subjects only cursorily dealt
with here, we shall be amply repaid for our labours.
We have endeavoured to indicate many of the more
important aids to study in short selected bibliographies;
but we have not felt it necessary to attempt to give
exhaustive lists of works on the various subjects
referred to.

We have deliberately omitted from our survey the most modern phase of Jewish literature, which may be said to date, roughly, from the time of Moses Mendelssohn (1729-1786). This is so essentially modern, and is divided off by so clear a line of demarcation from the older literature, that it seemed desirable to leave it out of account. We have limited ourselves to tracing out the literary development to the close of the mediæval period, which in the case of Jewish literature may be reckoned to have extended to the sixteenth century.

A word of explanation may be necessary as to the relation of the present book to our earlier work, *The Religion and Worship of the Synagogue* (second edition, 1911). Though to some limited extent the two books cover the same ground—viz. in the treatment of Rabbinical literature—yet they are essentially distinct and independent. We are here concerned *primarily* with the literature of Judaism, while in the earlier work this occupied only a subordinate place, Jewish religious life, custom, thought, and doctrine being the main themes. In consequence it will be noticed, if a comparison be made, that our treatment of the common element in this volume is on a larger and fuller scale ; while very many subjects dealt with in the earlier book are not even mentioned in the present one.

It will readily be understood that in the volume before us a certain amount of repetition of particular points is inevitable ; for we have endeavoured to survey the literature under distinct heads and classifications ; but as these necessarily shade off into each other some overlapping is unavoidable.

We have also found it impossible to be quite consistent in matters of spelling and transliteration, for there does not yet seem to be any generally accepted system, and in quoting from other writers we find variations in this respect. But we hope that no serious inconvenience will result from this cause.

Our earnest hope is that this strange and unfamiliar world of letters may become more widely known to the general reader. We shall be well content if our volume can assist in any real way towards attaining this end.

If only a society could be organised on an adequate basis, to be called (shall we say ?) " The Mediæval Hebrew Text Society," which would undertake to publish the original texts, with English translations (on opposite pages), of the best of these treasures, many a delightful book which is now buried in manuscript in European libraries would be given to the world.

Our warm thanks are due to Professor A. R. S. Kennedy of Edinburgh, who has kindly read through the proofs and made many valuable suggestions. The reader's attention is called to the list of Addenda printed on pp. 305–306.

W. O. E. OESTERLEY.
G. H. BOX.

CONTENTS

PART I

GENERAL HISTORICAL SURVEY

PART II

THE RABBINICAL LITERATURE

PART III

THE JEWISH LITURGY

PART IV

THE MEDIÆVAL LITERATURE

ABBREVIATIONS USED IN THIS VOLUME.

DB = Hastings' Dictionary of the Bible.

JE = *The Jewish Encyclopædia* (12 vols.).

JQR = *The Jewish Quarterly Review.*

MT = Masoretic Text.

*RWS*² = *Religion and Worship of the Synagogue*, by W. O. E. Oesterley and G. H. Box (second edition, 1911).

RV = Revised Version (of the English Bible).

Schürer *GJV* = *Schürer's Geschichte des jüdischen Volkes* (3 vols.), latest edition.

Singer = The Authorised Daily Prayer Book (Hebrew and English), edited by the Rev. S. Singer (for use in the Synagogues of the British Empire): published by Eyre and Spottiswoode.

TB = The Babylonian Talmud.

TJ = The Jerusalem (or Palestinian) Talmud.

Zunz *GV* = *Die gottesdienstlichen Vorträge der Juden*, von Dr. Zunz (1st edition, 1832 ; 2nd edition, 1892).

[In the transliteration of Hebrew words *ḥ* or *ch* represents ח, *ḳ*=ק, *ṣ* or *tz*=צ, and *ṭ*=ט.]

PART I

GENERAL HISTORICAL SURVEY

PART I

GENERAL HISTORICAL SURVEY

[LITERATURE (selected) : Josephus, *Antiquities*, bks. xiii.-
xx.; Reinach, *Textes d'auteurs grecs et romains relatifs au
Judaisme* (1895); Schürer, *Geschichte des Jüdischen Volkes*,
Band i. (1901); Stade, *Geschichte des Volkes Israel*, ii. (1888);
Edwyn Bevan, *The House of Seleucus* (1902); *Jerusalem under
the High-priests* (1904); Holtzmann, *Neutestamentliche Zeit-
geschichte*, pp. 1–69 (1906).

Milman, *History of the Jews* (1829); Jost, *Geschichte des
Judenthums und seiner Sekten* (1857 . . .); Karpeles,
Geschichte der Jüdischen Literatur (1886); Graetz, *History of
the Jews* (1891–1898); Cassel, *Lehrbuch der Jüdischen Geschichte und Literatur* (1896).

Lindo, *History of the Jews of Spain and Portugal* (1848);
Jacobs, *The Jews of Angevin England* (1892); Abrahams,
The Expulsion of the Jews from England (1895); *Jewish Life
in the Middle Ages* (1896); *Chapters on Jewish Literature*
(1899); *Maimonides* (1903); Hyamson, *A History of the
Jews in England* (1908); Rigg, *Select Pleas, Starrs, and
other Records from the Rolls of the Exchequer of the Jews*,
A.D. 1220–1284 (Selden Society) (1902). The many relevant
articles in *JE*.]

NO apology is needed if, as a preliminary to our
review of Rabbinical literature, we take a brief
glance at the historical background of the various
periods during which that literature was in growth.
It is probably true to say that in no other case has
the literature of a people been so conditioned by the
trend of historical events as in that of the Jews—a
fact which is perhaps to be accounted for by the

unique position which has always been occupied by
the Jews among the nations of the world.

It is over a stretch of many centuries that our task
will lead us; therefore, of necessity, our historical
survey can take account only of the more notable
landmarks. It is not our intention to attempt to
write history in the ordinary sense of the word; we
desire only to depict in outline the historical background of certain periods of Jewish history which
have been marked by special literary activity, or
have been the promising seed-field in which the later
harvest has germinated. We hope also to point out,
if possible, how the historical conditions of those
periods have affected and influenced the national
literature.

I

THE POST-EXILIC PERIOD

In the year 550 B.C., or thereabouts, Cyrus II.,
king of Persia, had conquered the entire Median
empire, and he proceeded then to deal with what
would have been a dangerous neighbour if un-
subdued—namely, the kingdom of Lydia. Crœsus
saw what was coming and tried to forestall the
blow by making alliances with Nabonidos, king of
Babylon, and Amasis, king of Egypt. It was in the
interest of both these monarchs to check the growing
power of the Persian conqueror. Cyrus, however,
struck too soon for them, and in a single campaign
(547 B.C.) defeated Crœsus before the allied armies
had been able to join him. Possibly as early as the
following year Cyrus, in continuation of his conquests, attacked Nabonidos; at any rate, within the
next few years, assisted by internal troubles in
Babylonia, he mastered this country too, and
entered Babylon, which he now made the capital of

his empire. From the so-called "Cyrus cylinder," on which the Babylonian priests recorded the doings of Cyrus, we learn that he respected the religion of the conquered country and himself accepted the worship of the gods of Babylonia.[1] This is fully in accord with his statesmanlike and broad-minded treatment of the Jews and their religion as recorded in the Old Testament, which enabled Ezra and Nehemiah to carry on their work—a work which had the most far-reaching effect on both the religious development and the literature of the Jews.

During the long period of Persian rule over the Jews there are but scanty records of their history; they were not sufficiently important to the outside world for historians to write about them, while the paucity of records—not always reliable—supplied by the Jews themselves must be accounted for by the restless and dangerous times through which they lived. Incessant wars went on around them; they did not, it is true, take any direct share in these, but it was inevitable that they should have been greatly affected by the turmoil which raged at their very doors; for during the long struggle between the Persians and the Egyptians (408–343 B.C.) Syria was the centre in which many a sanguinary battle was fought out, until, at length, in 343 B.C., Artaxerxes III. (Ochus) finally conquered the Egyptians. Although, as has just been said, the Jews did not take any direct share in this struggle, from two incidents which are on record it appears that they were tempted to make a bid for independence, for in 353 B.C., according to Orosius (III. vii. 6 f.), Jericho was attacked by the Persians and destroyed; a number of Jews were carried away captive to Hyrcania and Babylon. The other incident, somewhat obscure, is that recorded by Josephus (*Antiq.* XI.

[1] *cp.* Hommel, *Geschichte Babyloniens und Assyriens*, pp. 785 ff. (1885).

vii. 1) ; he tells of how Bagoses (*i.e.* Bagoas), one of the generals in Artaxerxes' army, punished the Jews because Jochanan slew his brother Joshua, the high-priest, in the Temple. It is not clear why the people as a whole should have been made to suffer for the individual outrage perpetrated by Jochanan, The story as given by Josephus is incomplete ; but, in view of the earlier incident, mentioned above, it is reasonable to suppose that it reflects some further attempt to throw off the Persian yoke. The date of this occurrence is uncertain, but it probably took place while Artaxerxes was preparing his third campaign against the Egyptians (348–346).

The downfall of the Persian empire, which was one of the results of Alexander's victories, did not, so far as we know, greatly affect the Jews at first. It is to be presumed that they recognised the Greek ascendancy and bowed to the inevitable. Not long after the death of Alexander, in 323, began the great conflict between the Seleucids and the Ptolemys, which continued, with interludes, during practically the whole of the third century B.C. During most of this time, again, the Jews do not seem to have suffered excepting in so far as the constant clash of warring elements around them necessarily brought hardships. They had to pay tribute to both Seleucids and Ptolemys, as these were alternately victorious ; but otherwise, so far as our scanty records give us information, they were not molested. They showed a preference, upon the whole, for the Ptolemys, since these had greater consideration for Jewish religious susceptibilities than the Seleucids.[1] But towards the end of the third century a great revulsion of feeling took place, and a considerable section of the Jews threw in their lot with the Seleucid ruler Antiochus III.

[1] For further details, see Oesterley, *The Books of the Apocrypha : their Origin, Teaching, and Contents*, pp. 28 ff. (1914).

The reason for this was, in all probability, due to the growth of Hellenistic influence among many of the Jews (*cp.* 1 Macc. i. 11 f.); though in 3 Macc. i. 10 f. it is accounted for by the fact that Ptolemy IV. attempted to enter into the Holy of Holies. Towards the close of our period a lamentable strife broke out between the aristocratic priestly families of Onias and Tobias in Jerusalem; it was concerned with religious as well as political questions, and ceased only with the rise of the Maccabees.[1]

In spite of both external and (to some extent) internal unrest during these centuries, there is reason to believe that the whole period was one of much growth and development among the Jews in more directions than one. Indeed, it is true to say that the seeds from which the Rabbinical literature grew (and this is here our main concern) began to be planted as early as the time of the Exile itself. One fact in particular is to be noticed here as being especially important from our present point of view, although its relevancy may not be immediately apparent: for an individual Israelite to be exiled from his native land was about as cruel a lot as could befall him, for it meant separation from his God and the snapping asunder of the tie which bound him to the communal life of his tribe, with all that these things signified. But in the case of the Babylonian Exile, not individuals, but whole families and tribes were taken away; when these, therefore, settled down in their new home they were able to continue to live under the same internal political and social conditions as in Palestine. To a large extent this was also the case regarding their religious life; the sacrificial system, it is true, could not be continued— a fact which resulted in consequences of the highest

---

[1] For a detailed account of this struggle, see Büchler's learned work, *Die Tobiaden und Oniaden* . . . (1899), where all the sources are thoroughly examined.

importance to the religion of the Jews. Moreover,
since whole families and septs went together into
exile, there was not, as would have been the case
with an individual, the same feeling of separation
from the national God, because, the family consti-
tuting, according to the old belief, a self-contained
unit for the purposes of worship, His presence was
believed to be assured, even in a strange land.
Besides, although the conception of "the God of the
land" still obtained to some extent, it is clear from
the books of Jeremiah and Ezekiel that a worthier
belief regarding the God of Israel had been attained ;
and there is especially this fact, that many priests,
and, above all, the heads of families, had come into
Babylon. According to very ancient belief and
custom, the heads of families were the religious, as
well as the political, leaders of the people ; their
importance and influence, which had been so cur-
tailed by the rise of the monarchy, were now
immensely increased, since the monarchy was no
more ; this is abundantly clear from the books of
Ezra and Nehemiah. They, therefore, took up their
old position of leaders of the people, both from the
point of view of politics and of religion.

Further, there are many indications which lead us
to the conclusion that the lot of the exiles in
Babylon was not a hard one. What the prophet
Ezekiel says does not suggest that the general
conditions were in any sense intolerable,[1] nor does
Jeremiah anticipate a time of cruel hardship for the
people, as is clear from his words : "Thus saith the
Lord of hosts, the God of Israel, unto all the captivity, whom I have caused to be carried away
captive from Jerusalem to Babylon : Build ye houses,
and dwell in them ; and plant gardens, and eat the
fruit of them ; take ye wives, and beget sons and
daughters, and take wives for your sons, and give

[1] Ezek. i. 3 ; viii. 1 ; *cp.* Ezra viii. 15-21.

your daughters to husbands, that they may bear sons and daughters; and multiply ye there, and be not diminished. And seek the peace of the city whither I have caused you to be carried away captive, and pray unto the Lord for it; for in the peace thereof shall ye have peace" (xxix. 4–7). Clearly, the people had reasonable freedom; they lived unmolested, and were able to carry on their various callings. But the most important factor was that they were permitted the unrestricted exercise of their religion. It was here that a deep and far-reaching change began to take place. Instead of the sacrificial system, which had hitherto been the chief religious expression in Israel, but which could now no longer be carried out, the people—or, at all events, their religious guides—were led to think of the deeper truths of religion: the problem of sin, personal responsibility, the meaning of suffering, a fuller conception of atonement; and there resulted a wider apprehension of God and of His relationship to man and to the world. Not that all the ancient and time-honoured external religious requirements were forgotten; circumcision and the observance of the Sabbath were more than ever emphasised; indeed, these came to be the distinguishing marks of the Jews. All these facts point to the Exile as being the period during which the foundations were being laid for that development of the Jewish religion the ultimate development of which is to be found in the Rabbinical literature. The later books of the Old Testament furnish us with many indications of how, in the practical religious life of the people, things were proceeding during the succeeding century or two; and before we conclude this section it will be well to refer quite briefly to some of the more important ways in which this is illustrated by these books.

From a liturgical point of view, it is of interest to note that, according to 1 Chron. xxiv. 1–19, the priests were divided into twenty-four courses, and from 2 Chron. xxiii. 4, 8, we learn that these courses changed every Sabbath.[1] It was the same with the Levites; see 1 Chron. xxiii. 3–32; xxiv. 20–31. That these arrangements were brought about during the post-Exilic period and were not part of the earlier practice is clear from the fact that neither in the Pentateuch nor in the earlier portions of the books of Ezra and Nehemiah is there any mention of them. Developments in the conduct of the services are of a still more far-reaching character. So far as the Temple singers are concerned, while they are unknown in the Pentateuch, their position is an established one, according to Neh. vii. 44; xi. 23; xii. 28; although here they apparently occupy a lower grade than the Levites. But, according to 1 Chron. xxv., they, too, were divided into twenty-four courses; and, what is more important, they were reckoned among the Levites (although occupying a lower grade), according to 1 Chron. xxiii. 3–5, for the leaders of the three choirs were Asaph, Heman, and Ethan (or Jeduthun, in 1 Chron. xv. 17, 19; xxv. 1–6; 2 Chron. v. 12), who belong to the "sons of Levi, Gershom, Kohath, and Merari" (see 1 Chron. vi. 16–32). These facts point not only to the importance placed upon the elaborating of the Temple services and to the consequent effect upon the Liturgy, but also to the far-reaching results which were ultimately brought about by the general body of worshippers being made to take part in the services, through being led by the Levitical choir, and by singing the Hallelujah and saying the Amen (cp. 1 Chron. xvi. 36; Ps. cvi. 48). The priests, of course, still continued to perform the main parts of the services, but they were no more in the position of entire separation from the congregation which had obtained in earlier days. We must see here, there-

[1] cp. pp. 147 ff.

fore, the beginnings of congregational worship in the
real sense of the word.

And, lastly, the Scribes of this period began to
form themselves into guilds (*cp.* 1 Chron. ii. 55); and
from the later book of Ecclesiasticus (xxxviii. 24–
xxxix. 11) we can see that they devoted themselves
exclusively to the study of sacred literature, the Law
being the centre of all their activities. The importance of this from our present point of view needs no
emphasis, since they were in the truest sense the
spiritual forbears of the Rabbis.

II

THE MACCABÆAN ERA AND THE HASMONÆANS; THE FALL OF JERUSALEM

The immediate cause of the Maccabæan rising was
the attempt of Antiochus Epiphanes, the Syrian
king, to enforce uniformity of religion and worship
throughout his kingdom (see 1 Macc. i. 41 ff.), and
therefore upon the Jews. He was doubtless encou-
raged to make this attempt owing to the presence
among his Jewish subjects of a strongly pro-
Hellenistic party (see 1 Macc. i. 13–15). The priestly
aristocracy in Jerusalem, headed by the usurping
high-priest Menelaus (of the house of Tobias), sided
with Antiochus; and it is evident that he was
followed by a considerable section of the people.
On the other hand, those Jews who were faithful to
their religion showed a very different spirit. They
first fled into the wilds east of Jerusalem; and on
being attacked on the Sabbath day they refused even
to defend themselves, lest they should desecrate the
Sabbath, and were slaughtered in cold blood—a
most striking illustration of the powerful effect
which insistence on the observance of the Law had

had upon many Jews. But this tame and useless attitude did not last long (1 Macc. ii. 39–41). Active resistance first took place under Mattathias, an aged priest from Modin. He, together with his five sons, organised a Jewish army whose watchword was to fight and die for the Law. Thus one of the most extraordinary religious wars in history came about (167 B.C.). Mattathias was the grandson of one named Hasmon, and it is from him that the Maccabæans took the family name of the Hasmonæans. The bold example set by Mattathias attracted many to his side, and especially the *Chasidim*, the "saints," as they are called in Ps. xxx. 4 (5) (1 Macc. ii. 42 ; *cp.* vii. 12–14). His first efforts were directed against renegade Jews, and he succeeded in re-establishing respect for the Jewish Law in Jewish lands. But he died in the following year (166 B.C.), and the leadership was taken by his son Judas, the " Maccabæan," who vigorously attacked the Syrians and succeeded in driving them from Jerusalem and the surrounding country. The Holy City thereupon became the religious centre of the revolt. The Temple was cleansed ; "blameless priests, such as had pleasure in the Law," were chosen ; the holy place was rebuilt ; and all the old services and sacrifices were reinstituted. A special ceremony of Dedication (*Chanukkah*)[1] took place in December, 165 B.C. (*cp.* Ps. xxx. title) ; and for a brief period there was peace (see 1 Macc. iv. 36–61). The war soon broke out again, however ; the Jews were attacked by some of the smaller peoples who had made common cause with the chief enemy ; while both in Gilead and Galilee the Gentiles menaced the Jews. But in all these theatres of the war Judas, greatly helped by his brother Simon, was successful. The high hopes now entertained by the Hasmonæans were but short-lived. We cannot enter here upon all

---

[1] This festival has been kept annually by the Jews ever since.

the details of the struggle.[1] Suffice it to say that, thanks to the leadership of Judas, religious liberty was gained ; but in 161 Judas fell, and his followers were filled with despair. Nevertheless, his brother Jonathan, nothing daunted, took up the struggle, and with success ; in 1 Macc. ix. 73 it is said : " And the sword ceased from Israel. And Jonathan dwelt at Michmash. And Jonathan began to judge the people ; and he destroyed the ungodly out of Israel." The struggle soon after was continued, but it entered upon a new phase owing to the activity of the rival claimants to the Syrian throne. The Maccabæan power, as it had now become, occupied the position of the deciding factor, and was thus courted first by the one and then by the other claimant to the throne. Jonathan was clever enough to utilise this for the advantage of his people. In 153 he was recognised as head of the Jewish people and was appointed high-priest of the nation.

From this point may be dated the real beginning of the Hasmonæan rule in Jerusalem. In 143 Jonathan was assassinated through Syrian treachery, and his brother Simon succeeded him as leader and high-priest. He continued the energetic and clever policy of his brother, and increased the nation's territory. Owing to him, Judæa became recognised as an independent country, and the Hasmonæan dynasty was formally established. Thus both religious and political freedom were gained for the Jews.

In 135 B.C. John Hyrkanos, the third[2] son of Simon, succeeded his father. On coins of his reign the inscription runs : " John the high-priest, head of the congregation[3] of the Jews." From this it is clear

---

[1] For these, see Oesterley, *op. cit.* pp. 427–438.
[2] The two elder sons had been treacherously slain with their father ; see 1 Macc. xvi. 11–17.
[3] The word is *Cheber*, meaning, in post-Biblical Hebrew, a " religious association."

that the official head of the Jewish state looked upon himself first and foremost as a religious personage. Nevertheless, the fact that John Hyrḳanos had his name inscribed on coins (he was, so far as is known, the first high-priest of the Jews to do so) indicates that he regarded himself as a temporal ruler as well as a high-priest. John Hyrḳanos's long reign (135-104 B.C.) was, according to Josephus, a prosperous one ; he says that Hyrḳanos "lived happily, and administered the government in the best manner for thirty-one years . . . he was esteemed by God worthy of the three greatest privileges, the government of his nation, the dignity of the high-priesthood, and prophecy ; for God was with him" (*Antiq.* XIII. x. 7). Hyrḳanos's son, Aristobulus I., was the first Jewish ruler to assume definitely the title of king. It is not necessary to go into the details of his reign, nor yet of those of the two following, viz. of Alexander Jannæus (103-76 B.C.) and of his widow Alexandra, or, according to her Jewish name, Salome (she died in 69 B.C.). But during the reign that followed altogether new conditions arose, for Palestine came under the suzerainty of Rome. The Roman power would, it is true, have asserted itself over Palestine in any case sooner or later ; but, as a matter of fact, circumstances in this country during the reign which followed that of Alexandra were such as to invite the intervention of Rome. At the very end of Alexandra's reign the Sadducæan party, which had been oppressed by the dominant Pharisaic party, broke out into revolt in Judæa. Of Alexandra's two sons, Hyrḳanos upheld the Pharisaic party, while Aristobulus sided with the Sadducees. The latter was the more vigorous of the two brothers and gained considerable success at the outset of this struggle. Alexandra died at the beginning of the civil strife. During her reign she had appointed her eldest son, Hyrḳanos, to the high-priesthood—he was, in any case, the rightful successor—but immediately upon her death her second son, Aristobulus, sought to gain the kingdom. He conquered his brother in battle near Jericho, and Hyrkanos fled to Jerusalem, and presently made peace by renouncing both the high-priesthood and the kingship in favour of Aristobulus. This, one would suppose, ought to have ended the strife ; but it was not so. Urged on by Antipater (the father of Herod the Great), governor of Idumæa (and, we may surmise, by the leaders of the Pharisaic party, too), Hyrkanos was induced to fight for his rights. An alliance, brought about by Antipater, was made between Hyrkanos and Aretas, an Arab prince. Together they attacked Aristobulus and overcame him. He, as his brother had done on a former occasion, fled to Jerusalem, where he was besieged.

Whilst this fratricidal struggle was going on, Pompey had been conducting his victorious campaign in Asia. In the year 65 B.C. he sent one of his generals, Scaurus, into Syria, where the latter heard of the civil war which was taking place in Palestine. Both brothers sent deputations to Scaurus and sought to gain him ; in the end he decided to uphold Aristobulus. For the time being, therefore, Aristobulus was master in Judæa. This did not, however, last long. Pompey himself arrived in Syria in 63 B.C., and while sojourning in Damascus he was approached by three deputations of Jews ; these represented the parties of Hyrkanos and Aristobulus, and a further one representing the Jewish nation ; this last wished to have nothing to do with the two others—an interesting fact, showing as it does that there was at least a considerable section of the Jews at this time which, presumably, stood apart from the Sadducæan and Pharisaic parties. As Pompey was about to undertake an expedition against the Nabatæans, he told his petitioners that they must wait until this had been accomplished, and that then he would decide upon what course he would follow. On his way south, however, he received news which gave him reason to suspect Aristobulus of treachery ; so he postponed his intended campaign. He now commanded Aristobulus to deliver up Jerusalem. Seeing that resistance was useless, Aristobulus submitted ; he left the capital and came to Pompey. Thereupon Pompey sent his general Gabinius to take possession of Jerusalem. Gabinius, however, returned without having accomplished his purpose, for the defenders of Jerusalem refused to give up possession of the city in spite of Aristobulus's surrender. So Pompey himself came against Jerusalem. Now in Jerusalem itself matters were in a deplorable state, for the supporters of Hyrkanos and Aristobulus were quarrelling amongst themselves ; those of Aristobulus determined to resist, while those of Hyrkanos wanted to submit because they regarded Pompey as their deliverer. These latter, being more numerous, had their way, and Pompey was admitted into Jerusalem without having to strike a blow. The supporters of Aristobulus, however, withdrew to the Temple mount, the position of which was very strong ; here they held out for three months, but were ultimately compelled to surrender. Jerusalem, together with the whole land of the Jews, became tributary to Rome. But, in addition to this, large portions of Judæa were cut off ; the whole of the coast-land on the west, and all the non-Jewish cities east of the Jordan, were taken from the Jews ; Samaria also, together with a large tract of the surrounding country, was separated from Judæa. What was left of Jewish territory was placed under the high-priesthood of Hyrkanos II., but he was not permitted to retain the title of king. It was not only the Jews who were affected, for the whole of Syria was made a Roman province.

From the taking of Jerusalem by Pompey in 63 B.C. to the year 47 B.C., when Cæsar became

actively interested in the Jews, the lot of the people
was a hard one. But things altered in consequence
of Cæsar's gratitude to them for supporting him in
his Alexandrine war; and he showed this in the
following way : In addition to being confirmed in the
high-priesthood, Hyrkanos was made temporal ruler
in Judæa with the title of ethnarch, which was to be
hereditary; the supreme court for the administration
of justice in all that related to Jewish law was also
placed under the immediate jurisdiction of Hyrkanos ;
a number of cities were given back to Judæa,
including Joppa on the coast ; Hyrkanos was permitted to rebuild the walls round Jerusalem ; and
many taxes were remitted. Further, Cæsar rewarded
Antipater, who had also been of assistance to him
during the Alexandrine war, by nominating him
procurator of Judæa. It is important to note that, by
receiving this office direct from Cæsar, Antipater was
no more subject to Hyrkanos, as he had been hitherto,
but was responsible to Rome alone. This is of
importance for the further history of Judæa, for
Antipater was thereby enabled to increase his power.
He managed, indeed, to procure important posts
for his sons, Phasael being appointed to administer
the district of Jerusalem, and Herod that of Galilee.
On the death of Antipater both his sons were made
tetrarchs, with the result that Hyrkanos to all intents
and purposes lost his authority as temporal ruler.
This happened in the year 41 B.C. In the following
year the whole condition of affairs in Judæa became
again altered owing to the invasion of Syria by the
Parthians. There is no need to go into the details of
this invasion ; the special point, among its various
consequences, that affected the Jews was that Herod
was made king of Judæa by the Roman power.
Under him the Hasmonæan dynasty came to an end
by the judicial murder of the aged Hyrkanos (31 B.C.).
Upon the whole, Herod left the Jews in peace so far

C

as their religion was concerned. His passion for gorgeous buildings is well known, and need not be further touched upon here excepting to say that the Jews benefited by it, especially by the way in which he beautified the Temple. On the death of Herod (B.C. 4) his kingdom was divided among his three sons. Archelaus became ethnarch of Judæa, Idumæa, and Samaria (*cp*. Matt. ii. 22); his lands (in A.D. 6) came under the immediate rule of the Roman procurators, of whom Pontius Pilate governed A.D. 27–37. Antipas, who is always called Herod in the New Testament, received the title of tetrarch (he is called "king" in Mk. vi. 14); he inherited from his father Galilee and Peræa. Philip became tetrarch of north-eastern Palestine. But while the arrangements regarding these divisions were being made in Rome bitter fighting broke out in Palestine, where the impossible project seems to have been entertained by some of throwing off the Roman yoke. Foremost among the Jewish leaders was a certain Simon, who was active in Peræa; in southern Judæa Athrouges, a shepherd, led the revolt; and, above all, Judas, in Galilee, by energetic action gained important initial advantages. But it was all useless; in a very short time Varus crushed every vestige of opposition for the time being. Nevertheless, the national spirit of the Jews and their yearning for freedom, fostered by the thoughts of the heroic and successful struggle of the Maccabees in bygone days against overwhelming odds, served to keep the embers of revolt from being extinguished. At last, in A.D. 66, the long-prepared conflagration broke out, and the fatal war against Rome began. The terrible details of this war cannot be entered upon here. It ended at last in the final overthrow of the Jews with the fall of Jerusalem in A.D. 70.

III

THE TALMUDIC PERIOD

The fearful struggle with Rome left the Jews physically prostrate. But it had the further and deeper effect of driving them from what had hitherto been the centre of their life and religion. Jerusalem no longer belonged to the Jews. A new phase of the Dispersion was about to commence which was going to make the words of Strabo true in a larger sense than he could ever have believed when he wrote: "Now these Jews are already gotten into all cities, and it is hard to find a place in the habitable earth that hath not admitted this tribe of men, and is not possessed by it."[1] Palestine itself was divided up; it was in part distributed among Roman soldiers and in part sold to the highest bidders; only a tiny remnant was left to the Jews. It is now that one is able to see the very far-reaching and abiding effect which, beginning with Ezra and Nehemiah, and continued by like-minded religious leaders through the centuries, the teaching of the Law had had upon the race. They had lost their country; as a self-constituted nation they were no longer in existence; even their religion was in danger. One thing left to them—the Law, together with a mass of traditional teaching on the Law which had been handed down for generations.

What we have called the Talmudic period includes the time during which the many elements of which the Talmud is made up were being gathered and welded together; and this period is divided into three well-marked divisions, which are known respectively as the times of the *Tannaim*, the *Amoraim*,

[1] Quoted by Josephus, *Antiq.* XIV. vii. 2 ; *cp. Sib. Orac.* iii. 271 : " Every land and every sea is full of thee."

and the *Saboraim* ; these names will be explained as we proceed.

(i) *The Tannaitic Period*

By the beginning of the Christian era there were recognised teachers of the Oral Law whose pronouncements were regarded as authoritative. Each such teacher received the name, or title, of *Tanna*, "teacher" (plur. *Tannaim*), from the Aramaic root *teni*, "to teach." These teachers all belonged to the Pharisaic party. After the destruction of the Temple (A.D. 70) the leaders of the Pharisaic party received permission from Titus to settle down in Jabne (Jamnia), a small place on the sea coast, not far from Jaffa. Here they established a new Sanhedrin, consisting of seventy-two "elders" (*Zekēnim*), under the presidency of the now aged Jochanan ben Zakkai. Jabne became a new centre for Palestinian Judaism, thus taking the place of Jerusalem in this respect ; and under the guidance of Jochanan ben Zakkai and his successors the Academy, or *Beth ha-Midrash*, of Jabne became so important that its pronouncements were recognised as authoritative not only among the remnant of the Jews in Palestine, but also throughout the Dispersion in the Western world. The head of this Academy soon came to be known as the *Nasi*, or "Prince." Later on the Academy was removed to Sepphoris, and afterwards to Tiberias. It will, therefore, be seen that the lot of the Jews under the Romans was at least tolerable ; though a subject race, they were not badly treated so long as they acquiesced in the new conditions ; what they most valued, religious freedom, was fully accorded to them.

In the meantime there were various scattered Jewish communities in the East, the descendants of the exiles in Babylonia and Mesopotamia. These had lived more or less unmolested for centuries, and had gradually established seats of learning in Babylonia. Over all these Eastern Jews there was a political head called the "Prince of the Captivity" (*Resh Gelutha*). Babylonia was destined to become the centre of Rabbinical Judaism; but before we come to this part of our survey we must continue briefly to follow the history of the Jews in Palestine. The period immediately following the destruction of Jerusalem was comparatively peaceful; certain hardships they had undoubtedly to bear, but it is evident that they were permitted full religious liberty, and intense activity in the Jewish schools of learning continued; communities were formed all over the country, and there can be no doubt that comparative security was enjoyed by the whole people; it would otherwise be impossible to account for the long and tenacious resistance offered later by the nation to Hadrian. During the reign of Trajan, whether on account of oppressions or owing to the yearning for independence, the Jews broke into open revolt both in Palestine and elsewhere. For the time being they were subdued. But when, some years later, Hadrian attempted virtually to stamp out Judaism as a religion, a really serious revolt against the Roman power burst forth under the leadership of Bar-Cochba ("son of a star"). For three years, A.D. 132–135, the fighting continued; but the power of Rome inevitably won the day at last. Hadrian founded a new city on the site of Jerusalem, in which he planted a colony of foreigners. He attempted to obliterate the very name of Jerusalem by calling his new city Ælia Capitolina; no Jew was allowed to enter it.

Among the religious leaders of this time the most prominent were the *Tanna* Rabbi Akiba,[1] who died about A.D. 132–135 probably, and Judah ha-Nasi;[2] the latter, as the redactor of the Mishnah, is certainly one of the most important figures in

[1] See further below, p. 95.
[2] See further below, pp. 44, 96 ff.

Jewish history. As religious leader of the Palestinian Jews he worked for many years in Beth She'arim (in Galilee), to which place he transferred the seat of the patriarchate and principal Academy. Later on he went to Sepphoris, where he lived for seventeen years, and died A.D. 220. From this time onwards, although the Palestinian teachers continued their work in the various Academies and finally completed the Palestinian Talmud, it was Babylon which became more and more the authoritative centre of Judaism.

(ii) *The Period of the Amoraim*

"Sherira Gaon, in his famous letter (the chief source for information on the Babylonian schools), wrote: 'No doubt, here in Babylonia public instruction was given in the Torah; but besides the exilarchs there were no recognised heads of schools until the death of Rabbi (Judah I.).' The principal seat of Babylonian Judaism was Nehardea."[1] But it was the nephew of Judah I., Rabbi Arika, known later as "Rab," who initiated a new epoch, for with him began the time during which for centuries the Academies in Babylonia played the leading *rôle* as the fountain-head of Judaism. This began approximately in A.D. 220. He founded a new Academy in Sura, leaving his friend Rabbi Samuel to preside at the ancient seat of learning in Nehardea. This latter city was destroyed in A.D. 259, and its place was thereupon taken by a town not far off called Pumbeditha. In these schools study was concentrated upon the Law and upon the various explanations and comments of earlier teachers on it which had accumulated in course of ages, and which to a large extent had been incorporated in the Mishnah. The scholar whose work during this period was of paramount importance was

[1] *JE* i. 145*a*.

Rabbi Ashi, the president of the Academy at Sura. He undertook the colossal work of gathering together and sifting the materials which were the outcome of two centuries of Rabbinical labour in the Academies of Babylonia. "The final editing of the literary work which this labour produced did not, it is true, take place until somewhat later ; but tradition rightly regards Ashi as the originator of the Babylonian Talmud. Ashi's editorial work received, indeed, many later additions and amplifications ; but the form underwent no material modification. The Babylonian Talmud must be considered the work of the Academy of Sura, because Ashi submitted to each of the semi-annual general assemblies of the Academy, treatise by treatise, the results of his examination and selection, and invited discussion upon them. His work was continued and perfected, and probably reduced to writing, by succeeding heads of the Sura Academy . . . from the Academy of Sura was issued that unique literary effort which was destined to occupy such an extraordinary position in Judaism."[1] The date of the completion of the Babylonian Talmud was approximately A.D. 500.

During the whole of this period work similar to that of the Babylonian Academies was being carried on in the Academies of Palestine ; here, too, a Talmud was by degrees being brought into existence. The centre from which this came forth was the Academy of Tiberias, and the foremost worker in connexion with it is Rabbi Jochanan ben Nappacha. All the teachers of this period, whether in Babylonia or Palestine, are known as *Amoraim*, the plural form of *Amora*, which means "a speaker"; but in the sense of "interpreter," it is used in reference to the interpreters of, or commentators on, the Mishnah. This period lasted to the year A.D. 500.

[1] *JE* i. 146a.

(iii) *The Period of the Saboraim*

This period was of much shorter duration than the two preceding ones. The scholars to whom the name of *Sabora* ("decision") was applied were those who gave the final touches to the Talmud (Babylonian); they added various decisions on many points which had been handed down from earlier teachers, but nothing that they added was of their own composition. They are to be regarded as the final redactors of the Talmud. This period closed, and with it the whole of what we have called the Talmudic period, about A.D. 550, or a little later.

It was a period which, speaking generally, was favourable to the Jews provided they acquiesced in what their rulers insisted upon. Both in Palestine, under the Romans (and later under the Byzantine Empire), and in Babylonia, under the Persians, there was (with one or two exceptions) no interference with the Jewish religion; this, from the point of view of Jewish literature, which is wholly a religious literature, was of paramount importance. The Jewish religious leaders, especially in Babylonia, had no wish to interfere in the world of politics; that they should be left in peace to continue their religious literary pursuits was their great desire; and that this was accorded them is evident from the results of their labours which have been handed down. The importance of Palestine as a Jewish centre continued to decrease, while that of Babylon gained more and more in authority and prestige; so much so that during our next period interest in Palestine becomes negligible.[1]

---

[1] Schools continued to exist in Palestine for several centuries, but their authority, as compared with that of the Babylonian centres of learning, was quite unimportant.

IV

THE GEONIC PERIOD

Gaon (plur. *Geonim*) means "Excellency" (*cp.* Ps. xlvii. 4), and was the title given to the heads of the two leading Academies in Babylonia, namely, Sura and Pumbeditha. They were the direct successors of the Amoraim and Saboraim; for, "while the Amoraim, through their interpretation of the Mishnah, gave rise to the Talmud, and while the Saboraim definitely edited it, the Geonim's task was to interpret it; for them it became the subject of study and instruction, and they gave religio-legal decisions in agreement with its teachings."[1] The Geonic period lasted from the latter part of the sixth century to the first half of the eleventh, about four centuries and a half;[2] throughout this period the Geonim were recognised as the chief religious authorities throughout Jewry—that is to say, not only in Babylonia, but also in northern Africa, Spain, and in those parts of Europe generally where Jewish communities were founded.

The great world-event of this period was the rise of Mohammedanism. When, early in the seventh century, it commenced its aggressive career in Arabia, the Jews were the first sufferers. There had existed here for many centuries an obscure Jewish community which does not seem to have had any relationship with either Palestine or Babylonia. When the Prophet raised his cry of " The Koran or the sword!" it meant bitter persecution for these Arabian Jews. But this formed an exception to the general treatment accorded by the Mohammedan rulers to the Jews. When once conquest was gained the Caliphs behaved tolerantly towards them; so

[1] *JE* v. 568a.   [2] See pp. 209 ff.

long as there was no active opposition the Jews were permitted the exercise of their religion without molestation. The Caliph Omar showed himself quite friendly to the *Geonim* in Babylonia; the schools of Sura and Pumbeditha, which had been closed for some time previously by the Persian government, were reopened, and .the heads of these Academies— known also by the name of *Kallah*[1]—gave themselves again uninterruptedly to the work which had been carried on by their predecessors. The most celebrated of the *Geonim* during the early part of this period was Jehudai ben Nachman, known also by the name of Judah the Blind; the influence of his teaching continued long after his death. The *Geonim* became by degrees the great authorities on all religious and legal questions, leaving all political matters, as we have seen, to the functionary called the *Resh Gelutha*, the origin of which dated from earlier centuries; he was originally an officer appointed by the suzerain power. But during Mohammedan ascendancy the *Resh Gelutha* lost more and more of his influence, and finally, in the tenth century, the office ceased to exist.

It was during this period that what is called the Karaite movement arose, a movement which owed its rise indirectly to Mohammedan influence. The founder of the sect which originated this movement was named Anan, who lived early in the ninth century. He and his followers called themselves *Benê Mikra*[2] ("sons of reading"), and they professed to follow the teaching of what they read in the Bible only, and ignored altogether the interpretations of the Rabbis and the teaching and practice

---

[1] Derived possibly from the Aramaic word for "garland," in reference to the teachers of the Academies, who formed a "circle" of adornment; but the origin of the word is obscure.

[2] From the same root as the word Koran. They were also called Ananites after the founder.

founded thereon. In fact, it was a repetition of that loyalty to the Written Law and repudiation of the Oral Law which in earlier ages had been championed by the Sadducees. The influence of the Karaite sect was in one respect far-reaching ; their main principle, *i.e.* regarding the Scriptures as the sole authority in matters of faith and practice, entailed on their part a minute examination of the text of the Bible in order to be able to refute the Rabbinical standpoint ; in order to counter this the Rabbis undertook a similar task. This critical study of the text of Scripture developed into a very keen contest between the Rabbinical and Karaite champions. There is no doubt that the bulk of the work of compiling an authoritative text, which was the outcome of this contest, must be assigned to the initiative of the Karaites. The result of this literary contest was of the highest importance, for it produced what is called the "Masoretic" text (from the Hebrew word *Massora*, "Tradition") ; this is the text of the Hebrew Bible at the present day, from which also the Authorised and Revised Versions of the English Bible were made. Apart from this, the Karaites exercised but little influence; they were never numerous. It is a curious thing that they, nevertheless, continued to exist, and are to be found even at the present day in Egypt and Eastern Europe, as well as in Jerusalem.

The most distinguished personality, from a literary point of view, in the Geonic period was Saadya. He was born in 892, in the Fayyûm (Upper Egypt), but spent many years of his life in Palestine. In 928 he was appointed Gaon of Sura, and under his guidance that Academy enjoyed a position of great importance and prestige, in spite of the fact that, owing to quarrels, Saadya had for part of the time to leave Sura and settle down in Bagdad. Saadya was not only the greatest Jewish literary light of his own time, but also the first great writer in post-Biblical Judaism since Philo; "as Philo had united the Hellenic language and culture with the Jewish spirit, so the language and civilisation of the Mohammedan Arabs gained a similar, but far more lasting, influence over the history of Judaism through the writings of Saadiah. He was, moreover, almost entirely a creator and an innovator in the scientific fields in which he laboured, although much of his work, even that which was written in Hebrew, is now known only from citations."[1] Of his many works, exegetical, grammatical, Halakic, liturgical, and polemical, the foremost is the *Emunoth we-Deoth* (" Articles of Faith and Philosophic Dogmas "), written in 933 ; it is " the first systematic presentation and philosophic foundation of the dogmas of Judaism " ever written ; it appeared originally in Arabic, and was twice translated into Hebrew. Ever since its publication, and right up to the present day, it has commanded the greatest respect and authority in orthodox Jewish circles.[2] He lived during the time of the Karaite movement, and was zealous in writing refutations of the teachings of this sect. Important, too, was his translation of the Hebrew Bible into Arabic, for it was "a potent factor in the impregnation of the Jewish spirit with Arabic culture."[3]

Though not confined to this period, but belonging to it in a special way, is an element in Jewish literature which is of a unique character, viz. the "Responsa Prudentum," or, according to the Hebrew form, *She'eloth u-Teshuboth* ("Questions and Answers"). These constitute a collection of replies, decisions, and comments, of various recognised teachers, and especially of the heads of Academies, in written form, to questions addressed to them by

---

[1] *JE* x. 580*b*.
[2] See further Jost, *Geschichte des Judentums*, ii. 279 ff. (1857).
[3] For details of his various works, see *JE* x. 581 ff.

Jewish inquirers in all parts of the world. "These *Responsa* constitute a special class of Talmudic and Rabbinical literature, which in form differs both from the commentaries and from the codifications of Rabbinical Judaism, yet in content is similar to both." They deal with subjects of every imaginable kind, and though many of them are of a theoretical character, the majority are concerned with practical matters of everyday life. The date of the earliest is subsequent to the completion of the Mishnah ; and though many belong to a time before the Geonic period, it is during this period specifically that the *Responsa* were written. The earliest were written in Aramaic ; later on Hebrew and Arabic took the place of Aramaic. The custom continued to much later times all over Europe ; but these later *Responsa* have neither the same importance nor interest as the earlier ones. Collections of the Geonic *Responsa* were made in the sixteenth century, and various further collections of them have been made since, the latest having been published in 1905 by Ginzberg, under the title "Genizah Studies."

The Geonic period coincides to a large extent with the centuries during which the Jews lived in much prosperity under the Ommeyade Caliphs in Spain ; it is, therefore, to this period that we must now turn.

V

THE JEWS IN SPAIN [1]

Not without reason has the period of the Jews' settlement in Spain from the eighth to the thirteenth century been called the "Golden Age of the modern Jews." [2] Communities of Jews had settled in Spain long before this time ; as early as the third century, so the evidence shows, they were already living in

[1] See further, pp. 209 ff.
[2] Milman, *History of the Jews*, iii. 267 (1829).

the country, the tombstone of a Jewish girl bearing a Latin inscription belonging to this century having been discovered at Adra,[1] a small town on the southern coast of Spain. Until the arrival of the Moors the lot of the Jews was not happy; both the civil and religious authorities oppressed them, though they enjoyed peaceful intervals at times. But by the beginning of the eighth century a very different prospect opened out before them. Under the Arab conquerors the Jewish population increased greatly, mainly through immigration from Africa; southern Spain especially became an asylum for oppressed Jews from other parts of the country. When the Caliphs began to establish themselves in the splendid state of peaceful sovereigns, the Jews found occasion to exercise their influence in teaching the less cultured people among whom they had settled the arts and luxuries of civilised life. "The Hebrew literature was admirably adapted to the kindred taste of the Arabians. The extravagant legends of the Talmud would harmonise with their bold poetical spirit; their picturesque apologues were probably the form of instruction in which the Arab tribes had ever delighted to listen to moral wisdom; even the niceties of their verbal disputes would not be without charm to their masters, who soon began to pay attention to the polish of their rich and copious language."[2] During the reigns of Abd al-Rachman, king of Cordova (called Al-Nasir), and his son, Al-Chakim (A.D. 912–961), the Jews rose to great importance; they devoted themselves whole-heartedly to the service of their masters, and were rewarded by being allowed absolute freedom and security, and were given posts of honour in the kingdom. These reigns constituted "a golden era for the Spanish Jews and Jewish science. Abd' al-Rachman's court

[1] Hübner, *Inscriptiones Hispaniæ Latinæ*, p. 267 (1869).
[2] Milman, *op. cit.* iii. 269.

physician and minister was Hasdai ben Isaac . . . the patron of Jewish scholars and poets. During his term of power the scholar Moses ben Enoch was appointed Rabbi of Cordova, and as a consequence Spain became the centre of Talmudic study, and Cordova the meeting-place of Jewish *savants*."[1] But things did not always go so well with the Jews even during this, generally speaking, prosperous period. The positions of authority and responsibility sometimes entailed being involved in political affairs, which, on occasion, brought disaster not only to a highly placed Jew, but also to his co-religionists. Such was, for example, the case towards the end of the eleventh and in the twelfth century during the bitter struggle between the Almoravides and Almohades in southern Spain. Under the Christian rulers in Spain the Jews again lived through very varied fortunes, at one time persecuted, at another favoured. A definite turning-point was, however, reached about the middle of the thirteenth century, under Ferdinand III., ruler of the united kingdoms of Leon and Castile, and James I., king of Aragon; owing to the power of the clergy, all Jews were forced to wear the yellow badge on their clothing. By this means the Jews were marked and differentiated from their fellow-subjects, with the inevitable result that they were regarded with suspicion and contempt. In 1250 a Bull was issued by the Pope, Innocent IV., to the effect that the Jews might not build a new synagogue without special permission; they were forbidden to make proselytes under pain of death and confiscation of property; they were not allowed to associate in any way with Christians; the latter were forbidden the use of any medicine prepared by a Jew—an exceedingly foolish provision, for the foremost physicians during the Middle Ages were Jews; the use of the yellow badge was again enjoined; no

[1] *JE* xi. 485*b*.

Jew was allowed to appear in public on Good Friday. Yet, in spite of this, there were periods during which life was quite tolerable for the Jews ; it depended mainly upon the attitude of the ruler for the time being whether they were tolerated or persecuted. But from the beginning of the fourteenth century their position became more and more precarious ; terrible massacres took place from time to time ; constant anti-Jewish enactments were put forth ; popular risings against the Jews were liable to take place at any time. By the end of the fourteenth century (the year 1391 was marked by one of the most bloody massacres) things had reached such a pitch that the ill-treatment of the Jews brought its own revenge upon the country. " The persecutions, the laws of exclusion, the humiliation inflicted upon them, and the many conversions among them had greatly injured the Jews, but with them suffered the whole kingdom of Spain. Commerce and industry were at a standstill, the soil was not cultivated, and the finances were disturbed. . . . In order to restore commerce and industry Queen Maria, consort of Alfonso V. and temporary regent, endeavoured to draw Jews to the country by offering them privileges, while she made emigration difficult by imposing taxes." [1]   And so the ups and downs went on from decade to decade, the details of which cannot be recounted here. The end came in 1492 with the edict of expulsion against the Jews issued by Ferdinand and Isabella, the Jewish population in Spain at that time being over a quarter of a million on a low estimate.

We have seen that during the long period in which the Jews lived in Spain it happened not infrequently that peaceable times of considerable duration were enjoyed, and this was especially the case up to about the twelfth century. During the eleventh and twelfth

[1] *JE* xi. p. 497*b*.

centuries Spanish Jewry had various centres of learning, from which issued scholars of great note ; indeed, all the foremost Jewish scholars of the Middle Ages came from this country: Among the large number of these, four stand pre-eminent ; of each of these a few words must be said.

The earliest is Ibn Gebirol (1021–1070). It is claimed for him that he was the first teacher of Neoplatonism in Europe, and that he exercised a considerable influence on mediæval Christian scholasticism. It is certain that he was one of the leading scholars and authorities in the Middle Ages on the philosophy of Greece, and that his learning was far more appreciated by Christian than by Jewish scholars, both during his lifetime and in succeeding ages. His most important works are the *Mekor Chayyim* ("The Fountain of Life") and his "Treatise on Ethics." In the former his main thesis is that "all that exists is constituted of matter and form ; one and the same matter runs through the whole universe from the highest limits of the spiritual down to the lowest limits of the physical, excepting that matter, the further it is removed from its first source, becomes less and less spiritual." In the latter work he attempts to show that ethics do not depend upon faith or dogma. Ibn Gebirol was also a poet of great renown ; he contributed many *piyyutim* [1] to Jewish literature ; of these the most celebrated is the *Kether Malkuth* ("The Kingly Crown") ; this has been incorporated in the Sephardic Ritual. A work of different character, but one which has enjoyed great popularity, is the *Mibchar ha-Peninim* ("The Choice of Pearls") ; this is a collection of aphorisms, reflections, and wise sayings, many of which are full of sound sense and practical value, *e.g.* : "What is a test of good manners ? Being able to bear patiently with

---

[1] Liturgical poems ; see below, pp. 272, 279–281.

bad ones." Comparatively short as his life was, Ibn Gebirol did much for his own and succeeding generations.

A contemporary of his was Judah ha-Levi (1085–1140), who likewise enjoyed with his brethren peace in the one country of Europe in which at this time the Jews were left unmolested. By profession ha-Levi was a physician, but his activity was mainly literary. Like all the great Jewish writers of these centuries, he was both an Arabic and a Greek scholar; much as he loved the ancient classics and the wisdom of the Greeks, he wrote characteristically of it that "it bears not fruit, but only blossom." Judah ha-Levi is best known as a religious poet; as such he probably stands foremost among post-Biblical Jewish writers. He was very deeply imbued with the religious spirit, and his poems breathe forth the most earnest piety. More than three hundred of his poems have been incorporated in the various forms of the Liturgy. But he was also a philosophical writer of great eminence. His chief philosophical work is the *Sepher ha-Kuzari*, written originally in Arabic, in about 1140. It is an "Apologia" of Judaism, which he vindicates in opposition to ancient philosophy, Christianity, and Mohammedanism. While not presenting a regular doctrinal system of Judaism, it deals with isolated doctrinal subjects; it is a book which has always enjoyed a great vogue in orthodox Jewish circles.

Another outstanding writer of these times was Abraham ibn Ezra (1092–1167), who wrote works on a large variety of subjects, of which the chief were his commentary on the Pentateuch, and the *Yesod Mora*, a study in religious philosophy. But the greatest of all the Jewish mediæval writers was Moses Maimonides (1135–1204), of whom the Jews say : "From Moses to Moses there hath arisen none like unto Moses." His life was a chequered one, but this is not the place for a biographical sketch,[1] as we are here concerned only with the literary activity of Maimonides. Of his many works the two outstanding ones are the *Yad ha-Chazakah* ("The Strong Hand") and the *Moreh Nebukim* ("Guide to the Perplexed"). The former, published in 1180 (its original title is *Mishneh Torah*), deals with the Jewish Law, written and oral ; the faith and practice of the Jews from the earliest times are presented, all the later authorities on the subject being taken into consideration. It is a work of immense research and industry, and has always been regarded as one of the most important Jewish literary productions. But in originality and independence of thought this work is far surpassed by the *Moreh Nebukim* ; this was originally written in Arabic ; it was published in 1191, and soon translated into Hebrew. The object of the work was to deal with the perplexities of religious belief, and in doing so Maimonides forsook all the old traditional lines of argument ; for, being steeped in the Aristotelian world-views, he sought to spiritualise the secrets of Holy Writ on the lines of Alexandrine allegorising. That his book called forth condemnation on the part of the orthodox cannot cause surprise, for, traditional Rabbinism being thus entirely set aside by Maimonides, the Rabbinical authorities of his day perceived at once the blow to orthodoxy which his views involved. Nevertheless, in spite of being condemned and publicly burned, the works of Maimonides received more and more recognition ; it is probably true that to-day no serious Jewish theologian would dispense with them. Maimonides was also a hymn-writer ; two of his hymns, *Adôn Olâm*

[1] See Geiger, *Nachgelassene Schriften*, iii. pp. 34–96, and the excellent article in *JE* by Lauterbach. See also Jost, *Geschichte des Judenthums und seiner Sekten*, ii. pp. 452 ff.; iii. 7 ff. (1857 . . .) ; and Abrahams, *Maimonides* (1903).

and *Yigdal*,[1] have been incorporated in the Jewish Liturgy.

All these writers, and many more (for we have mentioned only the most important), lived in Spain, and for the most part spent their whole lives there ; so that it is not without reason that this period is regarded as the " Golden Age " of Jewish literature. As we have already seen, Spain was for long the only country in Europe in which the Jews could live in peace. But the time came, in 1492, when they were driven even from Spain. They had been expelled from England in 1290, and in 1394 from France, where the great commentator Rashi lived during the latter part of the eleventh century. They were tolerated in parts of Germany, but this was only because they became, together with all their belongings, the absolute property of the Emperors, to be used as and when it suited them. Ultimately, however, there, too, life became unbearable for most of them, especially among the poorer classes, and they emigrated in large numbers to Poland, only a few settlements remaining in Germany. Some Italian cities (*e.g.* Rome and Venice) also permitted Jews to settle down in them ; but they were shut up in *Ghettos*.

It was not until the sixteenth and seventeenth centuries that Jewish literature began to flourish once more, especially in Holland, the foremost name being that of Spinoza, the Dutch philosopher (1632–1677). But with this later period we are not here concerned.

[1] On these see below, p. 157.

PART II
THE RABBINICAL LITERATURE

PART II

THE RABBINICAL LITERATURE

I

THE TARGUMS

[LITERATURE: Emanuel Deutsch, *Literary Remains*, pp. 319–403 (1874); Buhl, *Canon and Text of the Old Testament*, pp. 167–185 (1892); Zunz, *Die Gottesdienstlichen Vorträge der Juden*, pp. 65–86 (1892): Schürer, *GJV*, i. pp. 147–156 (1901); Dalman, *Grammatik des Jüdisch-Palästinischen Aramäisch*, pp. 11–35, with important bibliography (1905); the arts. "Targum" in Hastings' *DB* and *JE*, where a full bibliography is given. An English translation of the Targums to the Pentateuch was edited by Etheridge, *The Targums of Onkelos and Jonathan ben Uzziel on the Pentateuch, with the Fragments of the Jerusalem Targum* (1862, 1865). The Targums are printed by the side of the Hebrew text in the Rabbinical Bibles, and in Walton's Polyglot with Latin translation.]

(i) *Introductory*

SINCE the Targums are written in Aramaic, and not in the "holy tongue" of the Hebrews, a few preliminary words explaining how this came about will not be out of place.

Aramaic was the language of the Aramæans, the people who, during most of the Old Testament period, lived in the country to which the Greeks gave the name of Syria.[1] The Aramæans belonged to the Semitic race, whose primæval home was

[1] In the Septuagint the Hebrew *Aram* is always rendered *Syria*. The name *Syria* is first found in Herodotus.

Arabia;[1] they issued from here, in all probability, during the middle of the second pre-Christian millennium or thereabouts, and pushed northwards towards the Euphrates land. Shalmanassar I., king of Assyria (*circa* 1300 B.C.), refers frequently in the inscriptions of his time to the battles he was compelled to wage against the Aramæans. By this time they were constantly overrunning Mesopotamia, and when, soon after, the Assyrian empire came to an end (1275 B.C.), they succeeded in establishing themselves in the northern parts of this country; and it was not until over a century later that they were definitely driven into their natural element, the steppe. This was the work of Tiglath-Pileser I.,[2] the renewer of the ancient Assyrian empire; owing to the energy with which he combated the encroachments of the Aramæans, he succeeded in driving them off into the northern parts of what is now called Syria; at that time it formed part of the powerful empire of the Hittites. But even before the time of Shalmanassar I. it is highly probable that Aramæan invasions on a small scale had taken place not only into northern Syria, but even into Palestine. A distant echo of some contact between the Aramæans and the Israelites is to be discerned in Judg. iii. 8, where we read of the latter having been in bondage to Cushan-rishathaim, king of Aram-naharaim,[3] for eight years. This was approximately in 1200 B.C. Within a century of this time the Aramæans must, according to the *data* in the Old Testament, have been in possession of Damascus, the Hauran, and the districts east of the Jordan from the Lake of Tiberias

---

[1] This opinion regarding the origin of the Semites is now held by practically all authorities; see, *e.g.*, Paton, *Syria and Palestine*, pp. 3 ff., in "The Semitic Series" (1902).

[2] For details regarding the reign of this king, see Hommel, *Geschichte Babyloniens und Assyriens*, pp. 514 ff. (1885).

[3] *lit.* "Aram of the two rivers"; R.V. therefore renders it "Mesopotamia."

up to Mount Hermon. At any rate, by about 1000 B.C. the Aramæans[1] had become a powerful settled kingdom with Damascus as its capital. From this time onwards, *i.e.* approximately from the time of David, direct contact between them and the Israelites was frequent. This is abundantly illustrated in the pages of the Old Testament, and it continued until the final disappearance of the Aramæan (or Syrian) kingdom, towards the end of the eighth century B.C., through the conquests of the Assyrian kings.

But though the Aramæans as a nation ceased to exist, and by degrees became absorbed by other races, the results of their influence lasted on for many centuries ; this was through their language.[2] Commerce must have been the most potent cause at first of the spread of the Aramaic language among the Israelites ; to a less extent politics. But, whatever the various causes, it is quite certain that the Aramaic language came to be spoken more and more all over Palestine as time went on.[3] There was a constantly increasing tendency for it to become the common language of the ordinary people, while Hebrew was spoken by the more cultured classes and became the literary language. Added to this was the fact that from the comparatively early times of the first inroads of the Aramæans into Mesopotamia and neighbouring districts their language continued to be spoken there, with the result that during the Exile the Jews came more than ever into close touch with

[1] We are referring, of course, only to those who had by degrees worked their way northwards and westwards ; the Aramæan nation *as a whole* never formed a political unity.

[2] *cp.*, *e.g.*, Gen. xxxi. 47, where *Jegar-sahadutha* (Aramaic) and *Galeed* (Hebrew) occur side by side ; both mean " a heap of witness."

[3] "The opinion that the Palestinian Jews brought their Aramaic dialect directly from Babylon—whence the incorrect name ' Chaldee '—is untenable " (*Encycl. Bibl.* i. 282).

Aramaic. So that, even while absent from their own land, the Israelites used the same language, though a somewhat different dialect of it, to which they had been becoming more and more accustomed before the Exile.

Three main dialects of Aramaic existed from early times: Western, or Palestinian; Eastern, or Babylonian; and Mesopotamian. It is the two former which are of importance in the present connexion; for to one, or other of these belong the Aramaic portions of the Old Testament and the Targums, as well as the two Talmuds and a great deal of the Midrashic literature.[1]

As a literary language Aramaic appears for the first time, so far as we know, some time before 400 B.C.; for from Ezra iv. 8–22; v. 1–6, 12; vii. 12–26, we see that documents dealing with the history of the Second Temple were written in Aramaic; and a few short passages of the book itself are in Aramaic (iv. 23; v. 5; vii. 13–18).[2] A century or so later we have the book of Daniel, a considerable portion of which is written in Aramaic. "The employment of the two languages in these Biblical books well illustrates their use in those circles in which and for which the books were written. In point of fact, at the time of the Second Temple, both languages were in common use in Palestine: the Hebrew in the academies and in the circles of the learned, the Aramaic among the lower classes in the intercourse of daily life. But the Aramaic continued to spread, and became the customary popular idiom. . . ."[3]

Thus the knowledge and understanding of Hebrew were gradually lost by the people in general, and the

[1] The Talmuds and the Midrashic works contain a good deal of Hebrew as well as Aramaic; but it is Neo-Hebrew, not the classical Hebrew of the Old Testament.

[2] The Aramaic fragment of the Story of Aḥiḳar in the Assouan Papyri may be dated 420 B.C.

[3] *JE* ii. 69*a*. For the general use of Aramaic during the New Testament period, see Dalman, *Die Worte Jesu*, pp. 2 ff. (1898).

Scriptures, written in Hebrew, therefore threatened to become a sealed book to them. To avoid this the reading of the Scriptures in the synagogue was supplemented by translating the Hebrew into the Aramaic vernacular. This was, of course, done orally at first ; and that is the origin of the Targum.

(ii) *On the Targums generally*

The word *Targum* (the *u* is long) means "translation" or "interpretation"; the origin of the word is uncertain, but it is possible that it is related to an Arabic root used in connexion with forecasting the future, and which means "to unravel."[1] From it comes the word *Methurgeman*[2] (pass. part. form), which occurs in Ezra iv. 7 : ". . . and the writing of the letter was written in Aramaic and *translated* into Aramaic."[3] In Neh. viii. 8 we get what appears to be the earliest reference to the way in which the Targums first came into use : "And they read in the book, in the law of God, distinctly [or 'with an interpretation']; and they gave the sense, so that they understood the reading." Uncertain as the meaning of this text is,[4] there is no doubt that the Rabbis understood it in reference to the Targum.[5] Deutsch, in this connexion, appropriately quotes *Sanhedrin* 21*b* (Bab. Talmud)[6] : "Originally the Law was given to Israel in Ibri (Hebrew) writing and the holy language. It was again given to them in the days of Ezra in the Ashuri (Syrian) writing and the Aramaic language."

[1] Wellhausen, *Reste Arabischen Heidentums*, p. 207 (1897).

[2] The word "Dragoman" is a corruption of this.

[3] The text is obviously corrupt, but that does not affect the present point.

[4] See Batten, *Ezra and Nehemiah* (Intern. Crit. Com.), pp. 356 ff. (1913).

[5] Babylonian Talmud, *Megilla* 3*a*.

[6] *Literary Remains*, p. 321 (1874).

There can be little doubt that in its beginnings the Targum belongs to the time of the Second Temple, and, as already pointed out, it was originally delivered orally. The prohibition to commit the Targum to writing was due to the fear lest what was written down should come to be regarded as of canonical authority ; the *written* word and a *written* interpretation of it might, so it was. thought, easily involve the danger of each coming to be regarded as equally authoritative. For centuries, therefore, the explanation of the Scriptures in the Aramaic vernacular was handed down by word of mouth. But there is distinct evidence that by the beginning of the Christian era written Targums were in existence. Zunz goes so far as to say that "written Aramaic translations of most of the Biblical books certainly existed as early as the times of the Hasmonæans."[1] At any rate, it is reliably related of Gamaliel I.[2] that he caused a Targum on the book of Job to be walled up within the Temple.[3] There would doubtless have been other Targums extant before this, as the book of Job would certainly not have been the first to have been translated ; indeed, we know that this was the case, for the Targum of Onkelos (see below) to the Pentateuch belongs to the very beginning of the Christian era,[4] though in its permanent written form it belongs to a somewhat later date, in all probability. In the Mishnah (*Yadayim* iv. 5), which was redacted by Jehudah ha-Nasi at the end of the second or beginning of the third century A.D., rules regarding the manner of writing the Targums are given ; the practice must, therefore, have been in vogue long before this.

[1] *Die gottesdienstlichen Vorträge der Juden,* p. 65 (1892).
[2] He flourished at the beginning of the Christian era ; see Acts v. 34, 39.
[3] Bab. Talm. *Sabbath* 115*a* (Dalman, *op. cit.* p. 2).
[4] *cp.* Zunz, *op. cit.* p. 66.

The Targums, especially those which are more pronouncedly paraphrastic, come under the comprehensive term of Rabbinical literature, for, though the Rabbinical literature proper belongs to a rather later date, the Targums exhibit the traditional Rabbinical conception of the written text of the Scriptures, and especially of the Pentateuch. The Targums were used primarily for Biblical instruction, but they also had their place in the synagogal Liturgy. There were special rules which guided the reading of the Targum in the synagogue, and these varied according to the importance of the Targum which was being read. These rules are given in the Mishnah, *Megilla* iv. 4, where it says: "He who reads the Torah may not read less than three verses (at a time); but to a Methurgeman [1] not more than one verse may be read (at a time). But when the prophetical sections (are read) three (verses may be read at a time)." This means that in the ordinary reading of the Pentateuch not less than three verses should be read at a time; but when it is officially read in the synagogue, where it has to be translated into Aramaic for the congregation to understand, then only one verse is read at a time in the original and immediately translated. In the case of the prophetical books the translation is given after every three verses, these books not being so important as the Pentateuch (Torah). The reading of the Hebrew was never done by the Methurgeman; in the case of the Pentateuch there had to be one reader and one interpreter; in the case of the Prophetical books one reader, but there might be more than one interpreter.

By a strange irony of fate, it was the written Targum which became the cause of abolishing the use of the Targums in the synagogue. It was ignorance of Hebrew which called the Targum into

---

[1] The Hebrew was read to the Methurgeman, the official translator, and rendered by him in Aramaic to the people.

existence ; but Aramaic, in course of time, shared the same fate as Hebrew and was as little understood. Even where Aramaic continued to be the spoken language it altered its character, so that the Aramaic of the Targums, having become archaic, was no more understood. Among the Jews of the Diaspora, who did not know any Aramaic at all, it was, of course, worse. The rise of Islam tended to make Arabic the language of the Jews in the Oriental lands. In Babylon, however, the stronghold of Judaism for many centuries after the destruction of the Jewish state, the ancient Targum was used in the synagogue, in spite of its not being understood, up to about A.D. 1000 ; then it was given up, as had been the case for long previously among the Jews elsewhere. Among the Jews in Europe the Targums have never been in use in the synagogue ; [1] in spite of the desire, which existed for centuries, that after the reading of the Law it should be translated into the vernacular, this was not actually carried out until 1845, and then only in America and Germany.

(iii) *The Doctrinal Teaching of the Targums*

The doctrine of God in the Targums is based upon that of the Old Testament ; but there is this difference, that in the Targums a very pronounced transcendentalism is taught ; so much so that the thought of the divine working in the hearts of men directly seems to be almost entirely eliminated. Moreover, this one-sided doctrine of God is in so far antagonistic to the Old Testament teaching in that it altogether does away with the belief in God as the God of history ; for the divine transcendence as taught in the

[1] An exception to this was the reading of the Targum (which nobody understood) on the seventh day of Passover, and during the Feast of Weeks, in France and Germany (Elbogen, *Der jüdische Gottesdienst in seiner geschichtlichen Entwickelung*, p. 191).

Targums is such that God is represented as One
who is too holy and of necessity too separate from
human affairs to take any interest in man and his
doings. In accordance with this teaching the
Targums avoid everything that appears to savour
of anthropomorphism and implies any direct personal communion between God and man; the effort
is, therefore, made, for example, to soften down or
explain away everything that in the Old Testament
is represented as a likeness between God and man.
An interesting illustration, and one of the most
pointed which could be given, is the paraphrase in
the Targums of the words: "Let us make man in
our image, after our likeness" (Gen. i. 26). In the
earliest Targum, that of Onkelos,[1] the softening-down
process is not so marked as in the later Palestinian
Targum;[1] nevertheless, the tendency referred to is
quite distinct, for it is implied that the "image" and
"likeness" are between man and the angels rather
than God Himself. But in the Palestinian Targum
the paraphrase runs: "In the likeness of the presence
of the Lord created He them"; the likeness, that is to
say, is represented as being not to the Lord Himself,
but to the divine presence which, as it were, comes
between God and man. Interesting, too, is the way
in which the anthropomorphisms of the Old Testament are avoided, though here again this is more
characteristic of the Palestinian Targum than that of
Onkelos. For example, in Gen. xviii. 8 it is said:
"And he (Abraham) stood by them under the tree,
and they did eat"; in the Targum of Onkelos this is
given verbally, but the Palestinian Targum para-
phrases: "And he served before them, and they sat
under the tree; and he quieted himself (to see) whether
they would eat"; the direct assertion of their eating
is avoided. But both Targums constantly paraphrase

[1] On these see the next section. The tendency referred to is
more marked in the Palestinian Targum throughout.

anthropomorphisms by the expression "He manifested Himself," or something like it, *e.g.* Gen. iii. 5 ; Ex. iii. 8 ; xi. 4, etc. Examples could be given to any extent, but one more must suffice : Gen. xxxii. 28 runs : "Thy name shall be called no more Jacob, but Israel ; for thou hast striven with God and with men, and hast prevailed." For this the Targum of Onkelos has : "Thy name shall no more be Jacob, but Israel ; for a prince art thou before the Lord, and with men hast thou prevailed."[1] In the Palestinian Targum the elimination of the anthropomorphisms is even more pronounced ; there it says simply : "And an angel contended with him in the likeness of a man " ; a few verses further on the angel is spoken of as Michael.

Closely connected with what has been said is the doctrine of the *Memra* (the Word of God) in the Targums. The central point here is that the *Memra* takes up an intermediate position between God and men, thus making the divine relationship with man indirect. For example, in Gen. ix. 12, 13, it is said : " And God said, This is the token of the covenant which I make between Me and you and every living creature that is with you, for perpetual generations : I do set My bow in the cloud, and it shall be for a token of a covenant between Me and the earth " ; for this the Targum of Onkelos (the Palestinian Targum is practically the same [2]) has : " And the Lord said, This is the token of the covenant which I make between My Word and you and every living creature that is with you, for perpetual generations : I do set My bow

---

[1] It is, however, interesting to note that this rendering comes close to that of the Septuagint and the Vulgate : " . . . thou hast had power with God, and thou shalt prevail against men."

[2] In the Targum of Onkelos the term *Memra* is invariably used for the "Word," while in the Palestinian and so-called "Fragment" Targums (on this latter see the next section) the term *Dibbura* is also frequently used ; both terms come from roots meaning " to speak."

in the cloud, and it shall be for a token of a covenant between My Word and the earth." It may be regarded as a general rule that in the Targums *Memra* is used whenever it is desired to avoid the idea of a *direct* relationship between God and man. Another way of emphasising the divine transcendence in the Targums is by making the *Shekinah* (*i.e.* the visible glory which indicates the divine indwelling) take the place of God Himself; thus while in Gen. xviii. 33 it is said : "And the Lord went His way, as soon as He had left communing with Abraham," in the Targum of Onkelos this is paraphrased by the words : "And the glory (*Shekinah*) of the Lord ascended when it had ceased speaking with Abraham"; the Palestinian Targum is identical with this.[1]

One other point of special doctrinal interest is the teaching of the Targums concerning the Messiah. Here the fact of main importance is the stress laid upon the kingship of the Messiah ; indeed, in the Targums He is almost always spoken of as "King Messiah," or else this is implied, as, *e.g.*, in the Targum of Onkelos to Gen. xlix. 10, which reads : "He that exerciseth dominion shall not pass away from the house of Judah, nor the sceptre from his children's children for ever, until the Messiah come, whose is the kingdom and whom the nations shall obey." In the Palestinian Targum the expression "King Messiah" is used, and the following comment is there added : "How beauteous is King Messiah, who will arise from the house of Judah ! He hath girded His loins and hath descended, and hath set in array the battle against His adversaries. . . ." The Targums offer much that is of great interest on the subject of the Messiah, of which the following are examples ; they are taken from the so-called Targum of Jonathan

[1] For further details regarding these intermediate agencies between God and men, see Oesterley and Box, *The Religion and Worship of the Synagogue*, pp. 195–221 (1911).

(see next section) to the Prophets: in reference to Is. x. 17 this Targum says that at the coming of the Messiah He will annihilate the Gentiles. The paraphrase of Micah iv. 8 runs: " But Thou, Messiah of Israel, who hast been hidden because of the sins of Israel, Thine shall be the kingdom." In the paraphrase of Zech. iv. 7 the same Targum says : " And he will reveal the Messiah, whose name hath been uttered from all time, and He shall rule over all kingdoms."

Some general ideas regarding the Targums and their doctrinal tendencies will now have been gained. It remains to enumerate the various Targums at present extant, and to give a brief account of them.

(iv) *A Short Account of the Different Targums*

There exist Targums to the Pentateuch, to the Prophetical books, and to the Hagiographa, of which the third category is the least important, while the other two are of great importance for the study of Jewish exegesis and doctrine as well as for the light they throw on much that is concerned with Christian origins.

The Targum of Onkelos.[1] There are various references in the Talmud to Onkelos, and they are of a somewhat confusing character. What may, however, be regarded as certain is that he was a proselyte to Judaism, and that he lived about the middle of the first Christian century. His translation of the Pentateuch into the Aramaic vernacular was, therefore, undertaken in all probability during the lifetime of Christ, certainly not long after. Most authorities are agreed that the Targum of Onkelos originally came from Palestine, but, owing to the many marks of Babylonian influence which it contains in its present form, it is evident that it was at some time or other re-edited in Babylon, which became the centre of

[1] Best edition, *Targum Onkelos*, ed. Berliner (Berlin, 1884).

Jewry soon after the break-up of the Jewish state.
For this reason this Targum is often spoken of as the
Babylonian Targum (*Targum Babli*). Of all the
Targums this is the most literal in its translation, and
therefore the least paraphrastic. The deviations from
this literalness are most marked in poetical passages,
e.g. Gen. xlix.; Num. xxiv.; Deut. xxxii., xxxiii.;
thus in the Old Testament Num. xxiv. 7 runs:
" Water shall flow from his buckets, and his seed shall
be in many waters"; this is interpreted in the
Targum in the following way: " The king anointed
from his sons shall increase, and have dominion over
many nations." Smaller variations from the Old
Testament occur frequently, and there are not a few
discrepancies and fanciful interpretations and render-
ings; but in spite of these this Targum, in the words
of Deutsch, " never for one moment forgets its aim of
being· a clear, though free, translation *for the people*,
and nothing more." He goes on to say that " wherever it deviates from the literalness of the text, such
a course, in its case, is fully justified—nay, necessitated
—either by the obscurity of the passage, or the wrong
construction that naturally would be put upon its
wording by the multitude. The explanations given
agree either with the real sense or develop the current
tradition supposed to underlie it." [1]

The language of the Targum of Onkelos is in
the main Eastern Aramaic, though the Palestinian
dialect is very often to be discerned.[2] What has been
said above as to the avoidance of anthropomorphisms
in all the Targums applies, of course, here. This
Targum became greatly venerated from early times,
and manuscripts of it exist in great numbers. Its
popularity is seen from the fact that men were urged
to read it every Sabbath in their homes. There can,
moreover, be no sort of doubt that it has exercised a
great influence upon Jewish exegesis. A Jewish sage,

[1] *op. cit.* p. 355.   [2] See Dalman, *op. cit.* p. 67.

E 2

Sar Shalom, writing in the ninth century about the Targum of Onkelos, says : " The Targum of which the sages spoke is the one which we now have in our hands ; no sanctity attaches to the other Targumim. We have heard it reported as the tradition of ancient sages that God wrought a great thing [miracle] for Onkelos when He permitted him to compose the Targum." [1] The great twelfth-century Jewish teacher, Maimonides, also refers to this Targum as of high importance, the composer being described as "the bearer of ancient exegetic traditions, and as a thorough master of Hebrew and Aramaic." [2]

The Palestinian Targum. This, too, is a paraphrase of the Pentateuch only. In Jewish literature it is usually referred to as the Jerusalem Targum (*Targum Jerushalmi*). Formerly it was known as the " Targum of Jonathan ben Uzziel on the Pentateuch," but this was owing to a misunderstanding of the abbreviated form—" Targum J "—by which it was known ; the " J " was thought to stand for Jonathan, who was the author of the Targum to the Prophets (or believed to have been), while as a matter of fact it represented " Jerushalmi." It is, therefore, now sometimes spoken of as the " Targum of pseudo-Jonathan." As will have been noticed in the few quotations given in Section iii., this Targum is far more paraphrastic than that of Onkelos ; it is therein that the main difference between the two chiefly consists. As a further illustration of this, one example may be added here from Gen. iv. 8 (Targum Onkelos is practically identical with the Old Testament), viz. : "And Cain spake with Abel his brother ; [3] and it came to pass while they were in

---

[1] Quoted in *JE* xii. 59*a*.   [2] *Ibid.*

[3] It is worth noting that the literalness of the translation here is such that the corruption of the Hebrew text is followed. The Septuagint and other ancient authorities read : " And Cain said unto his brother Abel, Let us go into the field." (*cp.* the

the field that Cain rose up against Abel his brother,
and slew him." In the Palestinian Targum we have
a great expansion giving the details of the conversation between the brothers: "And Cain said unto
Abel his brother, Come and let us two go forth into
the field. And it came to pass when they two had
gone forth into the field, that Cain answered and
said unto Abel, I perceive that the world was created
in goodness, but it is not governed according to the
fruit of good works, for there is respect of persons in
judgement; therefore it is that thy offering hath
been accepted, and mine not accepted with good
will. Abel answered and said unto Cain, In goodness was the world created, and according to the
fruit of good works is it governed; and there is no
respect of persons in judgement; but because the
fruits of my works were better than thine, my
oblation hath been accepted with good will before
thine. Cain answered and said unto Abel, There is
neither judgement, nor judge, nor another world; nor
will good reward be given to the righteous, nor
vengeance be taken on the wicked. And Abel
answered and said unto Cain, There is a judgement,
and there is a judge, and there is another world; and
a good reward is given to the righteous, and vengeance is taken on the wicked. And because of
these words they had contention there in the field.
And Cain rose up against Abel his brother, and
drave a stone into his forehead, and slew him."

As to the date of this Targum there are some
clear indications; its comparatively late date is
shown, _e.g._, by the mention of Constantinople in
Num. xxiv. 19, 24; but more important is that in
Gen. xxi. 21. Mohammed's daughters Hadidiah and
Fatima are mentioned, showing that the date must
be later than the time of Mohammed; it cannot well

Palestinian Targum given below.) It is quite obvious that
something has fallen out of the Hebrew text.

have reached its final form before the middle of the seventh century. Its language differs from that of Targum Onkelos with its approximation to Biblical Aramaic, the Palestinian Targum being written in the idiom of the common people of Palestine. In spite of its late date, this Targum is valuable on account of the considerable quantity of ancient material embodied in it; "it is one of those late compilations in which the more ancient and the later tradition is stored; it forms, when used with critical caution, a very abundant source for the presentation of the religious conceptions of old Palestinian Judaism."[1]

The "Fragment" Targum. This work, which also deals with the Pentateuch, is closely connected with the foregoing; it has received its name in modern times, as it consists of isolated pieces. It represents, in all probability, a kind of preparatory work for the developed Palestinian Targum, but it often differs considerably from this. The two are of different authorship, but of the authors nothing is known. A striking characteristic of both is the developed angelology they exhibit.

The Targum of Jonathan ben Uzziel. This is a paraphrase of the Prophetical books; but it must be remembered that among these are included what are called the "former prophets," *i.e.* the books of Joshua, Judges, 1 and 2 Samuel, 1 and 2 Kings, and the "latter prophets," *i.e.* the books of Isaiah, Jeremiah, Ezekiel, and the Minor Prophets. This Targum as we have it now belongs possibly to the third century A.D.; some scholars place it a century later. That it is subsequent in date to the Targum Onkelos is evident, since various passages are quoted *verbatim* from it.[2] Jonathan ben Uzziel[3] was a pupil of the

---

[1] Weber, *Juedische Theologie*, p. xxi. (1897).
[2] Zunz, *op. cit.* p. 67, note.
[3] He was such an ardent student of the Law that the Talmud

celebrated Hillel; his name is attached to this Targum because there are good grounds for believing that he was the original author who laid the foundation upon which this Targum in later years was built up.[1] This is also borne out by the language, which is Eastern Aramaic, showing that in its present redacted form it belongs to Babylon, not Palestine, Jonathan's home. This Targum differs greatly from that of Onkelos both in its theological standpoint and in its free paraphrase; in fact, it is rather a Haggadic commentary than a Targum, and contains an immense amount that is of interest from the point of view of folk-lore. Deutsch goes so far as to say that "the Semitic fairy and legendary lore which for the last two thousand years—as far as we can trace it—has grown up in East and West to vast glittering mountain-ranges is to a very great extent to be found, in embryo state, so to say, in this our Targum."[2] Somewhat of an exaggeration as this is, there is no sort of doubt that it is largely true; the tales of wonder which it contains, and the activities of angels of which it tells,[3] certainly seem in numerous cases to be the basis of many of our fairy stories.

The Targums to the Hagiographa. There are three classes of these: first, the *Targums on the Psalms, the Proverbs, and Job.* These all belong approximately to the same period, viz. the seventh or eighth century A.D., and from their similar style would

(*Baba Bathra* 134a, *Sukka* 28a) relates of him that "when he sat studying the Torah, every bird that flew over his head was burned," the reason being that many angels gathered around him in order to hear the words of the Law which proceeded from his mouth (Weber, *op. cit.* p. xx).

[1] For details see Deutsch, *op. cit.* pp. 364 ff.

[2] *op. cit.* p. 374.

[3] The idea, *e.g.*, of Elijah hearing the voices of angels singing in silence (paraphrase to 1 Kings xix. 11–13) is interesting.

appear to have come from the hand of one author. They are all believed to have originated in Syria. The Targums to the Psalms and Proverbs have not much that is paraphrastic; they are mainly translations, and not of much value. That on Job is more interesting, and contains much Haggadic material. We have already referred to the existence of a Targum on Job in much earlier times; what relation there is between these, if any, it is, of course, impossible to say now.

The Targums to the Song of Songs, Ruth, Lamentations, Esther, and Ecclesiastes belong to another class, for they can scarcely be called Targums in the ordinary sense; they are picturesque commentaries, the commentary having often little or nothing to do with the text. An excellent English translation of the Targum to the Song of Songs has been edited by Prof. H. Gollancz (1908), and it gives one an intimate idea of this class of Targum; it contains much of great interest.

Lastly, there are the *Targums to Daniel, 1 and 2 Chronicles, and Ezra;* these, too, are comparatively late in date; they are of minor importance.

The great value of the Targums, though this applies mainly to those on the Pentateuch and the Prophetical books, is that they constitute a most important source for the early phases of Judaism before it became stereotyped and hardened into Rabbinical Judaism proper. They are, therefore, exceedingly interesting, and also important, for the study of the New Testament, and not infrequently throw light on this. For the history of Jewish exegesis they are, of course, invaluable.

II

THE MIDRASHIM

[LITERATURE (selected): Hoffmann, *Zur Einleitung in die Halachischen Midraschim* (1886); Zunz, *Die gottesdienstlichen Vorträge der Juden, passim*, especially pp. 37–61, 87–102, 195–283 (1892); Weber, *Juedische Theologie . . .*, pp. xxiv–xxx (1897); Bacher, *Die aelteste Terminologie der jüdischen Schriftauslegung* (1899); Schürer, *GJV*, i. pp. 138–146, ii. pp. 392–414, where a full bibliography will be found (1901); Oesterley and Box, *The Religion and Worship of the Synagogue*, pp. 77–100 (1911); Theodor's art. in *JE* viii. 548–580.]

(i) *Introductory*

The word *Midrash* (plur. *Midrashim*) is a Biblical one, though, it is true, it occurs but twice in the Bible, viz. 2 Chron. xiii. 22; xxiv. 27. It comes from a root (*darash*) meaning, in the first instance, " to resort to," " to seek out," which occurs frequently in the Hebrew Bible, *e.g.* Deut. xii. 5: *But unto the place which the Lord your God shall choose out of all your tribes to put His name there, even unto His habitation* (*i.e.* the place where He dwells) *shall ye seek (darash), and thither shalt thou come.* Later this root came to be used of searching out, or studying, the Law, *e.g.* Ezra vii. 12: *Ezra had set his heart to seek (darash) the Law of the Lord* When the Neo-Hebraic word *Midrash* was formed it meant the searching out, or investigating, of a book with a view to its interpretation; then, by a very natural development, the word was applied to the result of such investigation.[1] In

[1] In speaking of the variety of meanings attaching to different Hebrew technical terms Deutsch says : " Thus Midrash, from the abstract 'expounding,' came to be applied, first to the 'exposition' itself—even as our terms 'work,' 'investigation,' 'inquiry,' imply both process and product ; and finally, as a special branch of exposition—the legendary—was more popular than the rest, to this one branch only and to the books that chiefly represented it " (*Literary Remains*, p. 13 [1874]). We

the Targums and in the Talmud the root means "to examine," then "to expound," or "to interpret," and finally "to teach" and "to lecture" on, the Law and on the Old Testament generally. There is also the technical word *darshan*, from the same root, which means an "interpreter" of, or "lecturer" on, the Law.

This searching out of the Law was undertaken with the object of discovering hidden meanings, or such as could be derived by implication, a very different thing from the primary and obvious sense of a passage which could be readily understood by the simple. "In contradistinction to literal interpretation, subsequently called *peshaṭ*,[1] the term *Midrash* designates an exegesis which, going more deeply than the mere literal sense, attempts to penetrate into the spirit of the Scriptures, to examine the text from all sides, and thereby to derive interpretations which are not immediately obvious."[2]

The earliest evidence that we have of this deeper searching of the Scriptures is contained in Neh. viii. 2–8, where it is told how Ezra the Scribe, together with a number of other Scribes[3] who are mentioned by name, "caused the people to understand the Law; and the people stood in their place. And they (*i.e.* the Scribes) read in the book, in the Law of God, distinctly (R.V. marg. 'with an interpretation'), so that they (*i.e.* the people) understood the reading." The passage is obscure and the text is certainly not in order, but it is clear that the "interpretation" gave the people something more than the literal, primary meaning which could be easily grasped. We are,

shall come to deal presently with this one branch and the books represented by it.

[1] *i.e.* "simple"; *cp.* the word *Peshitta*, the Syriac equivalent to the Latin "Vulgate." [2] *JE* viii. 548*b*.

[3] They are called Levites in the text, but their procedure shows that they were *Sopherim*, or Scribes, as well. The earlier *Sopherim* (from Ezra to Simon the Just) were all members of the Levitical priesthood.

therefore, justified in regarding this passage as referring to the subject under discussion, and as seeing in it the earliest reference to *Midrash* in its abstract sense. The explanations and comments which these *Sopherim* gave were not written down, but were transmitted by word of mouth from teacher to pupil. But there was another type of *Midrash* which *was* written down in, comparatively speaking, very early times. This is proved by a reference to 2 Chron. xiii. 22 ; xxiv. 27 ; in the former of these passages the Chronicler speaks of a "commentary of the prophet Iddo"; in the latter he refers to the "commentary of the book of Kings." In both cases the Hebrew word for "commentary" is *Midrash*. So that at least as early as the middle of the third century B.C.[1] we find the Chronicler utilising written historical Midrashic works as sources for his history. Their historical value was almost certainly insignificant, but that is immaterial from our present point of view ; the important thing is that these *Midrashim* were already in existence as written documents in the third century B.C., and were regarded as sufficiently authoritative to be consulted in compiling a history of the nation. The character of these written *Midrashim* can, to some extent, be gathered by comparing the books of Samuel and Kings with Chronicles ; for this latter itself partakes of the nature of a *Midrash* (in certain passages) on the former ; instructive examples of this are : 1 Chron. xv. 1–xvi. 43 compared with 2 Sam. vi. 12–20 ; 1 Chron. xxii. 2–19 with 2 Sam. vii. 1–3, 13 ; 2 Chron. iii. 1–v. 1 with 1 Kings viii. ; 2 Chron. xii. 1–16 with 1 Kings xiv. 21 ff. ; 2 Chron. xiv. 9–15 with 1 Kings xv. 23 ; and many others.[2]

[1] Most modern authorities are agreed that the books of the Chronicles were compiled about 250 B.C. or slightly earlier.
[2] A more developed form of this type of *Midrash* can be seen, *e.g.*, by comparing the book of Jubilees with Genesis, or the additions to Esther with the canonical book of Esther.

In quite early times, therefore, we meet with two types of *Midrash* ; Neh. viii. 2–8 refers to interpretations of the Law given by the *Sopherim*, and the two passages 2 Chron. xiii. 22 ; xxiv. 27 refer to written historical *Midrashim*. In one case explanation of the Law, in the other narrative expansion, form the content of the Midrashic comment. In each it is a case of searching with the object of interpreting ; in the former the interpretation of the Law is meant to give guidance, in the latter the narrative is intended for edification. As these two elements give the keynotes to the entire body of Midrashic works which subsequently came into being, it will be well to say a word about them before speaking of these Midrashic works themselves.

(ii) *Midrash Halakah and Midrash Haggadah*

The vast Midrashic literature may broadly be divided into two main classes : the *Halakic* (*Midrash Halakah*) and the *Haggadistic* (*Midrash Haggadah*). The earliest written *Midrashim* which have been handed down, the *Mekilta*, *Sifra*, and *Sifre*, which in their oldest elements go back to the second century A.D., exhibit a mixed character containing Haggadah interspersed with Halakah. But they may be regarded as predominantly Halakic. The great mass of the Midrashic literature, apart from these examples, is essentially Haggadistic in character. The term *Halakah* (="rule," "binding law") is applied to the traditionally received rules of practice which were of a binding or legal character. This legal element in the Oral Law, together with the Rabbinical discussions and decisions which depend upon it, are embodied in the Mishnah, the Talmuds, and the compendiums of Rabbinical Law based upon the latter. The method of the Talmud is to group and classify the various Halakoth, and to comment on them, tradition by tradition, giving the Scriptural proofs for each, and otherwise elucidating them. On the other hand, the Halakic *Midrashim* are cast in the form of exegetical commentaries on particular books of the Bible, viz. part of Exodus, Leviticus, Numbers, and Deuteronomy. The Scriptural text determines the order of the exposition, and the various Halakoth dealing with the traditionally received rules of life and ritual are deduced from the Biblical text directly. The resultant *Midrashim* may be regarded as due to an attempt on the part of the teachers of the Law to justify in a popular way the Halakah against the objection of the Sadducees.

Of course, there is a large amount of Haggadistic material scattered about the pages of the Talmud, and this has been worked up in separate form and embodied for the most part in the Haggadic *Midrash.* It should be noted that the term *Midrash Halakah* is applied not merely to the verification of currently received practice from the text of Scripture, but also to the development of new Halakoth and legal enactments from the Biblical text.

An example of the method employed will serve to illustrate what has just been said. Thus, with reference to the verse (Ex. xii. 4) : *And if the household be too little for a lamb, then shall he and his neighbour next unto his house take one according to the number of the souls.* The *Midrash Mekilta, ad. loc.,* comments as follows . "*According to the number* (מכסת) *of the souls.* The word מכסת is to be understood only as (meaning) *number,* viz. that one must slaughter it (the lamb) according to the number (of persons) assigned to it. But if one have slaughtered it not for the number (of persons) assigned to it, one has transgressed a commandment." In other words, the Passover lamb cannot be legally slaughtered till the slaughterer is aware of the number of persons who are going to partake of it. This example is taken from the older and simpler Halakah, based upon a simple and direct exegesis. The later Halakah is more complicated and artificial in its methods.[1] Though the

---

[1] For details see the article "*Midrash Halakah*" in the *Jewish Encycl.* viii. 571.

line between independent collections of Halakoth as contained in the Mishnah and Tosefta and the Halakic *Midrashim* is not always sharply drawn (*e.g.* many sections in the Mishnah and Tosefta are Midrashic Halakoth,[1] and on the other hand the Halakic *Midrashim* sometimes contain independent Halakoth, without reference to the Scriptural text in support [2]), yet on the whole the broad distinction remains that the Halakic *Midrashim* are in form exegetical, following the text of certain books of Scripture. The occasional confusion between the two forms is explained by the fact that the redactors of the two kinds of collections borrowed from each other.

The term *Haggadah* means primarily "narration," "telling," and in its original application as a technical term connoted the recitation or teaching of Scripture; *cf.* the formula, frequently found in ancient Rabbinical literature, מַגִּיד הַכָּתוּב, "the Scripture teaches." Thus *Haggadah* probably had at first a general application, "but at an early date was restricted to denote a non-Halakic explanation." It thus came to mean the exegesis of Scripture, not included in the Halakic, *of a freer and more edifying tendency*, with stories and illustrative matter, drawn from popular custom, tales, and beliefs. In the *Midrash Haggadah* it expressed itself in a rich development, first in the form of homiletic commentary on Biblical books, and then independently as finished homily or popular discourse, not primarily exegetical in character. The popular preacher who delivered homiletic discourses in the synagogue of a Haggadic character was termed *Maggid, i.e.* "expounder of *Haggadah*." The characteristic features of this kind of oratory have been well summed up by Zunz: "The Haggadah, which is intended to bring heaven down to the congregation, and also to lift man up to heaven, appears in this office both as the glorification of God and the comfort of Israel. Hence religious truths, maxims, discussions con-

---

[1] *e.g.* Berakoth i. 3, 5.
[2] *e.g. Sifra Wayyiḳra Hobah* i. 9–13 (ed. Weiss, p. 16 *a*, *b*).

cerning divine retribution, the inculcation of the laws
which attest Israel's nationality, descriptions of the
past and future greatness, scenes and legends from
Jewish history, comparisons between the divine and
Jewish institutions, praises of the Holy Land, encou-
raging stories and comforting reflections of all kinds,
form the most important subjects of these discourses." [1]
The Haggadic literature thus reflects the highest and
deepest thoughts of the Jewish teachers on religion
and ethics embodied in popular form. Its aim was
to work upon the mind, conscience, and heart of the
Israelite in such a way as to inspire a passion for
religion ; and it sought to do this by using the past
and present experiences of the race as symbols and
illustrations designed to justify the ways of God to
man, and to kindle enthusiasm and devotion for the
ideals of Israel's religion, and a passionate belief in
Israel's vocation and destiny.

The literature in which the Haggadah is embodied,
i.e. the Haggadic Midrashic literature, is of vast
extent, and its production in literary form covers a
considerable period of time. It may be said to have
flourished from the second to the tenth centuries A.D.
But the beginnings of the Haggadah go back to a
much earlier period. Much material of this kind is
contained in the Apocryphal and Pseudepigraphical
literature, and it can be traced in the works of
Josephus and Philo. Its richest period of development may be placed in the period when the Mishnaic
and Talmudic literature grew up, *i.e.* between A.D. 100
and 500. The compilations which were produced
subsequently were largely in the nature of a reshaping of material already in existence (the epoch
of the revisers and collectors).

For a time (during the third and at the beginning
of the fourth century A.D.) " the masters of Halakah
were also the representatives of the Haggadah : but

[1] Cited *op. cit. ibid.*

side by side with them appeared the Haggadists proper (בעלי אגדה), who subsequently became more and more prominent, attracting with their discourses more hearers than the Halakists. The highest product of the Haggadah, the public discourse drawing upon all the arts of Midrashic rhetoric—sentence, proverb, parable, allegory, story, etc.—now received its final form."[1] Examples of the latter, furnished with proems and properly constructed, can be seen best in the *Pesikta* homilies (*Pesikta de Rab Kahana* and *Pesikta Rabbati*) and in the *Tanchuma* collection (for details of these works, see below).

(iii) *A Short Account of the Different Midrashic Works*

We can now proceed to enumerate the more important Midrashic works, and to give a short account of them. In his articles on the *Midrashim* in the *Jewish Encyclopædia* Theodor classifies the whole body of these writings in the following way:

A. Midrash Haggadah: *Mekilta; Sifra; Sifre* to Numbers; *Sifre* to Deuteronomy.

B. The earliest exegetical Midrashim: *Bereshith Rabbah; Ekah Rabbati.*

The homiletic Midrashim: *Pesikta; Wayyikra Rabbah; Tanchuma Yelammedenu; Pesikta Rabbati; Debarim Rabbah; Bemidbar Rabbah; Shemoth Rabbah; Aggadath Bereshith; We-Hizhir (Hashkem).*

The later exegetical Midrashim: *Shir ha-Shirim Rabbati; Midrash Ruth; Midrash Koheleth; Midrash Megillath Esther.*

The other exegetical Midrashim not dealing with the Pentateuch: *Midrash Shemuel; Midrash Mishle; Midrash Tehillim; Midrash Yeshayah; Midrash Yonah; Midrash Iyyob.*

[1] *op. cit. ibid.*

Special Haggadic Midrashim: *Pirke de Rabbi Eliezer ; Seder Elijahu ; Yalkut Shimeoni ; Yalkut ha-Makir ; Midrash ha-Gadol.*
A number of other small and unimportant Midrashic writings are enumerated ; but they do not call for notice here.

This scientific classification will be found valuable for reference. For readers, however, who are entirely unfamiliar with this class of literature it will probably be found useful if, in giving a short account of the different works, we enumerate them under the English names, and in the usual order, of the Biblical books with which they deal. In most cases a *Midrash* deals with one specific Biblical book ; but some of them include comments, etc., on two or more books. We will deal with the former first as being, generally speaking, though not always, older and more important.

A. GENESIS. Quite one of the most important of all the Midrashic writings is that called *Bereshith Rabbah,*[1] the great *Midrash* on Genesis. It is valuable on account both of its age and of its contents. It belongs approximately to the sixth century A.D., but contains materials of much earlier date. Indications pointing to its date are the following : Authoritative Babylonian teachers are cited who lived during the latter years of the third century A.D. Further, not only does it contain a story about the Emperor Diocletian,[2] but Rabbis who lived

---

[1] *Bereshith* (= " In the beginning ") is the Hebrew name of the book of Genesis. *Rabbah* (= " great ") is added as this *Midrash* belongs to the great collection of *Midrashim,* called " Midrash Rabbah," which comprises *Midrashim* on each of the books of the Pentateuch and on each of the five " Scrolls," as they are called, viz. Canticles, Ruth, Lamentations, Ecclesiastes, Esther. Best text, the critical edition issued in parts and edited by J. Theodor (Berlin), not yet complete.

[2] In § 63 it is said that in his earlier years he lived as a swineherd in Tiberias.

F

during his reign, and earlier, are frequently mentioned by name. Again, a list of a succession of seven Rabbis is enumerated, beginning with Rabbi Akiba (he lived at the beginning of the second century A.D.) and Rabbi Jehudah ha-Nasi (second half of the second century A.D.), of each of whom it is said that at the death of his predecessor a sun went down and a sun rose ; the meaning is that when God permits the sun of a righteous man to set (*i.e.* when he dies) He permits the sun of another righteous man to rise.[1] As Zunz[2] points out, even if this saying is not to be taken literally, and we suppose it to refer to generations of teachers, the date of the last-mentioned Rabbi in the list (Rabbi Abba Hoshaya) is only a few years before the reign of the Emperor Julian (A.D. 361–363). Lastly, the frequent occurrence of Greek words in this *Midrash* points to an early date, as well as the fact that its place of origin is Palestine.[3]

Bereshith Rabbah is a continuous commentary of Haggadic character on the whole of Genesis ; the sayings and explanations of many authorities, a large number anonymous, are quoted ; not infrequently the compiler adds long narrative passages illustrative of some verse under discussion. References are often given to contemporaneous historical events, and it. is characteristic of this *Midrash* "to view the personages and conditions of the Bible by the light of contemporary history." Although this *Midrash* is a commentary on Genesis, it must be confessed that, so far as elucidation of the text is concerned, it is not often illuminating ; over and over again one finds, on seeking for some explanation of a difficult text, that the *Midrash* offers little that is of help. There are, of course, exceptions to this ; but, generally speaking, the use and interest of it are of a different kind.

[1] The passage occurs at the beginning of § 58.
[2] *op. cit.* p. 185.   [3] See further Zunz, pp. 185 ff.

One or two examples of what we mean may be given :

Gen. iv. 15, *And the Lord appointed a sign for Cain* : The comments on this are as follows : "According to Rabbi Jehudah, the Lord caused the sun to rise on his behalf [*i.e.* that all the world might see that Cain was forgiven]. According to Rabbi Nechemiah, on the contrary, the Lord did not cause the sun to rise for this sinner, but made leprosy to come upon him (Ex. iv. 8). Rab said, He (the Lord) gave him a dog. According to Abba Jose bar Kisri, the Lord made the horn (of salvation) to sprout from him ; according to Rab, the Lord made him a sign of warning for murderers ; according to Rabbi Chanina, the Lord made him a sign for the repentant ; finally, according to Rabbi Levi, speaking in the name of Rabbi Simeon ben Lakish, the Lord caused him to be suspended in the air, and afterwards he was swept away by the Flood (Gen. vii. 23)."

Comments like this, which do not really throw any light on the subject, often occur. While exegetically this *Midrash* is not often helpful, in other respects it offers much that is useful and interesting ; the following example is taken from the passage about Abraham being commanded to sacrifice Isaac :

"Sammael[1] came to our father Abraham and said to him : 'Old man, old man, hast thou lost thy wits ? Art thou indeed about to sacrifice a son who was given to thee in thy hundredth year ?' Abraham answered : 'Even so.' Then Sammael continued : 'How if God should prove thee still further, wouldst thou still remain steadfast ?' Abraham said : 'Even if (God proved me) still further.' Again Sammael spoke : 'But to-morrow He will say to thee, Thou art a shedder of blood, thou hast murdered thy son.' Abraham answered : 'Even so [some words such as 'I will carry out my purpose' are understood]. When Sammael saw that he could do nothing with Abraham, he turned to Isaac and said to him : 'Unhappy child, he is going to kill thee.' Isaac answered : 'Even so, I will follow him. . . . '"

On the difficult words "Until Shilo come," in xlix. 10, the only comment is that it refers to "King Messiah."

[1] The angel of death ; identical with Satan in Rabbinica literature.

For the rest, there are numberless points of doctrine and practice, interesting archæological details, fables, and parables, as well as controversial passages against heretical opinions, all of which go to show that this *Midrash* is of marked importance.

Aggadath Bereshith. This *Midrash* is of later date and of much less value. It contains a collection of homilies on various set passages from Genesis. Each homily is in three sections, "so arranged that the first one connects with a *seder* ('section') from Genesis, the second with a prophetic section, and the third with a psalm." The contents of these homilies are for the most part taken from *Tanchuma* (see below), according to Theodor, who speaks of them as being "notable for artistic composition." This *Midrash* deals in the main with Genesis, but it comments also on passages from the Prophetical books and on some of the Psalms. (Best edition of text, Buber's, Cracow, 1903.)

EXODUS. Two Midrashic works on this book exist: *Mekilta*[1] and *Shemoth Rabbah.* The former and more important one, which contains both legal (Halakic) and narrative (Haggadic) material, is a commentary on Ex. xii.–xxiii. 19, the main legal portion of Exodus; it deals also with the two passages, xxxi. 12–17, xxxv. 1–3, which contain the law concerning the Sabbath. It appears, therefore, that the original intention of the compiler of this *Midrash* was that it should be purely legal in character; as a matter of fact, however, it contains just about as much Haggadic matter as Halakic. Like *Sifra* and *Sifre* (see below), this *Midrash* in its

---

[1] The word means "measure," "rule," or "form," equivalent to the Hebrew *Middah*; this title was given to the *Midrash* because the fixed Rabbinical rules of Scriptural exegesis are the basis upon which the comments, etc., it contains are constructed. The best editions of the Hebrew text are those of Weiss (Vienna, 1865) and Friedmann (Vienna, 1870).

original form goes back to the beginning of the second century A.D. " The disciples of Rabbi Jochanan ben Zakkai, viz. Ishmael, Akiba, and Eleazar of Modin, appear to have redacted the principal contents of the exposition on the basis of the still older and anonymous *stratum* of exegetical tradition. *Mekilta*, for the greater part, contains the comments and sayings of Rabbi Ishmael and his pupils. It will, therefore, be seen that a *Midrash* which embodies so much ancient material possesses a high value and interest ; and this is especially the case from the point of view of New Testament study, for it reflects the Jewish religious standpoint as this existed in the time of the Apostles. As an illustration we may give the following parable, which occurs among the comments on Ex. xx. 2 :

"It is like a king who had two stewards ; one was placed in charge of the straw (supplies) ; the other was set over the gold and silver treasure. He that was placed in charge of the straw (supplies) came under suspicion (of unjust dealing) ; thereupon he made complaint that he had not been set over the gold and silver treasure. Then he who had been set over the gold and silver treasure said unto him : 'Foolish man, having come under suspicion of unjust dealing regarding the straw (supplies), how shouldest thou be trusted with gold and silver?'"[1] (*cp* Luke xvi. 10.)

The other *Midrash* on Exodus, *Shemoth*[2] *Rabbah,* is of much later date ; it belongs in its present form, according to Zunz, to the eleventh or twelfth century A.D., though it has embodied a good deal from earlier *Midrashim*, especially *Tanchuma Yelammedenu* (see below). It contains a large number of parables, taken in the main from earlier works ; the thirtieth section alone contains nineteen.

[1] *lit.* "Thou didst lie concerning straw ; how much more (concerning) gold and silver?"
[2] *Shemoth* (= "Names") is the Hebrew title of Exodus ; it is shortened from *Elleh Shemoth* ("These are the names"), the opening words of the book.

LEVITICUS. On this book, likewise, there are two *Midrashim*, both of considerable importance. The first is called *Sifra* (= " the Book "); it is also known by the name *Torath Kohanim*[1] (= "the Law of the priests "). The authorities quoted in this *Midrash* belong, at the latest, to the first half of the third century A.D. ; it is almost wholly Halakic in content, as one would expect in a commentary on Leviticus ; the small Haggadic portions correspond with the historical passages in Leviticus. *Sifra* emanates from Babylonia, as its ancient title (see foot-note above) implies ; but Rab came originally from Palestine, so that we may take it that much of the Palestinian exegetical tradition is embodied in this *Midrash*. An example of Halakic commentary from this work is the following :

" *Thou shalt not be resentful.* What is meant by being resentful ? When one person says to another, ' Lend me your axe,' and he will not lend it ; then on the following day the latter says to the former, ' Lend me your sickle ' ; whereupon he says, ' Here it is ; I am not like you, who refuse to lend me your axe.' Therefore it is written : *Thou shalt not take vengeance*, and *Love thy neighbour as thyself.* Rabbi Akiba says : ' This is the great principle of the Torah.' Ben Azzai says : ' This is the book of the generations of man (Gen. v. 1, Hebrew), which is a still greater principle.' "[2]

The other *Midrash* on Leviticus is *Wayyikra*[3] *Rabbah* ; this is one of the older of the Midrashic works, though not so ancient as *Mekilta, Sifra, and Sifre* ; Zunz dates it in its present form about the middle of the seventh century A.D. ; it embodies, of course, material of much greater antiquity. A striking characteristic of this *Midrash* is its large

[1] Another ancient title is *Sifra debe Rab* (= "The Book of Rab's Academy") ; Abba Arika, the leading Babylonian Amora, is distinguished by the title " Rab," *i.e.* the teacher *par excellence.*

[2] Quoted in *JE* viii. 555*b*.

[3] *Wayyikra* (= " And He called") is the Hebrew name of Leviticus, being the word with which the book begins.

collection of proverbs, *e.g.* "If you have knowledge, what do you lack? If you lack knowledge, what do you possess?" (i. 6). "If one knot is unravelled, then two knots are unravelled" (xiv. 3).[1]

NUMBERS. The ancient and valuable *Midrash* called *Sifre* = ("Books") deals with Numbers, from chap. v. to the end, and the whole of Deuteronomy. The authorship is clearly dual; the portion which is concerned with Numbers is almost entirely Halakic, and it is full of the tedious and long-drawn-out discussions which are characteristic of the Talmud; the polemical element also is pronounced. The Deuteronomy portion is, likewise, in the main Halakic, but it is also in part Haggadic. The whole belongs to the third century A.D. It is a very important source for dogmatic Judaism; the following are a few examples:

"There is not a single commandment the fulfilment of which does not at once bring with it its corresponding reward (35*b*).
The words of the Torah are to be compared with water. Just as water is life to the world, so, too, are the words of the Torah life to the world (84*a*).
Wherever God is called Jehovah, there it is implied that He is the God of mercy; wherever He is called Elohim, there it is implied that He acts according to strict justice (71*a*).
Lord of the world, why did the first Adam[2] die? He (God) answered them (the angels): Because he did not fulfil My commands (141*a*)."[3]

The other *Midrash* on Numbers is called *Bemidbar*[4] *Rabbah.* This composite work is made up largely of quotations from *Tanchuma* (see below). It belongs to the twelfth century A.D., and is of much less importance than *Sifre.*

[1] Quoted in *JE* viii. 560*b*.
[2] With the expression "the first Adam" *cp.* 1 Cor. xv. 45 f.
[3] These quotations are from Weber, *Juedische Theologie*, *passim.*
[4] *Bemidbar* ("in the wilderness") is the Hebrew name for Numbers; it is the important word in the opening sentence of the book.

DEUTERONOMY. Of the more important of the two *Midrashim* on this book, *Sifre*, we have already spoken. The other is *Debarim* [1] *Rabbah*; this is of late date, about A.D. 900 according to Zunz. Like *Bemidbar Rabbah*, it has many extracts from *Tanchuma*. A short quotation may be given:

> "Our Rabbis say that the Torah may be compared with five things: with water, with wine, with honey, with milk, and with oil. . . . As this oil gives life to the world, so also do the words of the Torah give life to the world; as this oil gives light to the world, so also do the words of the Torah give light to the world" (§ 7).

SAMUEL. The *Midrash Shemuel* is a late work belonging to the first half of the eleventh century, and there are interpolations of still later date.[2] Of the thirty-two sections into which the work is divided, only the last eight deal with the second book of Samuel, all the rest being concerned with the first book. This *Midrash* is mentioned for the first time by Rashi (1040–1105); it emanates from Palestine, and the compiler drew his material for the most part from early Palestinian authorities whose comments, etc., are already quoted in the Mishnah and earlier *Midrashim*. This work does not offer much that is not found in earlier writings; its value, therefore, is small.

PSALMS. The *Midrash* on the Psalms, called *Midrash Tehillim*,[3] is a commentary on Pss. i.–cxviii., to which was added later an appendix dealing with the rest of the Psalms. Although late in date

[1] *Debarim* (= "words") is the Hebrew name for Deuteronomy; it is shortened from *Elleh ha-Debarim* ("These are the words"), the opening words of the book.

[2] Zunz, *op. cit.* p. 282. Edition of Hebrew text by Buber (Cracow, 1893).

[3] The Hebrew for "Psalms"; this Midrash is also known by the name of *Shocher tob* (= "He that diligently seeketh good," Prov. xi. 27), the opening words of the book. Best Hebrew text, Buber's *Midrasch Tehillim* (Wilna, 1891).

(not later than the eleventh century), it contains a great mass of interesting and valuable material, partly homiletic and partly exegetical, much of which is ancient. It is important as containing the traditional Palestinian exegesis of the Psalms. This *Midrash* contains a number of "stories, legends, parables, proverbs, and sentences, with many ethical and Halakic maxims. Of the interesting myths may be mentioned that of Romulus and Remus, to suckle whom God sends a she-wolf (*Midr. Teh.* to Ps. x. 6); and the legend of the Emperor Hadrian, who wished to measure the depth of the Adriatic Sea (*Midr. Teh.* to Ps. xciii. 6)."[1] The following is an example of a parable; it occurs in the comment on Ps. ii. 12, *Kiss the son lest he be angry, and ye perish from the way* :

"Whereunto is this to be compared? It is like a king who was wroth against the inhabitants of a city ; these, therefore, went unto the king's son and made their peace with him, in order that he might go to the king and make peace on their behalf. So he went and pacified the king. When the inhabitants of that city knew that the king had been propitiated, they desired to sing a song (of thanksgiving) to him ; but he answered and said: 'Do ye wish to sing a song (of thanksgiving) to me? Nay, but go and sing it unto my son ; for had it not been for him, I should have destroyed the inhabitants of the city.'"

PROVERBS. The *Midrash* on this book, which has not come down to us in its entirety, is called *Midrash Mishle* (= "Proverbs").[2] Opinions differ as to its date. Zunz places it as late as the middle of the eleventh century ; others regard it as belonging to the eighth century. Its place of origin is believed to be Babylonia, but this cannot be stated with certainty. Lauterbach says of this *Midrash* that it "is different from all other Haggadic *Midrashim* in that its interpretations approach the simple exegesis then in vogue, being brief and free from the prolixity found in the other *Midrashim*, so that this work is in

[1] *JE* x. 250a   [2] Best Hebrew text, Buber's (Wilna, 1893).

the form of a commentary rather than in that of a *Midrash*. The interpretations follow immediately upon the words of the text, without the introductory formulas found in the other *Midrashim*, 'as Scripture says,' or 'Rabbi N. N. began'; the latter formula, however, occurs at the beginning of the *Midrash*."[1]

JONAH. The *Midrash* on this book, called *Midrash Yonah*, which contains a Haggadic account of the Biblical story, is read in the synagogue on the Day of Atonement. It consists of two parts; the first part is the *Midrash* proper, while the second contains the story of Jonah allegorically referred to the soul. Zunz says it contains extracts from the Talmud and long passages from the *Baraitha* of Rabbi Eliezer, but does not offer anything original.[2] It is of late date, having been compiled subsequently to the *Midrash* on the books of Samuel.

Evidence is forthcoming that at one time *Midrashim* on Ezra, the books of Chronicles, and Job existed, as quotations from these are found in Rabbinical writings.

THE FIVE MEGILLOTH. The *Midrashim* on Ruth, Ecclesiastes, Song of Songs, Lamentations, Esther form a special group, with the exception of Lamentations (see below); they are called the five *Megilloth* (= " Rolls "):

Midrash Ruth. In its present form this little work belongs to the eleventh or twelfth century; but, like so many of the *Midrashim.* it embodies a great deal of much earlier material. Thus many passages from the Jerusalem Talmud, *Bereshith Rabbah*, and *Pesikta* are found in this *Midrash*; and it is likely enough that other ancient writings have been laid under contribution; so that the value of many of these later *Midrashim* is not necessarily diminished because their date of compilation is late. *Midrash Ruth*, which consists of eight divisions, is a running

[1] *JE* x. 231*b*.　　[2] *op. cit.* p. 282.

Haggadic commentary on the book of Ruth, which is preceded by a special introduction containing various proems (on these see below). There are many interesting matters dealt with, archæological and dogmatic points being of frequent occurrence, and, according to the Jewish traditional method, parables and stories often illustrate subjects of discussion ; the following is an example :

" A king was journeying from place to place ; and a pearl fell from his head (*i.e.* from the crown on his head). Then the king and all his following arose (and sought the pearl). And the people who were passing by said : 'What is the king, with his following, seeking here ?' They were answered : 'Do ye not see that a pearl has fallen from the king's head ?' So what did (the king) do? He caused the soil to be heaped up and had sieves brought ; then they put the soil of one heap through the sieves, but found nothing ; they did the same with a second heap ; all in vain. At last, at the third heap he found (his pearl). Then said the people : 'The king has found his pearl again.'"

This parable is spoken in reference to God seeking Abraham (§ viii., beginning).

Midrash Koheleth. This *Midrash* on Ecclesiastes is late, but, like the one just considered, contains a great deal of early material, and is Haggadic in character. Its interpretation of the text of Ecclesiastes is largely allegorical ; *e.g.* such passages as Eccles. ii. 24 ; iii. 13 ; v. 17 ; viii. 15, where an Epicurean and hedonistic view is expressed, are interpreted allegorically and given a religious significance, viz.: "Wherever eating and drinking are spoken of in this way, the pleasure is meant which the study of the Bible and the performance of good works afford." [1]

Midrash Shir ha-Shirim Rabbati. This *Midrash* to the Song of Songs is called also *Aggadath Chazitha*, from the opening Hebrew words. The comments and explanations, often clothed in the

[1] Quoted by Theodor, *JE* vii. 530a.

garb of a homily, are free and untrammelled; "the words of the text are treated in very diverse ways, being made to apply now to historical events, now to practical life with its religious needs. . . . Extraordinarily rich in colouring is the picture of the 'Woes of the Messiah,' *i.e.* the tragic period which is to precede the advent of the son of David."[1] The work is full of interesting matter, many parables and well-told stories, as well as fables and legends, occurring in it. The Song of Songs is throughout interpreted allegorically. Like the other *Midrashim* in this group, this one, which is a much bigger work than *Midrash Ruth*, not only has many extracts from earlier writings, especially *Bereshith Rabbah*, the Jerusalem Talmud, etc., but also contains material anterior to these. Its date in its present form is earlier than the two foregoing, as it belongs to a time previous to the ninth century; a more exact date cannot be determined. As an example of allegorical interpretation the following may be cited: i. 5, "I am black, but comely . . ." (supposed to be said by Solomon); this is explained thus:

"I appear black in my deeds, but comely in those of my fathers. The congregation of Israel says, I appear black unto myself, but comely in the eyes of my Creator." See Amos ix. 7.[2]

Ekah Rabbati. This *Midrash* on Lamentations is so called on account of its opening word *Ekah* (= "How"). *Rabbati* is added for the similar reason that *Rabbah* is added to certain other *Midrashim* (see above). It occupies a special position in this group because it belongs to the oldest of the Midrashic works; it was compiled from a mass of ancient material in the second half of the seventh

---

[1] Wünsche, *Der Midrasch Schir ha-Schirim*, p. v.

[2] Am. ix. 7 runs: "Are you not as the children of the Ethiopians unto Me, O children of Israel? saith the Lord." It is a good instance of the mechanical use the Rabbis make of the *words* of Biblical texts, no matter how inappropriate the use of the text itself may be.

century, according to Zunz.[1] "The Haggadic explanation of this book (Lamentations)—which is a dirge
on the fall of the Jewish state and the extinction of
the national splendour—was treated by scholars as
especially appropriate to the Ninth of Ab,[2] to the
day of the destruction of the Temple, and to the eve
of that fast-day."[3] The character of the contents of
this *Midrash* is similar to that of the others in this
group. (The best edition is that of Buber, Wilna,
1899.)

Midrash Megillath Esther. This *Midrash* on the
book of Esther (Megillath = "Roll") is also called
Haggadath (= "Narrative") *Megillah.* It was compiled before the eighth century, as it is often cited
in Rabbinical writings subsequent to that date.[4]
Like the other *Midrashim* of this group, it borrows
largely from the Jerusalem Talmud, *Bereshith Rabbah*,
and *Wayyikra Rabbah.*

B. Among the *Midrashim* which deal with more
than one book of the Old Testament the first which
claims attention is

Pesikta.[5] This word means "Section," and the
Midrash is so called because it is based on the
Scripture sections which form the lessons read in
the synagogue on Sabbaths and festivals. As these
lessons are taken from the Pentateuch and the
Prophetical writings, this *Midrash* deals with a
number of different Biblical books. It is an important work on account of its age, since it belongs to
approximately the same period as *Bereshith Rabbah*,
or even earlier. But, as Theodor[6] points out, "the
proems (see below) in the *Pesikta*, developed from
short introductions to the exposition of the Scripture
text into more independent homiletic structures, as

---

[1] *op. cit.* p. 191.   [2] One of the chief Jewish fast-days.
[3] Theodor in *JE* v. 85*b*.   [4] See Zunz, *op. cit.* p. 276.
[5] Known also as *Pesikta de-Rab Kahana*, from the name of
the compiler; but see Zunz, *op. cit.* pp. 204 f. Text by Buber
(Lyck, 1868); German translation by Wünsche, 1885.
[6] *JE* viii. 560*a*.

well as the mastery of form apparent in the final formulas of the proems, indicate that the *Pesikta* belongs to a higher stage of Midrashic development." Each of the sections of which the *Midrash* is composed forms a self-contained whole, the subject of which is the particular Scriptural lesson for the Sabbath or festival in question ; this is haggadically developed and ramifies into a mass of topics in relation, more or less, to the original subject. A good deal of the *Midrash* is identical with parallel passages in *Bereshith Rabbah*, *Wayyikra Rabbah*, and the Jerusalem Talmud.

Pesikta Rabbati.[1] This *Midrash*, like the one just considered, is also a collection of homilies on the lessons from the Pentateuch and the Prophets for Sabbaths and festivals. It is called *Rabbati* (" Larger ") to distinguish it from the earlier and more important *Pesikta*. Although the names are similar, the contents of these two *Midrashim* differ entirely. Zunz assigns the second half of the ninth century as the date of its compilation.

Tanchuma Yelammedenu. Two originally distinct *Midrashim* have become amalgamated under this name: (1) the *Midrash Tanchuma*, the work of a celebrated Palestinian Rabbi, named Tanchuma, who lived during the latter half of the fourth century ; and (2) a *Midrash* called *Yelammedenu*, an abbreviation of *Yelammedenu Rabbenu* (= " Let our Master teach us "), the formula with which the Halakic exordium begins.[2] Of these two the *Midrash* of Tanchuma is the more ancient, belonging to the fifth century in its present form ; it is one of the most important of the Midrashic writings. The *Yelammedenu* is later, having been compiled during the eighth or ninth century. This amalgamated *Midrash* contains a collection of homilies dealing with all five books of the Pentateuch.

[1] Hebrew text edited by M. Friedmann (Wien, 1880).
[2] Theodor, *JE* viii. 560a.

Midrash Hashkem. This, in the main, Haggadic *Midrash* on the Pentateuch is so called after the second word of the opening sentence, taken from Ex. viii. 20 (verse 16 in the Hebrew), with which it begins: "Hashkem," *i.e.* "Rise up early." It also has the name *We-Hizhir ;* this is abbreviated from the standing formula: *We-hizhir ha-Kadosh, baruk Hu* ("And may the Holy One—Blessed be He!— instruct [lit. illuminate]"), with which most of the sections in the *Midrash* begin. It used to be thought that these two names indicated the existence of two distinct *Midrashim* ; but Zunz has shown that they are really one and the same work, and his conclusion is now generally accepted. This *Midrash* is defective ; it is assigned by Zunz to the middle of the tenth century. It is one of the less important among the Midrashic works.

Finally, mention may be made of four special Haggadic works which partake of a Midrashic character :

Pirke[1] *de Rabbi Eliezer.* This contains lengthy Haggadic discussions on all the most important events described in the Pentateuch. According to Zunz, it cannot have been composed before the eighth century (see also Gerald Friedlander's translation, pp. liii ff.).

Yalkut[2] *Shimeoni.* This is a great collection of Midrashic material ranging over the entire Old Testament. Shimeon was presumably a Rabbi who lived in Frankfort[3] in the Middle Ages, but the date of this work cannot be determined. Its chief value is text-critical, for the comparison between it and the ancient Midrashic works helps towards determining the correct text of the latter.

Yalkut ha-Makiri. This is a later work than the foregoing, but also useful for text-critical purposes.

[1] *Pirke* = "Sections." An English translation by Gerald M. Friedlander was published in London in 1916.

[2] *Yalkut* = "Collection."

[3] This is stated in the preface to the printed edition of the work (1709) ; but there seems to be some doubt about it.

It is not known when the author, Machir ben Abba Mari, lived. The collection of Midrashic material which Machir gathered seems to have dealt with the Prophetical books and the Hagiographa ; but we do not know what the original extent of the work was.

Midrash ha-Gadol.[1] This is a still more comprehensive work than the two foregoing, as it includes quotations from the Targums and Kabbalistic writings (which the other collections do not), in addition to those from the *Midrashim* and *Talmudim.* It is later in date than the others. The name of the author is not known.

There are, in addition to the writings which have been enumerated, many other small and unimportant Midrashic works. It is not necessary to mention these by name. All that are of real value have been dealt with above.

A final word must be said about what are called the *Proems.* These are introductions, or prefatory remarks, which in all the more important Haggadic *Midrashim* precede the expository matter proper. They occupy, as Theodor insists, " an important position in the entire *Midrash* literature . . . they are the clearest evidence of the existence of a deliberate technical arrangement in the Haggadic *Midrashim*, and constitute both in name (*petichah*) and in nature an introduction to the exposition of the lesson proper ; to this, however, they lead up by means of the interpretation of an extraneous text, the proemial text, which must not be taken from the lesson itself ; and the proems may be as different in structure and finish as in contents. The proems are either *simple*, consisting of a simple exposition of the proem text, often amplified by quotations, parables, etc., and connected throughout, or at least at the end, with the lesson or with the initial verse thereof ; or *composite*, consisting of different interpretations of the

[1] *Ha-Gadol* = " The Great." The Hebrew text of the part on Genesis was edited by Schechter (Cambridge, 1902).

same extraneous verse, by one or by various authors, and connected in various ways, but always of such a nature that the last interpretation, the last component part of the proem, leads to the interpretation of the lesson proper."[1] The proems are often of great length, sometimes longer than the whole of the interpretations which follow ; in some cases there is more than one proem. It often happens that proems, or parts of them, belonging to earlier *Midrashim* have been incorporated into the expository portions of others ; by this means the dependence of one *Midrash* on another can be established. The proems are also important on account of the ancient material which they so often embody.

III

THE TALMUDIC LITERATURE

[LITERATURE : " The Talmud," an article published in the *Quarterly Review*, October, 1867, by E. Deutsch, and reprinted in his *Literary Remains* (London, 1874) ; the articles " Talmud " in *JE* xii. pp. 1–27 (by Bacher), and in the extra volume of Hastings's *DB*, pp. 57–66 (by Schechter), also in the *Encycl. Britt.* (by Schiller-Szinessy). Useful compendiums of information on the subject are Mielziner's *Introduction to the Talmud* (Cincinnati and Chicago, 1894) and Strack's *Einleitung in den Thalmud* (Leipzig, 4th ed. 1908). See also *RWS³*, pp. 52–76.

A *new edition of the Babylonian Talmud* (based upon a rearranged and abridged text) in an English translation, by Michael L. Rodkinson, was published by the " New Talmud Publishing Company," in New York, in 16 vols. (18 vols. in 16), together with an introductory volume on the *History of the Talmud* (2 vols. in 1 ; 1896–1903).

Various " Selections " from the Talmud have been published in English ; the following may be mentioned here :   Hershon's *Talmudic Miscellany* (1880); his *Treasures of the Talmud* (1882) ; and his *Genesis with a Talmudic Commentary* (1883) ; Polano, *The Talmud* (in the "Chandos Classics ") ; Montague, *Tales from the Talmud* (London, 1906) ; Gerald Friedlander,

---

[1] *JE* viii. 553a.

G

Rabbinic Philosophy and Ethics (an excellent volume ; London, 1912).

Reference may also be made to Schürer, *HJP* I. i. pp. 117 ff., and to I. Abrahams, *Short History of Jewish Literature*, chaps. i. and iii. (London, 1906).

Other literature is referred to below under the separate sections.]

(i) *Introductory*

The term "Talmud" is applied generally to the vast *corpus* of Jewish traditional literature which has been preserved in two independent collections, viz. the "Talmud Jerushalmi" (T.J.), *i.e.* the Jerusalem or Palestinian Talmud, and the "Talmud Babli" (T.B.), or "Babylonian Talmud." Both collections are the product of the Jewish schools, the former representing the work of the Palestinian schools, and completed some time in the fourth century A.D., the latter embodying the work of the Babylonian schools, and completed about a century later than the Jerusalem Talmud. Both may be regarded as amplifications of the Mishnah, which, in the form that was officially sanctioned by R. Judah I. about A.D. 190 or 200, was simultaneously adopted in Palestine and Babylonia as the basis for the discussions of the schools. Consequently the Mishnah is regarded as a component part of both Talmuds ; and even those parts of the Mishnah which have no Talmudic amplification are included in the text of editions of the Babylonian Talmud.

It is important to realise that both the Mishnah and the later Talmudic amplifications, which rest upon it, represent an *oral* tradition, transmitted for centuries in an oral form, until finally it was redacted in a fixed written shape. When exactly these works were reduced to writing is uncertain. A third-century prohibition forbids the committal of the teaching of tradition to writing, or the use of any written form of such by the teachers in lecturing (T.B. Giṭṭ. 60*a*,

Tem. 14*b*). In a reply addressed to the scholars of Kairwan, Sherira Gaon (A.D. 900—1000) alludes to this prohibition as follows:

> "In answer to your question asking when the Mishnah and Talmud were respectively committed to writing, it should be said that neither of them was thus transmitted, but both were arranged [redacted] orally; and the scholars believe it to be their duty to recite them from memory and not from written copies." [1]

It is clear from Sherira's words that even in the tenth century the scholars of the Jewish Babylonian Academies abstained from using written copies of the Talmud in their lectures; they were, it would seem, sufficiently familiar with its text to be able to recite this from memory. On the other hand, the Gaon's words certainly imply that written copies were already in existence. Such manuscripts, though their public and official use was interdicted, were doubtless employed for purposes of private study. At an earlier period still, during the time of the Amoraim (third to fifth centuries A.D.), it is probable that the Mishnah and the allied traditional literature of the Tannaim had already been reduced to writing. It may be added that, owing to the persecution of the Jews in the Middle Ages, and the consequent destruction of their MS. literature, only a comparatively small number of MSS. of the Talmud have survived. Most of these are fragmentary, codices of single sections ("Sedarim") or even of single tractates ("Massektoth"), which are preserved in various European libraries. The only known complete MS. of the Babylonian Talmud, written in A.D. 1369, is in the possession of the Royal Library of Munich. A fragment of the tractate *Pesaḥim*, of the ninth or tenth century, is preserved in the University Library

[1] Cited in *JE* xii. 19*b* (art. "Talmud").

of Cambridge, and an edition of this, with autotype facsimile, was issued at Cambridge in 1879, under the editorship of W. H. Lowe. The same editor was also responsible for a printed edition of the text of *the Mishnah on which the Palestinian Talmud rests*, from a unique MS. preserved in the University Library of Cambridge (1883). This is the most important extant authority for the text of the Mishnah.

The first printed editions of this literature were issued at Naples and Venice. At Naples as early as 1492 the Mishnah, with the commentary of Maimonides, appeared. The first complete edition of the Babylonian Talmud was published by Daniel Bomberg in twelve folio volumes, at Venice, in 1520–23. It contains not only the text, but also the commentary of Rashi, the Tosaphoth, the compendium of Asheri, and the Mishnah-commentary of Maimonides. This *editio princeps* has become the model for all subsequent editions, which reproduce its pagination by which reference to the Babylonian Talmud is made. It is also important critically, because it is free from the mutilations introduced into later editions by the Christian censorship. The first edition of the Jerusalem Talmud was also issued by Daniel Bomberg, at Venice, in 1523–24, in one folio volume, without any commentary.

The technical term "Talmud" has undergone a certain amount of development in meaning. Originally an old scholastic term of the Tannaim (*i.e.* the Rabbis mentioned in the Mishnah), its primary meaning is (1) "teaching" (from the Hebrew לָמֵד "teach"), although it also signifies "learning."[1] In this latter sense it sometimes denotes "the study of religion," and is contrasted with "practice" (מעשה), *i.e.* the practice of religion. In the sense of "teaching" it frequently occurs in Tannaitic terminology, *e.g.* in the phrase *talmud lomar*, to denote teaching

---

[1] *e.g.* in the phrase *Talmud Torah* = "study [learning] of the Law."

based upon the text of the Bible and the exegetic deductions made therefrom, and especially "teaching" which takes the form of a Halakic principle deduced by exegesis from the Biblical text. The term "Talmud" thus denotes primarily, in the Tannaitic phraseology, the exegetic confirmation of the Halakah, or binding religious rule.

It further (2) came to be applied, in a more restricted sense, to the exposition of the Halakah when this had been formulated into an independent code of Law (the Mishnah). In this more restricted sense it is distinguished from study of the Bible text (*Mikra*), and also from that of the Mishnah.

In a story referring to the Patriarch Judah I. (the compiler of the Mishnah in its present form) the three branches of study, as thus developed, are clearly distinguished. The members of the Academy are classified as follows (T.B. *Baba bathra* 8*a*, according to the true text of the passage): those who devoted themselves to the study of the Bible-text (בעלי מקרא) ; those who gave themselves principally to the study of the Mishnah (בעלי משנה) ; and those who mainly studied the Talmud (בעלי תלמה).

With this special development of Talmud study the term "Talmud" (3) began to acquire a larger meaning. The Mishnah became an integral part of the "Talmud," which also gradually incorporated into itself a large portion of the old Midrashic literature.[1] The term occurs in this comprehensive sense, as a designation of the entire *corpus*, in the Babylonian Talmud itself.[2]

As distinguished from the Mishnah, the commentary on it is termed "Gemara," a word derived from Babylonian Aramaic which has the meaning "what has been learned," *i.e.* the learning that has been transmitted by tradition, and then, in a restricted sense, applied specially to the exposition of the Mishnah. In this technical sense it seems to have been a comparatively late substitution for the term "Talmud."

While the Mishnah was written in pure Hebrew, the language of the Gemara, both of the Palestinian and of the Babylonian Talmud, is predominantly Aramaic. The Aramaic of each Talmud is, however, different, that of the Babylonian being a dialect of Eastern Aramaic (akin to "Syriac"), while the Aramaic of the Palestinian Talmud is Western in

---

[1] Of course, the Midrashic literature has been edited in separate and independent collections (see Part II., section ii., above). But many passages have parallel versions in the Talmuds. [2] See Bacher in *JE* xii. 2*b* for details.

character, and approximates to the dialect of the Palestinian Targum. The contents of the two Gemaras are also largely independent.[1]

The Talmud is in many respects unique among the literary monuments of the world. "In form a commentary, it became an encyclopædia of Jewish faith and scholarship, comprising whatsoever the greatest representatives of Judaism in Palestine and in Babylon had regarded as objects of study and investigation and of teaching and learning during the three centuries which elapsed from the conclusion of the Mishnah to the completion of the Talmud itself."[2] With the incorporation of the Mishnah the Talmud became a vast record of the gradually developed and enriched oral tradition. As we study its pages we hear the debates, often minutely recorded, that went on through successive generations in the Jewish schools. Its astonishingly varied contents, and wealth of detail on all sorts of subjects, show that, academic as it is in spirit, the Jewish scholars were in contact with the popular life, details of which are often minutely described. It thus constitutes an important source for the history of civilisation, not to speak of its excursions into the most varied branches of human knowledge— astronomy and medicine, mathematics and law, anatomy and botany—which furnish valuable data for the history of science.

The Talmud, in its finally redacted form, bridges the Judaism of the Bible and of the later period. But it did not remain a mere literary monument. It became a formative factor of the most decisive kind in the further development of Judaism in the post-Talmudic period. It acquired high authority as a religious thesaurus, "equal to the Bible itself as a source of instruction and decision in problems of

---

[1] For details see below, pp. 131 ff.
[2] Bacher in *JE, ibid.* 24*b*.

religion." It thus became the basis for systematic epitomes or expositions of religious duties and truths adapted to the needs of later times. The study of it determined, to a large extent, for centuries the very fibre of Jewish thought and the forms of Jewish intellectual activity. Its subtleties served to sharpen to an extraordinary acuteness the minds of its devoted students. Nor has it, even yet, lost its historical importance for Judaism. Though many Jews have, during the last century, absorbed modern culture and neglected Talmudic studies, the Talmud is to-day, for masses of Jews, the supreme authority in religion. The ministers and Rabbis of modern Jewry must possess a competent knowledge of their traditional literature, and, above all, of the Talmud, which is still, with the Bible, the most venerated religious authority among orthodox Jews.

It has already been pointed out that the Talmud (with the Mishnah) was in its origin a compilation of the *oral* Law. As such it was clearly marked off from the canonical Scripture, which was handed down in *written* form. The distinction was clearly marked in Rabbinical terminology, "the Torah by mouth " (תּוֹרָה שֶׁבְּעַל פֶּה) being distinguished from "the Torah in writing" (תּוֹרָה שֶׁבִּכְתָב), which was embodied in the canonical Pentateuch.[1]

The Oral Law was regarded by the later Rabbis as going back to Moses himself. Thus a saying attributed to R. Simeon ben Lakish (third century A.D.) runs :

"What is that which is written : *I will give thee tables of stone, and the Law, and the commandment which I have*

---

[1] In the first instance the Pentateuch formed the sole contents of canonical Scripture. Later the Prophets and Hagiographa were added, but were not put on the same level of authority, being regarded as " Tradition " (*Kabbalah*), though of course in a written form.

written to teach them (Ex. xxiv. 12)? 'Tables,' these are the ten words; 'Law,' that is the Scripture; 'and the commandment,' that is the Mishnah; 'which I have written,' these are the Prophets and Writings (Hagiographa);[1] 'to teach them,' that is the Gemara: thus instructing us that all these were given to Moses from Sinai" (T.B. *Ber.* 5*a*).

The real beginnings of the Oral Law are, no doubt, to be placed in the early post-Exilic period, when the written Torah of Moses, as canonical Scripture, was read and expounded in the synagogues. From small beginnings this gradually grew, being developed and modified from time to time to meet the exigencies of changing circumstances, till, after being subjected for some centuries to these varying influences, it first assumed a fixed and official form in the Mishnah promulgated by the patriarch Judah I. about A.D. 190–200. This final form of the Mishnah, it must be remembered, had been preceded by earlier attempts at codification, which prepared the way for R. Judah's work. The later developments of the oral tradition, which took the text of the Mishnah as the basis for further discussions and commentary, have already been referred to above.

Reference has been made to the extraordinarily varied contents of the Talmud. A broad distinction is drawn, in this connexion, between the Halakah and Haggadah.[2] The former term, which means "rule," is applied primarily to laws which are of a binding character, but in an extended sense it embraces not only the laws themselves, but also "all expositions, discussions, and reports which have the object of explaining, establishing, and determining legal principles and provisions."[3] Hence it comprises all the legal portions of the Talmudic literature. The actual Halakah includes, of course, all that belongs to the strictly legal or ritual element in Scripture, or can be deduced therefrom. "The term extends also to the

---

[1] Notice that the Prophets and Hagiographa are distinguished here from "Scripture," *i.e.* the Pentateuch.

[2] *cp.* what is said on this point above, pp. 60 ff.

[3] Mielziner, *Introduction to the Talmud*, p. 56.

usages, customs (*Minhāgîm*), ordinances (*Teḳanôth*), and decrees (*Gezērôth*) for which there is little or no authority in the Scriptures."[1] The Mishnah, which is essentially an independent codification of law, is almost exclusively Halakic in character. On the other hand, "Haggadah" (or *'Aggada*),[2] a term which in its original significance meant, apparently, *recitation* (*sc.* of the Scriptures), acquired a very extended meaning, embracing all that was not included in the Halakah. Hence the Haggadah comprises "all historical records, all legends and parables, all doctrinal and ethical teachings, and all free and unrestrained interpretations of Scripture"[3] which are non-Halakic in character. It is also applied to such subjects as astronomy, medicine and magic, theosophy and mysticism, and everything connected with folk-lore.

Before we proceed to discuss the different *strata* which make up the Talmudic literature, something must be said about the Jewish scholars who are referred to as authorities in this literature. These may be classified into two main groups, viz. (*a*) those referred to in the Mishnah and the allied literature, and (*b*) those referred to in the Talmuds.

(*a*) AUTHORITIES REFERRED TO IN THE MISHNAH AND THE ALLIED LITERATURE

The Mishnah and the Rabbinical literature more or less contemporary with it, *i.e.* the Tosephta and the Baraithas,[4] which embody the earliest compilations of the traditional material, mention the following as authorities: (i) The *Sopherim* or "Scribes"; (ii) the *Zugôth* or "Pairs"; and (iii) the *Tannaim* or "Teachers."

(i) THE SOPHERIM. This term is traditionally applied to the authorities who transmitted and

---

[1] Schechter in Hastings's *DB* v. (extra vol.), p. 58*a*.

[2] The Hebrew and Aramaic forms are הַגָּדָה אַגָּדָה and אַגַּדְתָא. The Hiphil (Aram. Aphel) of the verb נגד = *to narrate*; hence the noun = *recitation, narration*, and may be applied to a tale or anything related which has no binding authority.

[3] Mielziner, *op. cit.* p. 56 f.

[4] See below for details of these branches, pp. 108 ff., 111 ff.

expounded the Law from the days of Ezra to the time of Simon the Just (who flourished about 300–270 B.C.). The name "Sopher" (plur. "Sopherim") means "Bookman," *i.e.* one who taught out of the "Book" (Heb. *Sepher*) of the Law. The name was given to the successors of Ezra, who not only guarded and transmitted "the Book of the Law" (*i.e.* the Pentateuch),[1] but were also its official interpreters and administrators. These "Sopherim" were originally priests; "scribe and priest" was a combination that persisted long after Ezra—in fact, as has been pointed out, down to the time of Simon the Just. The latter was himself high-priest and also head of the "Sopherim"; but at his death (*c.* 270 B.C.) the organisation of this closely knit priestly body seems to have broken down, and *as an official body* its activities probably ceased.

Doubtless *individual* priests were active in the work of transmitting the Law after this period, but only as individuals, animated by piety. It was perhaps during the interval 270–190 B.C. that a class of pious laymen arose, who became teachers of the Law, and were the progenitors of the later Pharisaic party. When it became necessary to set up a new authoritative body—the Sanhedrin—its members were composed of priests and *laymen*, with the high-priest as its official head. The Sanhedrin was probably organised about 190 B.C. Henceforth the Rabbinical teachers, who were laymen as a rule, were active and influential. They must be carefully distinguished, as, in fact, they are carefully distinguished in the Rabbinical literature, from the early "Sopherim," who were priests.[2]

[1] They were responsible for transmitting the text of the Pentateuch in the Scrolls.

[2] See further the article "Pharisees" (by G. H. Box) in Hastings's *ERE* ix. 831 ff., and also an article by the same writer in the *Expositor* for June, 1918, "Scribes and Sadducees in the New Testament," p. 402 f.

Simon the Just was the last of the old Sopherim acting as a close and authoritative body of priests. The evidence for this fact is contained in a sentence of the Mishnah tractate *Pirke Aboth* (i. 2), which, referring to Simon, states that he was "of the remnants of the Great Synagogue," *i.e.* among its last survivors. It is highly probable that "the men of the Great Synagogue" of Rabbinical tradition are to be identified with the "Sopherim." It is represented to have been a synod consisting of 120 members. It is doubtful, however, whether such an assembly ever really existed. The element of truth underlying the tradition may be that an authoritative body of priestly Sopherim did exist and was active during the period referred to above. To the "men of the Great Synagogue" many "sayings, ordinances, and decrees are attributed; such as the arrangement of the Old Testament Canon, the reading of the Law on certain days of the week, the arrangement [in its earliest form] of the daily prayers, saying of grace after meals,"[1] and other matters, and doubtless there is a substratum of truth in these statements.

The chain of tradition is described in the following passage, which forms the opening paragraph of the tractate *Pirke Aboth* (i. 1):

"Moses received the Torah from Sinai, and he delivered it to Joshua, and Joshua to the Elders (Josh. xxiv. 21 ; Judges ii. 1), and the Elders to the Prophets, and the Prophets delivered it to the men of the Great Synagogue. They said three things 'Be deliberate in judgement' ; and 'Raise up many disciples and 'Make a fence to the Torah.'"

The second of these sayings suggests that the Sopherim were active in the work of teaching and expounding the Law. Probably, however, their exposition of the Law was simple and plain in character, without any of the elaborate amplifications

[1] *cp. RWS*[2], p. 56 f.

and deductions that marked the work of the later Rabbinical teachers. No great amount of readjustment was required while the community was small and compact, and undisturbed by the invasion of new and revolutionary influences. These came later with the rising tide of Hellenism; and when they came necessitated a total reorganisation of the Jewish community.

The earlier Sopherim must be carefully distinguished from the "Scribes" of the New Testament period, who were the purely professional class who possessed an expert knowledge of the Law, and were able to administer it. Though some priests may have been included in the scribal class of the New Testament period, the Scribes were predominantly laymen of the class of the Rabbinical teachers.[1] Though the earlier Sopherim were primarily concerned with the Law (Pentateuch), which was regarded by them as Scripture *par excellence*, there is no reason to suppose that they refused to recognise the other collections of sacred writings embodied in the Prophets and Hagiographa. On the contrary, the evidence suggests that they took an active part in the formation of these collections and their embodiment in the Canon of Scripture. Only it must be remembered that these other parts of Scripture were never put by them on a level with the Law. It is not improbable that some of the work of the earlier Sopherim (*e.g.* Ps. cxix.) is included in these later collections. Their outlook was broad and humanistic—they seem to have been much influenced by the class of the "Wise." Ben Sira may, perhaps, be regarded as inheriting their tradition. His picture of the "Scribe" (Ecclus. xxviii. 34 ff.) shows that a broad culture and wide interests were the marks of the ideal Scribe. It is to be noted that Ben Sira quotes freely from all parts of the Hebrew Bible, not merely from the Pentateuch.

The chain of tradition is continued in *Pirke Aboth* with the mention of Antigonus of Soko, who is stated to have continued the tradition of Simon the Just.

"Antigonus of Soko received from Simon the Just. He used to say : ' Be not as slaves that minister to the lord to receive recompense ; but be as slaves that minister to the lord without a view to receive recompense ; and let the fear of Heaven be upon you.'"

---

[1] See further the *Expositor* article above referred to.

Of Antigonus nothing further is known. He may have been one of the pious laymen who continued the work of the Sopherim, and as such stands here in a representative capacity for many others whose names have not been preserved. He forms the connecting link between the Sopherim and the " Pairs."

(ii) THE " PAIRS." This name (Heb. זּוּגוֹת = Greek Ζυγόν) is given to the leading teachers of the Rabbinical class who flourished between the Maccabæan age and the Herodian epoch (c. 150–30 B.C.).

The following five "pairs" are mentioned, and in this order (bridging five generations): (1) Jose b. Joezer of Zereda and Jochanan of Jerusalem; (2) Joshua b. Perachya and Nittai of Arbela; (3) Jehuda b. Tabbai and Shim'on b. Shetach; (4) Shema'ya and 'Abtalyon; (5) Hillel and Shammai.

According to tradition, the two mentioned in each case occupied the position of heads of the Sanhedrin, the one mentioned first being the President (*Nasi*), the second mentioned in each case being the Vice-President (*Ab beth din*). This is certainly not true of the official Sanhedrin, which down to New Testament times, and, indeed, to the last days of Jerusalem (A.D. 66–70), was presided over by the high-priest *ex officio*. What underlies the tradition may possibly be the fact that the teachers enumerated in the " pairs " really stood at the head of the organised Rabbinical schools, and were, according to Rabbinical theory, the rightful bearers of the functions entrusted to the heads of the Sanhedrin. Several of these names are distinguished in the history of Judaism (especially Shim'on b. Shetach, Shema'ya and 'Abtalyon), but the most important are those of Hillel and Shammai. Both these great teachers founded schools, which were called after them "the school of Hillel" and "the school of Shammai" (*Beth Hillel* and *Beth Shammai*). The controversies between the latter figure prominently in the Mishnah. Both

teachers were active in the Halakic development of
the Torah, and it was Hillel who framed the first
exegetical rules (seven in number, afterwards extended to thirteen, and later still further expanded).

(iii) THE TANNAIM (תַּנָּאִים) or "Teachers," a
name given to the doctors of the Mishnah,[1] may be
traced from the rise of the rival schools of Hillel and
Shammai, *i.e.* from about A.D. 10,[2] down to the close
of the career of Judah I. (*c.* A.D. 220). The period,
however, of their greatest activity falls between the
years A.D. 70–200 (from the destruction of the
Temple). Between these dates some 120 of these
teachers flourished, who may be grouped con-
veniently into four generations. It will only be
possible to note under each generation a few of the
more prominent names.

(1) *The first generation* (A.D. 70–100). The greatest
figure at this time among the Rabbinical teachers
was the famous Jochanan ben Zakkai, who founded
the college at Jamnia where Judaism was recon-
stituted. Jochanan was one of the leaders of the
peace party in the disastrous war with Rome (A.D.
66-70).[3]

(2) *The second generation* (A.D. 100–130). Jochanan
b. Zakkai was succeeded as head of the Academy at
Jamnia by Rabban Gamaliel II. (perhaps a grandson
of Gamaliel I.), a man of masterful character. To
this period also belong the five famous disciples of
Jochanan b. Zakkai, viz. Eliezer ben Hyrkanus,
brother-in-law of Gamaliel II., and head of a school
at Lydda, Joshua ben Chananya,[4] Jose the Priest,

---

[1] *Tannā* ("Teacher") does not occur in the Mishnah itself.
It was applied to the scholars mentioned in the Mishnah by
later generations.

[2] Rabban Gamaliel I (mentioned in Acts v. 34, 39) flourished
in this earlier period. He was a grandson of Hillel.

[3] Jochanan b. Zakkai belonged to the school of Hillel.

[4] These two authorities are constantly referred to in the
Mishnah as "R. Eliezer" and "R. Joshua" respectively.

Simeon ben Nathanael, and Eleazar ben Arak. To this generation also belong R. Eliezer b. Jacob I., famous as an authority on matters connected with the structure and services of the Temple (in which he had participated), and Eliezer b. 'Azarya, who traced his pedigree to Ezra the Scribe. From the younger members of this generation sprang its most dominating figure—Akiba, who met a martyr's death in the later insurrection against Rome organised by Bar-Cochba (A.D. 131–135). Akiba, who compiled an earlier form of the Mishnah, which was afterwards expanded by Judah I., was the great champion of a severely literal exegesis. He maintained the principle that every detail of the sacred text, even the minutest, was significant.[1] Another famous contemporary was R. Ishmael b. Elisha, who founded a school at Usha where *Midrash* studies were cultivated, and from which various *Midrashim* emanated. Against Akiba he maintained the principle that the language of Scripture is to be interpreted by the standards of human speech, and that details are not to be unduly pressed. R. Ishmael also developed Hillel's seven rules of interpretation into thirteen. Other famous contemporaries were R. Tarphon, R. Jose of Galilee, Simon b. Azzai, the last of whom entered with Ben Zoma, Elisha b. Abuya, and Akiba into "Paradise," *i.e.* engaged in mystical and theosophic speculation. Elisha b. Abuya, who is often referred to as "Acher" (*i.e.* "the other one"), ultimately apostatised from Judaism. He may be regarded as the Faust of the Talmud.

(3) *The third generation* (A.D. 130–160). The most important of R. Ishmael's disciples were R. Josiah and R. Jonathan, who are often referred to in the early *Midrashim* (*Mekilta* and *Sifre*), but not in the Mishnah. The most important of Akiba's disciples

[1] Akiba's principles of interpretation influenced the new Greek translation of the Old Testament made by Aquila.

was R. Meir, who is mentioned no fewer than 330 times in the Mishnah and 452 times in the Tosephta. For a time Meir was a pupil of R. Ishmael, but afterwards of Akiba. He lived mostly at, or in the neighbourhood of, Tiberias. He was responsible for a redaction of the early Mishnah of Akiba, and it was Meir's edition of this which was ultimately worked up by Judah I. Other famous disciples of Akiba were: R. Simon b. Jochai—referred to in the Mishnah[1] always as " R. Simon" simply—R. Jose ben Chalaphta (in the Mishnah[2] always " R. Jose "), R. Jehuda ben Ilai (in the Mishnah[3] always " R. Jehuda" simply). Of these Simon ben Jochai is traditionally connected with the mystical literature. He figures prominently in the traditions of Oriental Judaism, especially in those of Persia. From Jehuda b. Ilai the groundwork of the early *Midrash Sifra* (on Leviticus) is derived. Mention may also be made here of R. Eliezer, son of Rabbi Jose of Galilee, who was a famous Haggadist, and R. Simon II., son of Gamaliel II. and father of the Patriarch Judah I.

(4) *The fourth generation* (A.D. 160–200). The great figure of this period was the Patriarch Judah the Prince (*Nasi*), often referred to as *Rabbi* without further qualification. He is famous as the compiler of the most authoritative form of the Mishnah, which, with some slight later additions, is identical with the one that has been handed down to later generations. Judah was a man of wide culture and sympathies, and dispensed a lavish hospitality. He is one of the most impressive and attractive figures in the whole history of Judaism. Himself the disciple of Simon b. Jochai and of Eleazar ben Shammua,[4]

---

[1] Some 325 times.   [2] Some 330 times.
[3] More than 600 times.
[4] Referred to in the Mishnah as " R. Eleazar " simply. He was born near Alexandria and was a disciple of Akiba, whom he visited in prison.

he surrounded himself with a band of able scholars and disciples. In virtue of his office he presided over the later (Rabbinical) Sanhedrin, which in his time seems to have moved about from place to place—from Usha to Beth Shearim, and thence to Sepphoris and Tiberias. Among the Patriarch's colleagues may be mentioned R. Nathan ha-Babli ("the Babylonian"), who had emigrated from Babylonia to Palestine. Possibly the recension of the tractate *Aboth* which underlies the text of the *Aboth de Rabbi Nathan* goes back to him. Symmachus ben Joseph, a famous Halakist and a disciple of Meir, also belongs to this period, as does the ascetic R. Pinchas (Phinehas) ben Jair, to whom miracles were attributed. He is the reputed author of a later *Midrash* known as *Tadshe*.

Some scholars, *e.g.* Strack, assign to a fifth generation the younger contemporaries of the Patriarch Judah who survived him, and who gave final authoritative recognition to the Mishnah. They form a group which is transitional to the Amoraim, and may be classed as "half-Tannaites." At their head stands Gamaliel III., the son and successor of Judah I. Others belonging to this group are : R. Chiyya, the disciple and friend of Judah, a Babylonian who, late in life, emigrated to Palestine and settled in Tiberias ; he took part in the redaction of the Halakic *Midrash* on Leviticus known as *Sifra* ; and bar Kappara, who presided over a school in Cæsarea.

The outcome of the labours of these various generations of Tannaim and of their predecessors was the Mishnah with its allied literature, to the consideration of which we now proceed.

(ii) *The Mishnah, Tosephta, and Baraithas*

[SPECIAL LITERATURE : (*a*) *Editions of the Mishnah Text.* The best text is that edited by W. H. Lowe, to which reference has been made above. A classical edition is that of Surenhusius, 6 vols., Amsterdam, 1698-1703 (Hebrew text with Latin translation and commentaries). An edition, with pointed Hebrew text and German translation in parallel columns, has been appearing (in Berlin) since 1885 (edited by Sammter and others).

H

Valuable editions of separate treatises have been edited by Strack, and an edition of the tractate *Pirke Aboth* ("Sayings of the Jewish Fathers") by Dr. C. Taylor (2nd ed., Cambridge, 1897); also an edition (with English translation and notes) of the tractate '*Abodah zara* ("The Mishnah on Idolatry") by W. A. L. Elmslie ("Text and Studies" series, Cambridge, 1911). The text of the Tosephta has been published complete by Zuckermandel (1880–82). An edition of the Tosephta tractate *Berakoth* (text, translation, and explanations) appeared in 1912 edited by Oscar Holtzmann (Giessen, Topelmann).

(*b*) *Translations.* Of English translations the following call for mention : *Eighteen Treatises of the Mishna*, translated by De Sola and Raphall (2nd ed., London, 1845); eighteen tractates translated by J. Barclay and published in a volume under the title *The Talmud* (London, 1878). A German translation of the Tosephta tractate *Berakoth* (by H. Laible) appeared in 1902.

(*c*) *Discussions, articles, etc.* Graetz, *History of the Jews*, English translation, vol. ii., chaps. 13–17 ; the article "Mishnah" in *Encycl. Brit.* xvi. 502 (9th ed.), by Dr. Schiller-Szinessy ; the articles "Tosefta" and "Baraita" (together with the literature cited) in *JE* xii. 207–209 and ii. 513–516. An important work has been published by Zuckermandel under the title *Tosefta, Mishna, und Baraitha in ihrem Verhältniss zu einander* (2 vols., Frankfort, 1908).]

(*a*) THE MISHNAH

The name "Mishnah" is a Hebrew term derived from a verb (*shanah*) which means "to repeat," and then "to learn" or "teach" by repetition. It thus came to mean "teaching" (by oral repetition).[1] The text of the Mishnah is arranged in six parts or *orders* (Heb. *sĕdārîm*, sing. *seder*). Each *order* (*seder*) is divided into *tractates* (*massektoth*[2]), and each *tractate* into *chapters* (*perakîm*[3]), and each *perek* into paragraphs, which are called individually a *Mishnah*.

[1] Such traditions (*Mishnay-Yoth*) are termed δευτερώσεις, *i.e.* "repetitions," in the Patristic literature, *e.g.* Jerome, *Ep.* 121 ("I would fail to tell of the multitude of the traditions of the Pharisees which are now called δευτερώσεις"). See *RWS*², p. 59, note.

[2] Plur. of *masseketh* (מסכת, Aram. מסכתא), from a root meaning "to weave" ; *cp.* Latin *textus.*

[3] *Perek* = "joint."

The six *sedarim* or *orders* are as follows :

(i) *Seder Zera'im*, or " Seeds," contains tractates dealing mainly with the laws connected with agriculture. But the opening tractate of this *seder* treats of prayer (*Berakoth* = " Blessings ").

(ii) *Seder Mo'ed* (*Mo'ed* = " Festival ") deals with the festivals, including the Sabbath.

(iii) *Seder Nashim* ("Women ") is mainly concerned with marriage laws, but includes two tractates on vows.

(iv) *Seder Nezikin* (" Damages ") is mainly concerned with civil and criminal law.

(v) *Seder Kodashim* (" Holy Things ") deals mainly with the laws of sacrifice. It includes an interesting and valuable tractate (*Middoth*) on the structure and dimensions of the Temple, based upon tradition.

(vi) *Seder Toharoth* (" Purifications ") deals with the laws of personal and ritual purification.

In all, the six Sedarim[1] contain sixty-three tractates, as follows :

(i) *Seder Zera'im* (eleven tractates)

1. *Berakoth* (ברכות = *Blessings* or *Benedictions*). This tractate treats of liturgical matters, at what times prayers should be offered, on what occasions, and in what places, etc. It contains nine chapters.

2. *Pe'ah* (פאה = *Corner*) deals with the questions relating to " the corners of the field " (Lev. xix. 9 ; *cf.* Deut. xxiv. 19, 21) and the rights of the poor in connexion therewith. It contains eight chapters.

3. *Demai* or *Dammai* (דמאי = *Uncertain*) discusses questions concerning corn and various fruits from which it is doubtful whether or not tithes should be given to the priests.

4. *Kil'ayim* (כלאים = *Mixtures*). This tractate discusses the problems involved in giving effect to the injunction of Lev. xix. 19 : *Thou shalt not let thy cattle gender with a diverse kind ; thou shalt not sow thy field with two kinds of seed; neither shall*

---

[1] Heb. ששה סדרים contracted to ש"ס, which in later editions of the Talmud is frequently substituted for גמרא. Hence *Shas* is a popular designation of the Babylonian Talmud.

there come upon thee a garment of two kinds of stuff mingled together (*cf.* Deut. xxii. 9–11). It contains nine chapters.

5. *Shebi'ith* (שביעית = *Seventh, i.e.* "Seventh" or "Sabbatical" year). The subject-matter of this tractate is concerned with the command of Ex. xxiii. 11 : *The seventh year thou shalt let it* [thy land] *rest and lie fallow* (*cf.* Lev. xxiii. 1–8) ; the last chapter deals with the question of the remission of debts at the end of this year (*cf.* Deut. xv. 1–3). It contains ten chapters.

6. *Terumoth* (תרומות = *Heave-offerings*). The whole subject of heave-offerings is explained and discussed in this tractate. The text for the discussion is Num. xviii. 8–20 (*cf.* Deut. xviii. 4). It contains eleven chapters.

7. *Ma'asroth* (מעשרות = *Tenths, Tithes*) deals with the tithes due to the Levites (*cf.* Num. xviii. 21–24). It contains five chapters.

8. *Ma'aser sheni* (מעשר שני = *Second Tithe*). The subject of this tractate—"second tithe"—is closely connected with that of the tractate immediately preceding (*cf.* Deut. xiv. 22–29 ; xxvi. 12–13). It contains five chapters.

9. *Challah* (חלה = *Dough*). In Num. xv. 21 the injunction is given : *Of the first of your dough ye shall give unto the Lord an heave-offering throughout your generations.* The subject-matter of this command is fully discussed in this tractate, and the use of leaven is fully dealt with. It contains four chapters.

10. *'Orlah* (ערלה = *Foreskin* [*buds, first-fruit*]) deals with the command not to eat the fruit of trees during the first three years, during which they are to be "uncircumcised" (*cf.* Lev. xix. 23 ff.). The last chapter refers to the prevalence of this custom outside the land of Israel (in Syria and elsewhere). It contains three chapters.

11. *Bikkurim* (בכורים, *First-fruits*) deals with the first-fruits which were to be brought to the Temple (*cf.* Deut. xxvi. 1 ff.; Ex. xxiii. 19). It contains three chapters.

(ii) *Seder Mo'ed* (twelve tractates)

1. *Shabbath* (שבת = *Sabbath*) is an elaborate tractate. It discusses fully the laws relating to the Sabbath, predominantly the prohibitions of work (*cf.* Ex. xvi. 22–30 ; xx. 10 ; xxiii. 12, etc.). It contains twenty-four chapters.

2. *'Erubin* (עירובין = *Combinations* or *Amalgamations*) is really an appendix to the previous tractate, dealing with one special aspect of Sabbath observance, viz. the ways in which localities can be artificially extended so as to enlarge the Sabbath boundary and evade the strict letter of the law regarding a Sabbath day's journey. It contains ten chapters.

3. *Pesachim* (פסחים = *Passovers*) sets forth the laws regulating the observance of the Passover—the search for and removal of leaven on the eve of the feast, the slaughter of the Passover lamb, its roasting, the service of thanksgiving, etc. It contains ten chapters.

4. *Shekalim* (שקלים = *Shekels*) has for its main subject the Temple-tax (*cf.* Ex. xxx. 11–16) and the various objects for which it was spent. It also touches on other matters. It contains eight chapters.

5. *Yoma* (יומא = *The Day*, sc. of Atonement). One of the most interesting and valuable of the tractates, dealing, as its name implies, with all that concerns the ritual of the Day of Atonement as celebrated in the Temple (*cf.* Lev. xvi.). It contains eight chapters.

6. *Sukkah* (סוכה = *Booth*). This interesting tractate deals, as its name suggests, with the laws concerning the observance of the Feast of Tabernacles or Booths, and other celebrations connected with the festival (*cf.* Lev. xxiii. 34 ff.; Num. xxix. 12 ff.). It contains eight chapters.

7. *Betzah* (ביצה = *Egg*), so called from its opening word ; but the nature of its contents is better indicated by the alternative title *Yom tob*, *i.e.* " Feast-day." It gives directions regarding the different kinds of work allowed or prohibited on the festivals (*cf.* Ex. xii. 10). It contains five chapters.

8. *Rosh ha-shanah* (ראש השנה = *Head of the Year*, *i.e.* New Year) deals with questions of the calendar, but more especially with the laws regarding the due observance of the beginning of the seventh month (*Tishri*), which is the Jewish (civil) new year (*cf.* Lev. xxiii. 24 ; Num. xxix. 1 ff.). It contains four chapters.

9. *Ta'anith* (תענית = *Fasting*) deals with the laws to be observed on the fast-days, together with the liturgical directions. It contains four chapters.

10. *Megillah* (מגלה = *Roll*). *Megillah* is the technical name of the " Roll" of the Book of Esther, which is read in the synagogue on the Feast of Purim (*cf.* Esther ix. 28). The tractate treats of the times appointed for the reading of the book, the manner in which it is to be written and read, and of other matters, such as the public reading of the Law on various solemn days and other topics. It contains four chapters.

11. *Mo'ed Kaṭan* (מועד קטן = *Minor Feast* or *Season*). This tractate contains directions regarding the observance of the middle days (*i.e.* the days between the two first and the two last days of the seven prescribed) of the Feasts of Passover and Tabernacles, setting forth the kinds of work allowed and prohibited on those days. At the end of the tractate there is a section on mourning customs. It contains three chapters.

12. *Chagigah* (חגיגה = *Festival offering*) treats of the duty of attending the pilgrimage feasts at Jerusalem (Passover, Weeks, and Tabernacles), the kinds of sacrifice to be brought on such occasions, and the different degrees of defilement against which the pilgrims must be on their guard. For the pilgrimage feasts see Ex. xxiii. 17 ; Deut. xvi. 16. It contains three chapters.

(iii) *Seder Nashim* (seven tractates)

1. *Yebamoth* (יְבָמוֹת = *Sisters-in-Law*, or possibly to be pointed יְבָמוּת = *The duty of Levirate marriage*). The main subjects dealt with in this tractate are (*a*) Levirate marriage (*cf.* Deut. xxv. 5–10 [Matt. xxii. 24]) ; (*b*) the ceremony of the " Chalitzah " (*cf.* Ruth iv. 7), and all that this involves. " Chalitzah " means the " drawing off " of the shoe (*i.e.* sandal). It symbolised renunciation of rights and possession on the part of the widow ; (*c*) the forbidden degrees in marriage (*cf.* Lev. xviii., etc.). It contains sixteen chapters.

2. *Kethuboth* (כתובות = *Marriage-deeds*), as the title implies, has for its subject marriage-deeds and marriage-settlements - (*cf.* Ex. xxii. 16). It also deals with the subject of divorce. It contains thirteen chapters.

3. *Nedarim* (נדרים = *Vows*) treats of the whole subject of vows and their annulment on the basis of Num. xxx. It contains eleven chapters.

4. *Nazir* (נזיר = *Nazirite*) deals with the subject of the Nazirites (*cf.* Num. vi.). It contains nine chapters.

5. *Sotah* (סוטה = *Adulteress*). The subject of the tractate is " the woman suspected of adultery " (*cf.* Num. v. 11–31). It contains nine chapters.

6. *Gittin* (גטין = *Divorces*) deals with the procedure involved in delivering in due form " bills of divorce," the preparation of such documents, their attestation, etc. (*cf.* Deut. xxiv. 1). It contains nine chapters.

7. *Kiddushin* (קדושין = *Betrothals*) deals with the subject implied by its title. It contains four chapters.

(iv) *Seder Nezikin* (ten tractates)

1. *Baba kamma* (בבא קמא = *First Gate*) ;
2. *Baba metzi'a* (בבא מציעא = *Middle Gate*) ;
3. *Baba bathra* (בבא בתרא = *Last Gate*). These three tractates originally formed a single treatise under the general title of *Masseketh Nezikin* (מסכת נזיקין), "Tractate of Damages." When the order was compiled, and other tractates had to be included, the one on Damages was subdivided into three, bearing the titles given above, and each containing ten chapters.

The three tractates are primarily concerned with questions of law ; the first deals with damages of various kinds caused by man or beasts for which he is responsible (*cf.* Ex. xxi. 18 ff. ; xxii. 5 ff.) ; the second gives directions regarding the disposal of property which has been found, trusts, the prohibition of usury, etc., the treatment of hired labourers (*cf.* Ex. xxii. ; Lev. xix. 13, etc.) ; the third is concerned with the laws of property, landed estates, boundary marks, sale of land, etc.

4. *Sanhedrin* (סנהדרין = *Courts*) and

5. *Makkoth* (מכות = *Stripes*) anciently formed a single tractate. The former deals with the constitution and procedure of the various courts of justice and the administration of the criminal law (capital punishment, etc.). The latter has for its subject the infliction of corporal punishment, the thirty-nine stripes prescribed in the Law (*cf.* Deut. xxv. 1–3), the punishment of false witnesses (*cf.* Deut. xix. 16 ff.), and the laws of the cities of refuge (*cf.* Num. xxxv. 10 ff.). *Sanhedrin* contains eleven, and *Makkoth* three, chapters.

6. *Shebu'oth* (שבועות = *Oaths*) deals with the subject implied by the title, viz. oaths taken in private or administered with judicial sanction (*cf.* Lev. v. 4 ff.). It contains eight chapters.

7. *'Eduyyoth* (עדיות = *Testimonies* or *Evidences*). This tractate is rather different in character from most of the others. It gives the testimony of later Rabbinical authorities as to the laws sanctioned by earlier teachers. It is largely concerned with the opposing opinions of the schools of Hillel and Shammai on a variety of subjects. It contains eight chapters.

8. *'Abodah zarah* (עבודה זרה = *Strange worship, Idolatry*) contains the principles and regulations which should govern Jews in their attitude towards idolatry and idolators. This is one of the most interesting of the tractates, discussing as it does the problems that confronted a pious community in a heathen environment. It contains five chapters.

9. *Aboth* or *Pirke Aboth* (פרקי אבות = *Sections of the Fathers*). This is not only the best known, but in many respects the most valuable of the Mishnaic tractates. The "Fathers" are the Fathers of Jewish tradition, and the treatise contains a collection of their ethical maxims. The Rabbis represented mostly belong to the Tannaim. It traces the "chain" of tradition, which was ultimately embodied in the Oral Law, from its beginning in Moses, and in this way justifies and safeguards its authority. The whole tractate is included in the Jewish Prayer Book, and at certain times is read in the synagogue service. It contains five chapters, with an appendix ("The Perek of R. Meir ").

10. *Horayoth* (הוריות = *Teachings, Decisions*) deals with wrong decisions given by authorities (or a court), and the sacrifices

thereby necessitated if the people acted on such wrong decisions (*cf.* Lev. iv.). It contains three chapters.

(v) *Seder Ḳodashim* (eleven tractates)

1. *Zebachim* (זבחים = *Sacrifices*) contains the laws relating to sacrifices and offerings. It is an important source of information regarding the sacrificial system generally and its doctrinal significance. It contains fourteen chapters.

2. *Menachoth* (מנחות = *Meal-offerings*) deals with meal-offerings and the laws regarding libations (*cf.* Lev. ii.; v. 11–12, etc.; Num. v. 11–31 ; vi. 12–20 ; xxviii. ; xxix.). It contains thirteen chapters.

3. *Chullin* (חולין = *Profane things*) is mainly concerned with laws and regulations concerning the slaughter of animals for ordinary domestic (*i.e.* non-sacrificial) use. It also deals with the general question of eating animal food, and other matters. It contains twelve chapters.

4. *Bekoroth* (בכורות = *First-born*) deals with the regulations regarding the first-born of men and animals (*cf.* Ex. xiii. 2, 12–16; Lev. xxvii. 26 f.'; Num. viii. 16–18, etc.). It contains nine chapters.

5. *'Arakin* (ערכין = *Estimations*) deals with valuations of persons and things dedicated to the Temple (*cf.* Lev. xxvii. 2–8). Some laws regarding the year of Jubile are also included (*cf.* Lev. xxv.). It contains nine chapters.

6. *Temurah* (תמורה = *Exchange*) deals with the laws regarding the substitution of a "common" (*i.e.* non-sacred or secular) animal for one already dedicated to the altar (*cf.* Lev. xxvii. 10, 33). It contains seven chapters.

7. *Kerithoth* (כריתות = *Excisions*). The sins which incur the punishment of "cutting off" from the people (*cf.* Gen. xvii. 14 ; Ex. xii. 15, etc.) are discussed in this tractate. It contains six chapters.

8. *Meʿilah* (מעילה = *Trespass*). The "trespasses" here referred to consist in applying to secular use things belonging to the Temple or altar (*cf.* Lev. v. 15 f.). It contains six chapters.

9. *Tamid* (תמיד shortened for עולת תמיד = *Continual Burnt-offering*). This interesting and valuable tractate gives details relating to the arrangement and ritual of the daily burnt-offering, which was offered morning and evening in the Temple (*cf.* Ex. xxix. 38–42 ; Num. xxviii. 3–8). It contains valuable information about the early Liturgy, and has seven chapters.

10. *Middoth* (מדות = *Measurements*). A valuable tractate, embodying much sound tradition about the structure, buildings, etc., of the Temple. It contains five chapters.

11. *Ḳinnim* (קנים = *Birds' nests*) gives information about the

dove-offerings (two turtle doves or two young pigeons [1]) which might be offered on account of poverty, instead of a lamb, by a woman for purification after child-birth (*cf.* Lev. xii. 8) ; the same might also be offered as a free-will burnt-offering (*cf.* Lev. i. 14–17). It contains three chapters.

(vi) *Seder Ṭeharoth* (twelve tractates)

1. *Kelim* (כלים = *Vessels*). A long and important tractate which has for its subject the different degrees of Levitical uncleanness that may attach to furniture, garments, and utensils of various kinds (*cf.* Lev. xi. 32 ; Num. xix. 14 f. ; xxxi. 20 f.). It contains thirty chapters.

2. *Ohaloth* (אהלות = *Tents*) treats of the Levitical uncleanness that may arise in connexion with tents and other kinds of habitation. A dead body makes unclean not merely (as in other cases) by contact, but by proximity ; as, *e.g.*, in the case of a man who finds himself in the same tent with a dead body (*cf.* Num. xix. 14). It contains eighteen chapters.

3. *Negaʿim* (נגעים = *Plagues, i.e.* leprosy). This tractate deals with leprosy in its various degrees (*cf.* Lev. xiii.–xiv.). It contains fourteen chapters.

4. *Parah* (פרה = *Heifer*) gives minute regulations regarding the "red cow" (or heifer) of Num. xix.—the age, required characteristics, preparation for slaughter, making ready of the ashes, and sprinkling of the water mingled with ashes, etc. It contains twelve chapters.

5. *Ṭoharoth* (טהרות = *Purifications*). The title is euphemistic for *Defilements*. Various degrees of minor Levitical uncleanness are dealt with that lasted till sunset. It contains ten chapters.

6. *Miḳwaʾoth* (מקואות = *Baths* or *Cisterns*) gives directions as to the proper requirements of the ritual bath (*cf.* Lev. xv. 11, 12). It contains ten chapters

7. *Niddah* (נדה = *Uncleanness* [menstruation]) deals with the Levitical uncleanness incurred by women under certain recurring physical conditions (*cf.* Lev. xii. ; xv. 19 ff.). It contains ten chapters.

8. *Makshirin* (מכשירין = *Things made ritually fit for certain purposes*) sets forth the conditions under which certain things, by coming into contact with liquids, become capable of defilement (*cf.* Lev. xi. 34, 37 f.). It contains six chapters.

9. *Zabim* (זבים = *Persons with fluxes*) deals with the impurity attaching to persons afflicted with running issues (*cf.* Lev. xv. 2 ff.). It contains five chapters.

---

[1] The one for a sin-offering, the other for a burnt-offering.

10. *Tebul Yom* (טְבוּל יוֹם = *Immersed on (during) a day*) has for its subject the condition of a person who has already taken the ritual bath, but has to await the coming of sunset before he can be regarded as completely free from defilement (*cf.* Lev. xv. 5 ; xxii. 6, 7). It contains four chapters.

11. *Yadayim* (יָדַיִם = *Hands*) is an interesting and important tractate, being concerned with the question of ritual uncleanness and its removal by washing of the hands (*cf.* Matt. v. 2, 20 ; xxiii. 25 ; Mark vii. 2–4 ; Luke xi. 38–40). It contains four chapters.

12. *'Uktzim* (עוּקְצִין = *Stalks*) deals with the question how far the stalks may be considered part of the fruit, and so capable of conveying impurity when touched by anything unclean. It contains three chapters.

The Mishnah is written in New Hebrew, an idiom which, though essentially scholastic in character, and cultivated as a learned language, was developed organically from the older language. It has a large admixture of Greek and Latin words.[1]

As has already been pointed out, the Mishnah, as we have it, has grown out of earlier compilations. The date of its final redaction may be fixed approximately some time before A.D. 220, and its present form is due (with the exception of some slight additions) to the Patriarch Judah I.

Possibly the first composition of such a collection of material was already begun by the early disciples of Hillel and Shammai. R. Akiba compiled an edition, which was continued and enlarged by his disciple R. Meir, and this was the principal source of Judah's work, though he also used other compilations of a similar kind (*e.g.* the Mishnah of Abba Shaul). Clear indications of these different *strata* are often discernible.

As Schechter well remarks, Rabbi Judah's work was undertaken and accomplished, "not with the

[1] There is a good discussion of the character of this idiom in M. H. Segal's essay, "Misnaic Hebrew and its Relation to Biblical Hebrew and Aramaic," published in *JQR*, July, 1908 (and also separately reprinted by Horace Hart, Oxford). For the grammar, see K. Albrecht, *Neuhebräische Grammatik* (in the "Porta Linguarum Semiticarum" series), 1913.

purpose of providing the nation with a legal code, but with the intention of furnishing them with a sort of thesaurus, incorporating such portions of the traditional lore as he considered most important. Hence the ground for his including in the work the opinions of the minority (*e.g.* of the school of Shammai), which only in a few exceptional cases were accepted as a norm for practice."[1]

Judah's compilation was accepted as a sort of canonical collection. But there were other collections of similar material, embodying the teaching of the Tannaim, parts of which have survived. Thus there are scattered about the Talmud certain sections known as *Baraitha* (see below) which are of this nature, and a sort of " apocryphal" Mishnah is extant under the name of *Tosephta* (see below).

Though the contents of the Mishnah are predominantly legalistic in character, there are other elements, which lend variety, such as the description of the architecture and administration of the Temple in *Middoth*, and the delineation of sacrificial rites and ceremonies as they were actually practised. Many of these elements are of earlier literary origin than the compilation of the collection, and in some cases much earlier.[2]

The style of the Mishnah is terse and compressed, almost to baldness. Brevity, for the sake of memorising, was aimed at. Only very occasionally does a flowing description emerge, such as the charming picture of a procession of first-fruits arriving in Jerusalem (*Bikkurim* iii. 2 f.). Some illustrative citations from the Mishnah will be given in the sections that follow to exemplify its relation to the Tosephta and Gemara respectively.

---

[1] Hastings's *DB*, extra vol. (v.), p. 61*b*.
[2] See Schechter, Hastings's *DB*, v. p. 62.

(b) THE TOSEPHTA

The name " Tosephta" means " Addition " or
" Supplement," and is given to a collection of
Halakoth parallel to the Mishnah proper. The
material embodied in it is largely of the same
character and covers the same ground as that in the
latter. Like the Mishnah, the Tosephta is divided
into six " orders," or *sedarim*, containing the corresponding tractates, with the exception of *Aboth* in
Seder Nezikin, and *Kinnim, Middoth,* and *Tamid* in
Seder Kodashim. The Tosephta, though it covers
the same ground as the Mishnah, deals with the
material in a much freer manner. It often illustrates
the theme by anecdotes, and sometimes gives the
Halakoth in fuller form. Consequently it is a valuable
supplement, especially for critical purposes, of the
official Mishnah.

The exact relation of the Tosephta to the Mishnah and the
Baraithas of the Talmud has not yet been satisfactorily determined. The relation with the Mishnah is undoubtedly very
close. The phenomena are complex. Parts of the Tosephta
apparently come from collections earlier than our Mishnah,
but in the collected form in which we know it, it presupposes a
knowledge of the Mishnah in its official shape. Other elements
may be of an even later date, presupposing the Gemara of the
Talmud, and having been recast in the New Hebrew of the
Mishnah. Schechter concludes, on the basis of these data,
that "the date of its final redaction falls in the later age of the
'Amoraim, though its composition may have been initiated by
R. Chiyya and R. Hoshaya, the disciples of R. Jedudah [the
Patriarch], to whom tradition attributes such a work, undertaken
in imitation of the Tosephta of R. Nehemiah, who is credited
with having collected 'additions' to the Mishnah of R. Akiba."[1]

The following brief extracts from the tractate
Sanhedrin will serve to illustrate the style of Mishnah
and Tosephta, and their relation to one another.
The paragraphs are taken from the Mishnah,

[1] *op. cit.* p. 62b.

Sanhedrin iv. 5 f., and the Tosephta, vii. 8–11, viii. 1, 2.[1]

Mishnah

:" The Sanhedrin sat in the form of a semicircle so that they might all see each other ; and two judges' clerks stood in front, one on the right and one on the left, taking down the evidence for the prosecution and the defence.   R. Jehudah [bar Ilai] holds that there were three : one taking down evidence for the prosecution, the second for the defence, and the third taking down both.   Before them sat three rows of disciples, each knowing his own place.   If it became necessary to appoint another judge, he was appointed from the front row, while one from the second row took his place, and one from the third row that of the second.   And for the third row one of the assembled audience was chosen.   He did not sit in the place just vacated, but in a place for which he was suited."

Tosephta

vii. 8. *When the Prince* [" *Nasi* "] *enters, all the people stand, and do not sit until he bids them do so. When " the Father of the Court " [" Ab beth din "] enters, they stand up on either -side to make a passage for him, until he has come to and taken his place. When a member of the court enters, one after another stands up to make room for him until he has come to and taken his place.   When the services of the children and disciples of the members of the court are required, they pass over the heads of the assembled people.   And although they say that it is not praiseworthy in a disciple of the wise to come in late, he may yet go out if necessity demand it, and come in again and take his place.*

[1] From the translation by H. Danby (in the series or " Translations of Early Documents "), pp. 75–77.

9. *The children and disciples of the members of the court, if they can understand the proceedings, turn their faces to their fathers; if not, they turn their faces towards the assembled people.* R. *Eleazar, the son of* R. *Zadok, says:* "*Also at a feast children are placed by the side of their fathers.*"

10. *When a member of the court comes in, his opinion is not asked until he has had time to make up his mind. Similarly a disciple should not be asked his opinion as soon as he comes in. If on his entering he finds the court occupied in some legal discussion, he may not break in upon their talk until he has sat down and discovered what is the subject with which they are occupied. If he should do so it is of such a one that it is said:* "*There are seven marks of the clod, and seven of the wise man,*" *etc.*[1]

11. *Seven rules of interpretation did the elder Hillel expound before the elders of Bethyra . . . . . .*
. . . .[2]

viii. 1. *Every Sanhedrin in which are two members competent to speak, and all to comprehend, is worthy of being a Sanhedrin. If there are three, it is an average assembly; if four, a wise one. The Sanhedrin was arranged in the form of a semicircle, so that they might all see each other. The Prince* ["*Nasi*"] *sat in the middle, with the elders on his right and left.* R. *Eleazar, the son of Zadok, said:* "*When Rabban Gamaliel* [*II.*] *sat in Jabneh (Jamnia), my father and another sat on his right, and the other elders on his left.*" *And why does one sit in accordance with age on the right? Because of the reverence due to age.*

2. *There were three rows of disciples sitting in front*

---

[1] This is cited from *Pirke Aboth*, v. 10, and the passage continues: "The wise man speaks not before one who is greater than himself in wisdom, and does not interrupt the words of his companion."

[2] The omitted lines give the technical designations of the seven exegetical rules (afterwards expanded to thirteen). See Singer, p. 13.

of them : the most important first, the second in importance next, and the third in the last row. After this there was no fixed order, except that each should be placed four cubits away from his fellow.

The officers of the court, the defendant, the witnesses and their refuters, and the refuters of their refuters, used to stand within the front row near the people. And it was always easy to know which was the defendant, since he was always stationed next to the chief witness.

It will be noticed, when the two parallel passages given above are compared, that the matter contained in the Tosephta is at once fuller, and also introduces elements that are not represented in the Mishnah text at all.

(c) THE BARAITHAS

The term " Baraitha " (בְּרִיתָא) is an Aramaic one meaning " outside," " external " (sc. Mishnah [1]), and designates a Tannaitic tradition not incorporated in the official Mishnah, or a collection of such.   It has been suggested [2] that this Aramaic designation may be an adaptation of the New Hebrew term *sepharim ha-chitzonim, i.e.* " the external books," which denotes apocryphal writings, and is employed by Akiba (*Sanh.* x. 1).   The relation between the official Mishnah and the Baraithas would thus be similar to that of the Apocryphal Books to the canonical writings of Scripture.[3]

In the Babylonian Talmud " Baraitha " is applied to very varied kinds of literature—in fact, to any Tannaitic traditions not contained in the official

---

[1] In Aramaic מתניתא.

[2] In *JE* ii. 513*b* (*s.v. Baraita*).

[3] Another explanation connects the term with the Tannaitic tradition taught in the private schools (designated *bara*, " outside ").

Mishnah, such as the collections known as Tosephta, and even the Tannaitic *Midrashim Sifra, Sifre,* and *Mekilta.*

A large amount of the material, however, which is properly termed "Baraitha" exists in the form of isolated sections, scattered about the Talmuds,[1] where they are distinguishable from the rest of the Gemara by the fact that they are cited in Hebrew, while the language of the Gemara is Aramaic. They are also introduced by a formula which runs: "Our Rabbis have taught" (*tenô rabbānan*), or "There is a tradition" (*tanyā*), or where an authority is cited by name: "Rabbi So-and-so taught" (*tenî R.*).

The material contained in the Baraitha sections embraces both Halakah and Haggadah, the latter element being often very considerable, while in the official Mishnah it is reduced to a minimum. The Baraitha material also may be broadly distinguished into two main divisions, viz. the pre-Mishnaic and post-Mishnaic, which fundamentally differ from each other. The former, for instance, has often preserved the older Halakah which was rejected by the official Mishnah.[2] In many cases also the reasons are given fully for a Halakah which is merely enunciated by the official Mishnah, and assumed as axiomatic without further discussion.

The Haggadic Baraithas are probably survivals of earlier collections of such material which have perished. That such collections, consisting of homiletic expansions with an admixture of legendary elements, and based on a continuous Biblical text, were early in existence is suggested by such a book as *Jubilees* or the so-called *Biblical Antiquities* of Pseudo-Philo. From such collections many of the

[1] It should be noted that these sections are often cited *from collections*, such as those referred to above.

[2] This applies particularly to the rejected Halakoth of the school of Shammai.

Haggadic Baraithas cited in the Talmud were probably drawn.

The later (post-Mishnaic) Baraithas differ altogether from the earlier. They presuppose the official Mishnah and supplement it, sometimes adapting its rules to the conditions of a somewhat later time. Occasionally views differing from those accepted in the official Mishnah, but unrecorded there, are given, with the names of the authorities. But even in these cases the motive for presenting such opinions seems to have been a desire to supplement the official text, and there is some reason to suppose that the disciples of Judah I. may have even been prompted to undertake this work by the Patriarch himself. Their work was probably embodied in collections of which only excerpts have survived, which have been preserved in the Talmuds and *Midrashim*, and the Tosephta.

In the period of the Amoraim there was some conflict of opinion regarding the authority of the Baraitha collections when these, in any of their *dicta*, contradicted the rules accepted in the official Mishnah. The rule ultimately laid down was that such opinions could lay claim to no binding authority. On the other hand, in the large number of cases where the Baraithas supplemented the official Mishnah without contradicting it they were cited and highly valued. The Baraitha collections were diligently studied by some of the Talmudic scholars—in Babylonia especially by Sheshet and Joseph b. Chiyyah, who belonged to the third generation of the Amoraim, and who prided themselves upon their knowledge of such collections. In general, however, the Palestinian scholars possessed a wider and more exact knowledge of these collections.

I

(iii) *The Talmuds*

[SPECIAL LITERATURE : A Latin translation of a large part of the Palestinian Talmud is given in Ugolini's *Thesaurus*, vols. xvii., xx., xxv., and xxx. A complete translation into French has been made by Moses Schwab (Paris, 1871 and following years) ; and an English translation of Schwab's first volume (*Berakoth*) appeared in 1885. The Haggadic portions are given in Wünsche, *Der jerusalemische Talmud in seinen haggadischen Bestandtheilen* (Zurich, 1880).

An edition of the Babylonian Talmud (Hebrew text and German translation), by W. L. Goldschmidt, which is not yet completed, has been appearing for many years past. The Haggadic passages have been translated by Wünsche, *Der babylonische Talmud in seinen haggadischen Bestandtheilen* (2 vols., 1886, 1888).

Translations of single tractates have appeared in Latin, German, French, and English. In English, the treatise *Chagigah*, translated, with introduction, notes, glossary, and indices, by the Rev. A. W. Streane (Cambridge, 1891).

For other literature, see the list printed on pp. 81 f. above.

A valuable conspectus of Talmudic archæology is contained in Dr. S. Krauss's *Talmudische Archäologie* (3 vols., Leipzig, 1910–12).

An invaluable aid to the study of the Talmuds is embodied in various works by Bacher, especially his *Agada der Tannaiten*, vol. i. (*von Hillel bis Akiba*), 2nd ed. 1903 ; vol. ii. (*von Akiba's Tod bis zum Abschlusz der Mischna*), 1890 ; and his *Die Agada der Palästinenischen Amoräer* (3 vols., 1892, 1896, 1899) ; also *Die Agada der Babylonischen Amoräer* (1878).

For Talmudic terminology, the following works may be mentioned : W. Bacher, *Die exegetische Terminologie der judischen Traditionsliteratur*, Part i., *Die Bibelexegetische Terminologie der Tannaiten* (Leipzig, 1899) ; Part ii., *Die Bibel- und Traditions-exegetische Terminologie der Amoräer* (Leipzig, 1905). In this connexion also Mielziner's *Introduction to the Talmud* (referred to above, p. 81) is useful.

The following grammatical and lexicographical works are important : G. Dalman's *Grammatik des Jüdisch-Palästinischen Aramäisch* (for the dialect of the Palestinian Talmud) ; C. Levias, *A Grammar of the Aramaic Idiom contained in the Babylonian Talmud* (Cincinnati, 1900), and Max L. Margolis, *A Manual of the Aramaic Language of the Babylonian Talmud* (Munich, 1910) ; Marcus Jastrow, *A Dictionary of the Targumim, the Talmud Babli and Yerushalmi, and the Midrashic Literature* (London : Luzac, 2 vols., 1903).

Though not strictly falling within our purview here, it may be useful to mention the following works on Rabbinic theology : *Some Aspects of Rabbinic Theology*, by S. Schechter (London, 1909) ; and *Jewish Theology Systematically and Historically Considered*, by Dr. K. Kohler (New York. 1918).]

I

With the completion of the work of the Tannaim, which is embodied in its most authoritative form in the official Mishnah, though it also embraces, as we have seen, the earlier *Midrashim* (*Mekilta, Sifre, Sifra*), as well as many Baraithas and the Tosephta, the work of the Jewish schools did not cease. On the contrary, the text of the official Mishnah became the basis for further discussion and amplification in the schools both of Palestine and of Babylonia ; and the outcome of all this activity is embodied in the two Talmuds. The authorities who were responsible for this work are technically designated "Amoraim" (Heb. אֲמֹרָאִים), *i.e.* "speakers" or "interpreters," and the term is applied to the scholars who flourished between A.D. 220 and about 500.

It is important to remember that during this period the principal centres of Rabbinical learning were not confined to Palestine (Tiberias, Sepphoris, Cæsarea), but existed also in Babylonia (Nehardea, Sura, and later Pumbeditha). In fact, the Babylonian Academies gradually took the place of the earlier schools in Palestine. "Palestine did not continue to offer a friendly welcome. Under the more tolerant rulers of Babylonia, or Persia, Jewish learning found a refuge from the harshness experienced under those of the Holy Land. The Babylonian Jewish schools in Nehardea, Sura, and Pumbeditha rapidly surpassed the Palestinian in reputation, and in the year 350, owing to natural decay, the Palestinian schools closed." [1]

It may be added that a difference of title distinguishes the Amoraim of Palestine from those of Babylonia. The former, who had been ordained by the Patriarch (*Nasi*), bore the title of

---

[1] Abrahams, *Short Hist. of Jewish Literature*, p. 20.

" Rabbi," while those who had received ordination in Babylonia were as a rule called " Rab."[1]

The "Amoraim," as their name implies, were originally "speakers" who rehearsed to the audience of the disciples the original discourse of the earlier *Tanna* or " Rabbi." They were not primarily independent teachers or authorities, though they did, indeed, develop a certain amount of independence and authority in dealing with the old material, which they made the basis for further development. Their function was "to interpret the often very brief and concise expression of the Mishnah, to investigate its reasons and sources, to reconcile seeming contradictions, to compare its canons with those of the Baraithoth, and to apply its decisions and established principles to new cases not yet provided for."[2] Their authorities were the earlier Tannaim and the literature embodying the Tannaite traditions, especially the Mishnah and Baraithas.

These teachers were active during the three centuries A.D. 200 to 500, and the results of their work are embodied in the two Talmuds. Like the earlier Tannaim, they were men of very varied character and antecedents. Some were rich and well-to-do, others were extremely poor. Very few were professional men of letters, and many of them combined some secular calling or trade with the pursuit of learning, being physicians, artisans, or even field-labourers, as well as teachers of the Law. In this way they combined scholarship—for their scholarship within their own domain was remarkable—with contact with the practical affairs of life. The variety of interest and outlook thus secured is reflected in the Talmudic literature. The Amoraim themselves

---

[1] The title " Rabban" is superior to both " Rabbi " and " Rab," being confined to the Patriarchs and heads of the Sanhedrin, *e.g.* " Rabban Gamaliel."

[2] Mielziner, *op. cit.* p. 40.

were also men of very varied character and achievement. The most important of these teachers, of whom several hundreds are mentioned in the Talmud, are the following, classified into five (or sometimes six) generations:

(1) FIRST GENERATION (220–280) : (a) *Palestine.* Perhaps the oldest of the Amoraim proper is Chanina b. Chama (A.D. 180–260), who migrated at a mature age from Babylonia to Palestine, and taught in Sepphoris. He was a friend and pupil of the Patriarch Judah I., who greatly esteemed him. He was famous as a Haggadist, and a master of pungent speech. To him is ascribed the aphorism : "Everything is in the power of Heaven except the fear of Heaven."

Another famous teacher of this generation who lectured at Sepphoris, and afterwards at Cæsarea, was R. Hoshaiah, one of the reputed compilers of the Tosephta. He also was a famous Haggadist, and, it is interesting to note, was often engaged in controversy with Christians in Palestine, and may even have met, in such circumstances, the famous Church Father Origen, who presided over a famous theological school at Cæsarea for some years following A.D. 231.

The principal centre of learning in Palestine was at Tiberias, where a great school was established by R. Jochanan b. Nappacha (A.D. 199–279), a pupil of Chanina. He is often referred to in the Talmud (usually as "R. Jochanan" simply), and may be regarded as the leading Amora of Palestine. Jochanan seems to have been a man of great attractiveness, with a sense of artistic beauty—he was a lover of Greek. He may, perhaps, be regarded as having laid the foundations of the Palestinian Talmud.

A contemporary of R. Jochanan was his brother-in-law Simon b. Lakish (A.D. 200–275), usually styled "Resh Lakish." The two men were closely associated during life and worked together, though Simon exercised a completely independent judgement in his interpretation of the Halakah. It is said of him by a contemporary that "when he discussed Halakic questions it was as if he were uprooting mountains and rubbing them together" (*Sanh.* 24*a*). He was also a great Haggadist. Some of his sayings are strikingly bold and pungent: "No man commits a sin unless struck by momentary insanity"; "Do not live in the neighbourhood of an ignorant man who is pious." Simon was a man of masterful personality, intensely courageous, and a genuine lover of truth.

Another famous contemporary was Joshua ben Levi (first half of the third century A.D.), who figures prominently in many legends. He presided over the school of Lydda, in southern Palestine. A man of wealth and public spirit, Joshua occupied a prominent position in the affairs of his time. His authority as a teacher was widely recognised, and he was eminent as both a Halakist and a Haggadist. He strongly insisted upon the importance of study, combined with piety. In character he was tender and sympathetic towards the poor and unfortunate, and a saying attributed to him declares that the Messiah when He comes will be found among the beggars and cripples of Rome.

Another eminent Haggadist of this period was R. Simlai, who belonged to both Palestine and Babylonia. He was probably born in the latter country (at Nehardea), but migrated to Palestine, settling in Lydda, and later going to Galilee. In Palestine he often engaged in friendly controversy with Jewish Christians.

With this generation ought strictly to be reckoned R. Eleazar ben Pedath (usually referred to as "R. Eleazar" simply), who died probably about A.D. 279. Born in Babylonia, where he studied under Rab and

Samuel, he migrated to Palestine, and became a colleague of R. Jochanan at Tiberias, succeeding the latter as head of the college. He was a fine example of a great scholar who accepted poverty proudly.

(b) *Babylonia.* The chief Babylonian Amora is Abba Arika (A.D. 175–247), commonly styled "Rab," *i.e.* "the Teacher" *par excellence* (*cf.* "Rabbi" applied to Judah I.). In youth he accompanied his uncle Chiyya to Palestine, and became a pupil of the Patriarch Judah I. After the death of the latter he returned to Babylonia and founded at Sura in A.D. 219 the famous Academy, which was destined to last eight centuries. This was attended by, it is said, some 1,200 pupils, and more than 100 of his disciples are mentioned by name in the Talmud.

A contemporary and fellow-disciple with Rab of the Patriarch Judah I. was Mar Samuel (180–254), under whom the school at Nehardea attained a high degree of prosperity. It was Samuel who laid down the principle, so important for Jewish communities living under non-Jewish governments, that "the law of the land is law."

Rab determined the form and method of the Babylonian Talmud. Taking the Mishnah of Judah I. as the basis, and adding to this the other Tannaitic traditions, he proceeded to derive from these sources the theoretic explanations and applications of the religious Law. "The legal and ritual opinions recorded in Rab's name and his disputes with Samuel constitute the main body of the Babylonian Talmud." [1]

To his manifold activities in the cause of learning Rab also added a warm interest in the welfare of the mass of the people. For their benefit he organised popular lectures to promote the study of Rabbinical learning generally. He was also deeply interested in the synagogue Liturgy, and was responsible for the

[1] *JE* ii. 30.

present form of one of its finest prayers.[1]   One of the
striking sayings attributed to Rab runs : " Man will
hereafter be called to account for depriving himself
of the good things which the world lawfully offers."

(ii) SECOND   GENERATION   (A.D.   280–320):
(a) *Palestine.* Abbahu, a native of Palestine, and
head of the Academy at Cæsarea, was the most
prominent Palestinian Amora of this period.   He
had been a pupil of R. Jochanan at Tiberias, and
was on terms of intimate friendship with the latter.
He was wealthy and popular, not only with his own
people, but also with the high Roman officials at
Cæsarea.   He frequently engaged in controversy
with the Christians of his day.   His interests were
wide (he was a good Greek scholar), and he was
eminent as both a Halakist and a Haggadist.
Popular, cultivated, and influential, he is one of the
most attractive figures among the Rabbis.   Among
his contemporaries were Chiyya bar Abba, Ammi,
and Assi (Ammi ultimately became head of the
Academy at Tiberias).

Another famous name that belongs to this
generation is that of Samuel ben Nachman
(Nachmani), pre-eminent as a Haggadist (born at the
beginning of the third, and died at the beginning of the
fourth, century).   He visited the Emperor Diocletian
at Paneas.   To him is ascribed the rule that during
the heat of the day instruction should be suspended.

(b) *Babylonia.* Rab Huna (A.D. 212–297) succeeded
Rab as head of the school at Sura, and completed
Rab's work in making this famous Academy the
centre of Jewish intellectual life.   A man of great
learning and wealth (though in early life he had been
very poor), he was also distinguished for piety and
open-handed hospitality.   He was equally eminent
as a Halakist and a Haggadist.

[1] The *'Alēnû* Prayer (see Singer, pp. 76–77, beginning " It
is our duty . . . ").

Another disciple, equally eminent, of Rab was Judah b. Ezekiel (A.D. 220–299). He often stayed in the house of Rab, whose son Chiyya was his pupil. Judah was a scholar of vast learning and possessed of great critical powers. He founded the Academy of Pumbeditha, and there introduced a new method of instruction, based upon critical principles. He may be regarded as the founder of Talmudic dialectics.

Two other Rabbis must be mentioned in this connexion, Chisda (died A.D. 309 at an advanced age) and Shesheth. Chisda, who had been a disciple of Rab and Huna, presided over the school at Sura for ten years (A.D. 299–309). He was a great casuist. Shesheth was a friend of Chisda, and ultimately founded a school at Shilhe. He possessed an extraordinarily retentive memory, which compensated for his blindness. It is said that he was able to recite the entire body of Tannaitic tradition, together with the Amoraic interpretations (T.B. *Shebuoth* 41*b*). He hired a scholar to read the Mishnah and Baraitha to him (*Sanh.* 86*a*). He was a great casuist.[1]

(iii) THIRD GENERATION (A.D. 320–370): (*a*) *Palestine.* During this period the Palestinian schools gradually decayed, and finally ceased to exist, owing to the persecuting policy of the Christian Emperors Constantine and Constantius. Perhaps the most important Palestinian Amora of the period was R. Jeremiah b. Abba (always referred to simply as " R. Jeremiah "), a Babylonian, who migrated to Cæsarea, where he made rapid progress in his studies. Among his teachers were Abbahu and his own countryman Ze'ira. The latter, a Babylonian, who had been a pupil of Chisda and Judah b. Ezekiel at

[1] Another Babylonian Amora of some importance belonging to this period is R. Nachman bar Jacob (died A.D. 320). He had been a pupil of Mar Samuel, and became head of the school at Nehardea. He is often referred to as " R. Nachman."

Pumbeditha, out of his love for the Holy Land emigrated to Palestine, where he became the intimate friend of Assi and Chiyya bar Abba. Ze'ira was highly regarded by Abbahu, the head of the school at Cæsarea, and was a pupil of the latter. On account of his piety he was known as "the pious Babylonian." Among his Haggadic sayings the following is notable: "He who has never sinned is worthy of reward only if he has withstood temptation to do so" (T.J. *Kidd.* 61*d*).

Jeremiah, as has been said, was Ze'ira's pupil, and astonished his contemporaries by his diligence in study. He ultimately became recognised as the leading scholar in Tiberias, and his fame as a scholar was equally great in both Babylonia and Palestine.

A famous pupil of Jeremiah was R. Jonah, who became a leading Amora in Palestine in the fourth century. With his schoolmate and lifelong colleague, R. Jose II., he had studied under Ze'ira. About A.D. 350 these scholars presided over the school at Tiberias. An elder colleague, and, like them, an eminent member of the Tiberias circle, was R. Haggai, who had likewise been a pupil of Ze'ira. It is reported that "Haggai opened the discourse and Jonah and Jose closed it" (T.J. *Rosh ha-shanah* ii. 58*b*). Jonah left a worthy son and successor in Mani II. (Mani is an abbreviation of Menachem), who was a pupil of Jose II. He lived and taught for the most part in Sepphoris.

One other famous Palestinian Amora calls for mention here, Tanchuma b. Abba, who, according to Bacher, resided in Nave, a town in Peræa. He was pre-eminent as a Haggadist, and may be regarded as completing the line of Palestinian Haggadic scholars. It was he who began the process of fixing the *Midrash* in literary form, and may be regarded as the founder of the *Midrash* literature. His collection of *Midrashim*, which is no longer extant in original form, probably formed the basis of the *Pesikta Midrashim* (*Pesikta de Rab Kahana* and *Pesikta Rabbathi*), as well as of the Tanchuma (" Yelammedenu ") *Midrash*. He often engaged in controversy with Christian scholars.

(*b*) *Babylonia*. Rabbah b. Nachmani (270–330) forms the connecting link between the fourth and the previous generation of the Babylonian teachers. He was a pupil both of R. Huna at Sura and of Judah b. Ezekiel at Pumbeditha. Though he belonged by birth to a distinguished priestly family of Judæa, he seems never to have left Babylonia. He is usually styled " Rabbah " simply. On the death of Judah, Rabbah was elected head of the Academy at Pumbeditha, and held this office till his death. A man of keen critical faculty, he was a master of dialectic, and on this account was styled " the uprooter of mountains." He and his family seem to have lived in great poverty, in spite of his fame as a teacher. A contemporary and pupil of Rabbah was Raba b. Joseph b. Chama (A.D. 280–352). He was born and died in Machuza, where his father was a wealthy and distinguished scholar. His companion in study was Abaye (A.D. 280–338), a man of about his own age. The two scholars developed the dialectic method of their master Rabbah. When, after the death of R. Joseph, Abaye was chosen head of the Academy at Pumbeditha, Raba founded a school of his own at Machuza, to which centre, when Abaye died (in 338), the Academy at Pumbeditha was transferred ; and during the lifetime of Raba, Machuza remained the only seat of Jewish learning in Babylonia. Raba ranks as a high authority in the chain of Halakic tradition ; but he was equally pre-eminent as a Haggadist. His Haggadic discourses seem to have been delivered, to a large extent, in public, perhaps in connexion with the Sabbath afternoon service. His controversies (on Halakic subjects) with Abaye contributed much to the development of the dialectic method of the Talmud.

Abaye was one of the first to draw a clear line of demarcation between the simple meaning of Scripture (the *Peshat*) and the Midrashic exegesis of it. It is also interesting to note that he defended the Apocryphal book Ecclesiasticus against the attacks of his teacher, Rab Joseph. The latter, belonging to the older generation (died A.D. 323), was styled by his contemporaries "Sinai," on account of his profound knowledge of the traditional Law. For two years and a half after the death of Rabbah he was head of the Academy at Pumbeditha.

A pupil of Raba and Abaye must be mentioned here, Papa (A.D. 300–375), who, after the death of his teachers, founded a school at Neres, a city near Sura. He engaged in the trade of brewing, in which he amassed considerable wealth, and is said to have been very avaricious. He was not a great scholar, and lacked independence of judgement. He, however, possessed considerable knowledge of the world, which he acquired by extensive travel, and was considered to be an authority on popular proverbs.

(iv) FOURTH GENERATION (A.D. 375–427): *Entirely Babylonian.* In the year that Raba, the head of the school at Machuza, died, one who was destined to play an all-important part in the perpetuation of the labours of the Babylonian Amoraim was born. This was Ashi (A.D. 352–427), who, at the age of twenty, reopened the Academy at Sura as its head, and presided over it for fifty-two years. It had been closed since Chisda's death (in 309), and under Ashi regained all its old prestige. Ashi's commanding position among his contemporaries is indicated by a saying of the time that since the days of the Patriarch Judah I. (the compiler of the Mishnah) "learning and social distinction were never so united in one person as in Ashi" (T.B. *Sanh.* 36a). He was the first really important teacher to arise in the Babylonian colleges since Raba's death.

Owing to the fact that he was *persona grata* with the Persian government, and also regarded with reverence by the authorities of the other Babylonian colleges (Nehardea and Pumbeditha), he was able to carry on his life-work undisturbed. This was the initiation of the task of compiling, sifting, and arranging the material which was afterwards embodied in the Gemara of the Babylonian Talmud. The work begun by Ashi was only completed under Rabina, the last of the Amoraim (died A.D. 499). It required immense powers of memory, great mental grasp, and mastery over the vast and varied material, which Ashi possessed in abundant measure. He not only made Sura a centre of intellectual life, but materially enhanced its prosperity by rebuilding at great expense Rab's old Academy and the synagogue attached to it.

Ashi's teacher was Rab Kahana, who afterwards became head of the Academy at Pumbeditha. Another senior contemporary and teacher of Ashi was Amemar II., who re-established the college at Nehardea, which had been destroyed over a century before, and for many years (A.D. 390–422) acted as its head. Together with Ashi and Mar Zutra he officially represented the Jews at the court of Yezdigerd II.

(v) FIFTH GENERATION (*Babylonian*) (427–500). During this period the Academies of Sura and Pumbeditha were active. Ashi's son, Mar bar Rab Ashi (Ṭabyomi), did not immediately succeed his father, on the latter's death, as head of the Sura Academy, but was elected to the office twenty-eight years later, and held it for the remainder of his life (A.D. 455–468). He continued his father's work on the arrangement and compilation of the Talmud. This work also went on under Rabba Thospia (or

Thospha'ah), who succeeded Tabyomi as head of Sura. His work on the text of the Talmud consisted of amplifications and explanatory additions to make the sense of certain obscure passages clear.

The last of the Amoraim, who completed the work of the schools in editing the Talmud, was Rabina[1] (died A.D. 499). Under him the great work was practically brought to an end. He was head of the school at Sura.

The finishing touches were given by the so-called "Saborai" ("explainers").[2] They were responsible for the final redaction of the text. As their name suggests, the "Saborai" did not venture to assume authority to give decisions on their own responsibility, but confined themselves to the task of elucidating the text, and making clearer doubtful cases where the Amoraic authorities disagreed. As a mediæval Jewish authority says: "They have added nothing of their own to the Talmud, nor have they expressed any divergent opinions, merely determining the arrangement of the text of the Talmud in all its chapters."

The Babylonian teachers to whom the designation "Saborai" is applied were the heads of the Academies at Sura and Pumbeditha between 500 and 540. There was no corresponding class of teachers in Palestine.

The connecting link between the Amoraim and Saborai was Rab Jose, who presided over the Academy at Pumbeditha during the years A.D. 475–520. "Flourishing still for a number of years after the close of the Talmud, he was at the same time the first of the Saboraim and must be considered as the most prominent among them."[3] Other prominent Saborai are Rab Achai b. Huma and Rab Samuel b. Abbahu.

II

As has already been pointed out, the Palestinian Talmud was completed some time in the fourth

[1] Rabina is a contraction of "Rab Abina." This Rabina is usually styled by historians Rabina II. to distinguish him from a former teacher of the same name who was a disciple of Raba. In the Talmud both are called simply "Rabina," which sometimes leads to ambiguity.

[2] The verb סבר means "to reason," "think," "suppose," or "conjecture," and from it סבורא is derived.

[3] Mielziner, *op. cit.* p. 55.

century, about a century before the Babylonian Talmud. But who was responsible for giving it its present shape we do not know. It was apparently not subjected to a final revision, and has reached us in an incomplete form. Possibly some portions have been lost.

In its present form it embraces thirty-nine of the sixty-three tractates of the Mishnah, but in some parts of these the Gemara is incomplete.

All the tractates of the *orders* ("sedarim") Zera'im, Moed, Nashim, and Nezikin (except 'Eduyyoth and Aboth) are included; but none in Kodashim and Teharoth (except Niddah).

In the Babylonian Talmud also the Gemara is incomplete, only thirty-seven tractates of the Mishnah being commented on—actually two less than in the Palestinian Talmud. But the bulk of the Babylonian Talmud is very considerably larger than that of the Palestinian.

The following are the names of the tractates which have a Gemara in the Babylonian Talmud. The number of pages folio in each tractate is given in brackets after each enumeration:

(i) *Seder Zera'im*

1. *Berakoth* (64). [All the other tractates of this Seder are without a Gemara in T.B.]

(ii) *Seder Mo'ed*

1. *Shabbath* (157).	7. *Rosh ha-shanah* (35).
2. *'Erubin* (105).	8. *Yoma* (88).
3. *Pesachin* (121).	9. *Sukkah* (56).
4. *Betzah* (41).	10. *Ta'anith* (31).
5. *Chagigah* (27).	11. *Megillah* (32).
6. *Mo'ed Katan* (29).	

(iii) *Seder Nashim*

1. *Yebamoth* (122).	5. *Nedarim* (91).
2. *Kethuboth* (112).	6. *Nazir* (66).
3. *Kiddushin* (82).	7. *Soṭah* (49).
4. *Giṭṭin* (90).	

(iv) *Seder Nezikin*

1. *Baba kamma* (119).	5. *Sanhedrin* (113).
2. *Baba metzi'ah* (119).	6. *Shebu'oth* (49).
3. *Baba bathra* (176).	7. *Makkoth* (24).
4. *'Abodah zarah* (76).	8. *Horayoth* (14).

(v) *Seder Ḳodashim*

1. *Zebachim* (120).	6. *Temurah* (34).
2. *Menachoth* (110).	7. *Kerithoth* (28).
3. *Bekoroth* (161).	8. *Me'ilah* (22).
4. *Chullin* (142).	9. *Tamid* (9).
5. *'Arakin* (34).	

(vi) *Seder Ṭeharoth*

1. *Niddah* (73). [All the other tractates of this Seder are without Gemara.]

It will be noticed that all the tractates in the first and sixth Sedarim are without Gemara, with the exception of one in each case. It is noteworthy that the Palestinian Talmud has a Gemara for all the tractates of the first Seder, thus (to some extent) supplementing the Babylonian Talmud. In the case of the second Seder the only tractate that is without Gemara in the Babylonian Talmud is *Shekalim*. The third Seder (*Nashim*) is complete. In the following Seder (*Nezikin*) *Aboth* and *Makkoth* have no Gemara, and this is also the case with the tractates *Middoth* and *Ḳinnim* in the fifth Seder (*Ḳodashim*).

The figures given above in brackets represent the pagination which is reproduced in all editions of the Babylonian Talmud, the two sides of each leaf being regarded as one page numbered *a* and *b* respectively. In accordance with this numeration, references to the Babylonian Talmud (T.B.) are made. Thus "T.B. Berak. 30*a*" means that the reference will be found in the Gemara of the Babylonian Talmud in the tractate *Berakoth* on the first side of the folio or page numbered 30.

In the case of the Palestinian Talmud references are sometimes made in the same way (ed. Krotoschin). It is more usual, however, to cite by the Mishnaic chapters, each of which together with the Mishnah text contains, immediately following, the corresponding Gemara, divided into paragraphs (usually styled "Halakah 1, 2, 3, etc.").

It may be added that the text of the Mishnah (as distinguished from the Gemara) is cited according to chapter and paragraph, *e.g.* "Berak. vii. 2" shows at a glance that the Mishnah (not the Gemara) is referred to ; and that the seventh chapter of the tractate *Berakoth*, and the second paragraph, are intended.

Besides the tractates enumerated above, which form the text of the Babylonian Talmud proper, a number of minor tractates, forming a sort of apocryphal collection, are appended in the editions, usually at the end of the fourth Seder, immediately following *'Abodah zarah*. The two first of these are of considerable value historically and in other ways. There are seven altogether.

1. *Aboth de Rabbi Nathan.* This work, which is written in New Hebrew, and contains forty-one chapters, forms a kind of Tosephta text to the Mishnah treatise *Pirḳe Aboth*, which, it will be remembered, possesses no Gemara. The general character of the treatise is similar to that of *Aboth*, but with considerable expansion and illustration of the ethical *dicta* therein contained. The R. Nathan to whom the work is attributed was a Tanna of the fourth generation (A.D. 160–200), and is usually styled "the Babylonian" (see above, p. 97), but in its present form the treatise is post-Talmudic.

A critical edition by Schechter, giving two recensions, appeared in 1887 ; a German translation (*Rabbi Nathans System der Ethik und Moral*) by Kaim Pollak in 1905 (Frankfort-on-the-Main); and an English translation is given in Rodkinson's *Talmud*, vol. i.

2. *Sopherim* (" Scribes ") : a treatise in twenty-one chapters, containing rules for the writing of the Pentateuch scrolls, as well as Masoretic and liturgical rules. The liturgical matter is of considerable importance (see pp. 149 f.).

The best edition is that of Dr. Joel Müller in 2 vols., containing a critical Hebrew text with elaborate notes in German; Leipzig, 1878.

3. *Ebel rabbathi* (sometimes called euphemistically *Semachoth*, " Joys ") : a treatise on mourning. It contains fourteen chapters, and deals with mourning and burial customs and rites.

An edition of the original text, with German translation and notes, has been edited by M. Klotz (Berlin, 1890). An English translation is given in Rodkinson's *Talmud*, vol. viii.

4. *Kallah* (" Bride ") : a small tractate consisting of one chapter, dealing with the subject of marriage (the obligation of chastity in married life, etc.).

5. *Derek 'eretz* (" Conduct of Life ") : a treatise containing eleven chapters; it deals with ethical, social, and religious themes.

6. *Derek 'eretz zuta* (" Conduct of Life ; minor treatise "), in ten chapters, of the same general character as the preceding.

English translations of the two last mentioned are given in Rodkinson's *Talmud*, vol. i.

7. *Perek ha-shalom* (" Chapter on Peace ") : a small tractate consisting of one chapter, which has for its theme the importance of peacefulness.

For further details regarding the above, reference may be made to Zunz, *GV²*, pp. 93 f.

Another collection of seven minor tractates (distinct from the above), edited, under the title *Septem libri Talmudici parvi Hierosolymitani*, by Raphael Kircheim from an ancient MS., appeared in 1851 (Frankfort-on-the-Main).

III

Besides the difference of language already referred to, the two Talmuds differ markedly in other respects. The Palestinian is much simpler and more direct in statement, and contains (in spite of its smaller bulk) a larger Haggadic element than the Babylonian. Though many authorities are cited equally in both, neither Talmud quotes directly from the other. Owing to the decay of the Palestinian schools in the fourth century, the Palestinian Talmud was never formally completed or subjected to a final redaction. Parts of it have probably perished, and what has survived is often fragmentary and incomplete. In these circumstances it naturally fell into neglect, and till recent times it was, as a rule, only known to special scholars among the Rabbis.

On the other hand, the Babylonian Talmud was formally completed and redacted, as we have seen, in the schools of Babylonia. Its development, before the final fixing of its text, went on for more than a century later than the Palestinian. As a consequence, it has a much larger and more richly developed dialectic and casuistic element.

Further, the study of it has been maintained continuously among the Jewish communities, and so it is, *par excellence*, to this day *the Talmud* for the mass of orthodox Jews. After its completion the study of it spread from Babylon to Egypt, northern Africa, Italy, Spain, France, and Germany—in a word, to the centres of Jewish communal life. It is true that there has been from time to time a certain amount of reaction against its predominance, as in the Karaite movement, which began in the eighth century, in Babylonia itself, and, later, in the growth of mysticism and mystical movements (Kabbalah). In the Middle Ages the greatest Jews, like Maimonides, combined the study of the Talmud with

K 2

that of philosophy. But from the sixteenth to the eighteenth century the Talmud was almost the exclusive preoccupation of the Jews, though a violent mystical reaction was marked by the rise of Chasidism in the eighteenth century.

" The Talmud," it has been said, " is not a book, it is a literature. It contains a legal code, a system of ethics, a body of ritual customs, poetical passages, prayers, histories, facts of science and medicine, and fancies of folk-lore. The Talmud is not exactly a national literature, but it was a unique bond between the scattered Jews, an unparalleled spiritual and literary instrument for maintaining the identity of Judaism amid the many tribulations to which the Jews were subjected." [1] In spite of its many faults— its massive incoherence, its lack of style and form, its over-refined subtleties and wearisome casuistry—it remains one of the great literary monuments of the world. The work embodied in it is immense. If its form is uncouth, it never lacks strength, and its grandeur is strange and arresting. " The very incoherence of the Talmud," a Jewish writer remarks with justice, " its confusion of voices, is an index of free thinking." [2]

Indeed, its defects must serve to endear it to Jewish eyes, for in it the pious Jew sees a true reflex of the labours and aspirations, the ideals and achievement of his race, as these expressed themselves throughout a fateful and fruitful epoch. If it lacks some of the qualities which mark great literature, it remains an arresting, an amazing, and a weirdly fascinating product of Jewish genius, a literary monument, unique in character, which faithfully exhibits many characteristic aspects of the life and thought of a gifted but peculiar people.

[1] I. Abrahams, *op. cit.* p. 25.
[2] I. Zangwill, *Chosen Peoples*, p. 24

ADDITIONAL NOTE

TALMUDIC COMMENTARIES AND COMPENDIUMS

Though the commentaries which appear in printed editions of the Talmud, and the compendiums of Talmudic law which have been compiled from time to time, belong properly to the mediæval literature of Judaism, it will be convenient to refer here to one or two of the more important examples. The text of the Talmud presents numerous difficulties and obscurities to the student; and without the aid of commentaries even the Jewish student would often be at a loss. As a consequence, many commentaries, written in Hebrew, have been produced, and a selection of these is usually printed, below the text, in the printed editions.[1]

The most famous of these is the commentary of Rabbi Shelomoh Yishaḳi of Troyes (A.D. 1040–1105), who is usually styled, from the initials of his name, "Rashi." This commentary, which embraces nearly all the tractates of the Babylonian Talmud, is always printed in editions of that work.[2] It is, indeed, indispensable for the study and elucidation of the Talmudic text. Remarkable alike for its brevity and lucidity, "by a few plain words it often sheds light upon the obscurest passages and unravels the most entangled arguments of the Talmudical discussions.

[1] The best complete edition of the Babylonian Talmud is the Wilna edition of the Widow and Brothers Romm (1880–86 in 25 vols.). In this a large number of commentaries are given, among others that of Rabbenu Chananel (ר״ח) of Kairowan (Africa), who flourished about A.D. 1050, and commented on a large part of the Talmud. A full list of Talmud commentaries will be found in the article "Talmud Commentaries" in *JE* xii. 27–30.

[2] An unfortunate exception to this rule is the text, accompanied by a German translation, of the Babylonian Talmud by Goldschmidt in several volumes (not yet complete). Goldschmidt's text is printed without any commentaries.

As if anticipating the slightest hesitation of the inexperienced student, it offers him at once the needed explanation, or at least a hint that leads him the right way. It has truly been said that, but for this peerless commentary of Rashi, the Babylonian Talmud would have remained as neglected as the Palestinian." [1] Rashi's comments also often indicate and establish the true Talmudic text, where this has been corrupted.

In addition to Rashi's commentary proper,[2] which is printed in the inner margins, the editions of the Babylonian Talmud have also a number of annotations and glosses, printed in the outer margins, which are called *Tosaphoth* (= " Additions "). They do not form a running commentary (like Rashi's), but take the form of separate notes, and often embody discussions of difficult passages, and occasionally criticise the explanation given by Chananel or Rashi. Often, too, they attempt to harmonise contradictory passages or meet possible objections, and are full of subtle dialectic. The authors of these additions, called Tosaphists (*cp.* pp. 231 f.), were numerous, and flourished in France and Germany during the twelfth and thirteenth centuries. They are partly identical with the authors who supplemented missing parts of Rashi's commentaries.[3]

Commentaries were also written on the Mishnah as

[1] Mielziner, *op. cit.* p. 66.

[2] Rashi's commentary, where incomplete, was supplemented by his relatives and disciples. Thus his son-in-law, R. Jehuda b. Nathan, completed the commentary on *Makkoth*, his grandson, R. Samuel b. Meir (" Rashbam "), that on *Baba bathra* ; while the commentary on *Nedarim* was completed by supplying the missing portion from the work of Rabbenu Gershom, a predecessor of Rashi.

[3] The פסק תוספות (" Decisions of the Tosaphoth ") which are appended in the editions of the Babylonian Talmud at the end of each tractate are the work of an anonymous compiler of the fourteenth century, who collected from the Tosaphoth the practical results of their discussions and decisions.

an independent work. The best known is that of
Maimonides (twelfth century), which was composed
in Arabic[1] and afterwards translated into Hebrew (by
several hands). The Hebrew translation is usually
printed in editions of the Talmud. Another well-
known commentary on the entire Mishnah is that of
R. Obadiah of Bertinoro, in Italy, who was Rabbi in
Jerusalem in the sixteenth century (died A.D. 1510).
Both these commentaries are given in a Latin translation in Surenhusius' great edition of the Mishnah
(6 vols., Amsterdam, A.D. 1698–1703).

Commentaries were also written by distinguished scholars on
separate tractates, especially on those which have no Gemara in
the Babylonian Talmud, and which are, therefore, not included
in Rashi's commentary. Thus R. Simson of Sens (twelfth
century), a famous Tosaphist, completed a commentary on all
the tractates of Seder Zera'im, except *Berakoth*, and on all
those of Seder Teharoth, except *Niddah*. A similar series on
the same tractates was completed by R. Asher b. Jechiel
(thirteenth century). An important commentary on the tractate
Middoth (for which there is no Gemara) was written by R.
Shemaya, who is supposed to have been a disciple of Rashi.

The commentaries on the Palestinian Talmud are few, none
older, apparently, than the sixteenth century. Some of the
more important are comparatively modern.

As the Babylonian Talmud possessed not only a
theoretic but also a practical interest for all orthodox
Jews, since it was the source of the laws which
regulated religious practice, it was inevitable that
attempts should be made to codify in systematic
form the rules and regulations which were binding
for practical life and conduct. In these epitomes or
codes the irrelevant elements, such as the Haggadic
material and the lengthy discussions, were either
wholly omitted or condensed, and the relevant
material was systematised.

[1] Maimonides commenced it in the twenty-third year of his
age in Spain, and finished it in his thirtieth year in Egypt.

The most important compendiums are those of

(*a*) R. Isaac Alfasi (born at Fez, in Africa, 1013 died 1103 in Spain), who is usually styled from the initials of his names " Rif."[1] This is a real compendium, being an abridgement of the Talmud, the style and language of which it retains.

(*b*) R. Asher b. Jechiel, already mentioned (died 1327), a German Rabbi, who died in Spain. R. Asher modelled his work on that of Alfasi, adding the opinions of later authorities. This compendium is printed in the editions of the Talmud at the end of each tractate.[2]

A codification of the Talmudic legal material in the strict sense was first accomplished by Maimonides in his great work *Mishneh Torah* (= " Repetition of the Law "). It embraces the material included in both Talmuds, or based upon such, with occasional references to the opinions of the post-Talmudic authorities, the Geonim. It is written in New Hebrew, in a lucid and attractive style, and is divided into fourteen books ; hence the popular name for the collection, *Sepher ha-yad* (" Book of the Hand "—the Hebrew word for " hand," יָד = numerically 14), and later, by way of distinction, *Yad ha-chazakah* (יד הַחֲזָקָה, " The Strong Hand "). Each book is divided into " Halakoth," and these again are subdivided into " sections " or " chapters " (*perakim*) and paragraphs. Maimonides' work also became the basis for later commentaries and annotations, which are usually printed with it.

A code which deserves mention here is that known as "the great Law-Book" (מצות גדול ס״ג) of R. Moses of Courcy, in France (thirteenth century). Here the Talmudic laws are grouped

---

[1] His work is often cited as ר״ף or אלפסי.
[2] Under the title רבינו אשר.

under 613 precepts (positive laws and prohibitions), which is the number of such enactments found, according to the Rabbis, n the Pentateuch.

Another important codification bears the title *Turim* (= " Rows," *i.e.* " rows of laws "). This was compiled by R. Jacob, son of the R. Asher b. Jechiel already referred to. It is divided into four parts, viz. *Tur orach chayyim*, dealing with liturgical laws ; *Tur yoreh de'ah*, dealing with ritual laws ; *Tur 'eben hā-'ezer*, dealing with marriage laws ; and *Tur choshen mishpaṭ*, dealing with civil laws. Each part is divided up into sections, with appropriate headings, according to subject-matter ; and each section is subdivided into smaller portions called *semānîm*. The *Turim* differ from the *Mishneh Torah* of Maimonides in that they deal only with those laws and customs which are in actual use, all others being disregarded. It thus embraces rites and customs which are of post-Talmudic origin.

The printed editions usually give the commentaries on the *Turim* by R. Joseph Karo (this commentary being styled *Beth Joseph*) and by R. Moses Isserles (*Darke Mosheh*).

The most famous of all the codifications, and the one that has established itself as authoritative among orthodox Jews, even down to the present day, is the work of the Joseph Karo already referred to (sixteenth century). Taking the *Turim* and his own commentary thereon as a basis, and retaining its four divisions with their titles, he remodelled the entire contents so as to give it the character of a text-book of law. This remodelled work is known as the *Shulchan 'Aruk* (" The Prepared Table "), and is widely used by orthodox Jews. The author's con-temporary, R. Moses Isserles (רמ״א), added numerous annotations ; and these, with a number of commentaries which have been produced, are usually printed with the text in the folio editions.

A word may here be added as to the collections of Haggadic material from the Babylonian Talmud. A well-known one which is very comprehensive is the *'En Ja'aḳob* ("Well of Jacob") of R. Jacob ibn Chabib (beginning of the sixteenth century). Vol. I. of an English translation has recently been published (by S. H. Glick) in New York (1919). A similar collection made from the Palestinian Talmud was published, with a commentary, by R. Samuel Japhe (Vienna, 1590, reprinted Berlin, 1725-26) under the title *Yepheh mar'eh* (יפה מראה).

PART III

THE JEWISH LITURGY

PART III

THE JEWISH LITURGY

[LITERATURE (selected) : Zunz, *Zur Geschichte und Literatur* (1845) ; Zunz, *Synagogale Poesie des Mittelalters* (1855) ; Zunz, *Die Ritus des synagogalen Gottesdienstes geschichtlich entwickelt* (1859) ; Baer, *Seder Abodath Israel* (1868) ; Zunz, *Die gottesdienstlichen Vorträge der Juden, historisch entwickelt* (1892) ; M. Friedländer, *The Jewish Religion* (1900) ; Morris Joseph, *Judaism as Creed and Life*, pp. 177–318 (1903) ; Seeberg, *Die Didache des Judentums und der Urchristenheit* (1908) ; Duchesne, *Les Origines du culte chrétien* (1910) ; Oesterley, *The Psalms in the Jewish Church* (1910) ; Oesterley and Box, *The Religion and Worship of the Synagogue* (1912) ; Elbogen, *Bemerkungen zur alten jüdischen Liturgie*, in " Studies in Jewish Literature, issued in honour of Prof. Kaufmann Kohler " (1913) ; Elbogen, *Der jüdische Gottesdienst in seiner geschichtlichen Entwickelung* (1913) ; Schwaab, *Historische Einführung in das Achtzehngebet* (1913) ; Srawley, *The Early History of the Liturgy* (1913) ; Abrahams, *Annotated Edition of the Authorised Daily Prayer Book* (1914) ; Rendtorff, *Die Geschichte des christlichen Gottesdienstes unter dem Gesichtspunkt der liturgischen Erbfolge* (1914). The relevant articles in Hamburger's *Realencyclopädie des Judenthums* and in the *Jewish Encyclopædia*.]

I

SOME PRELIMINARY CONSIDERATIONS

THE importance and interest of the Jewish Liturgy —especially, of course, in its earlier elements—for the study of Christian origins is not generally recognised ; not that this is a matter for surprise, for the Jewish Liturgy, in whatever forms at present existent (and they are various), is so complex and involved to the uninitiated that the ordinary reader of it, even as it exists in its English and much abbreviated form, is not unnaturally somewhat overwhelmed when he first comes to read it. Nevertheless, there is an immense deal in the Jewish Liturgy which is of profound importance and interest for the student of Christian origins; and that interest must be greatly enhanced when it is realised that in the Jewish Liturgy are embedded the prayers, praises, and thanksgivings offered up by Our Lord Himself, by His disciples, and by the Jewish-Christians of the first century. The earliest accounts which we have of the Christian Liturgy—fragmentary and incomplete as they are— show clearly enough that the worship of the early Church was influenced by that of the synagogue. In the primitive Church Order contained in the *Didaché*,[1] chaps. vii.–xv., the prayers are distinctly Jewish in character and reveal many phrases and ideas which are to be found in the Jewish Liturgy. The same is true of certain passages, dealing with the worship of the early Church, in the epistle of Clement of Rome to the Corinthians;[2] concerning them Srawley says: " These passages, then, suggest that certain ideas and stereotyped phrases had found a place in the language of Christian worship, and that a certain defined type of prayer had become current, based upon Christian terminology, the Old Testament, and the forms of the synagogue worship."[3] The same writer, in speaking of Justin Martyr's account[4] of the Sunday Eucharist, points out that it shows that " the separation of the Eucharist from the Agapé had already been effected, and 'the service of the word,' which in later times was known as the *Missa*

---

[1] First half of the second century.
[2] Written about A.D. 95.
[3] *The Early History of the Liturgy*, p. 31 (1913).
[4] *Circa* A.D. 150.

Catechumenorum, consisting of lessons from the Old and New Testaments, a sermon, and prayers, had established itself as the introductory portion of the liturgy. This preliminary 'service of the word' shows the influence of the religious services of the Jewish synagogues, which included the same three elements, prayers, lessons, and homily." [1]

But, even apart from this, there are two considerations regarding the Jewish Liturgy which should commend it at least to the sympathetic notice of all students of religion. As has been truly pointed out,[2] it is the earliest form of divine service which was offered with great regularity not only on Sabbaths and festivals, but on every day throughout the year; with the result that the whole life of the nation became influenced by religious thought and the religious spirit, and a national unity was brought into existence which nothing else could have effected.[3] And there is also this consideration, that nowhere is the history of the growth of religious ideas more clearly revealed than in the modification or development of liturgical forms; therein are reflected ultimately the religious thoughts and conceptions which through centuries perhaps had been growing in the minds of a people; there they become stereotyped; and there they remain until a further advance in religious conceptions demands some modification. In the Jewish Liturgy we have an excellent example of this; and the observation of the changes which it has undergone has its advantages for the Christian student of religion, inasmuch as in studying the phases of religious ideas as reflected in a liturgy other than one's own one can

[1] *op. cit.* p. 37.
[2] Elbogen, *Der jüdische Gottesdienst in seiner geschichtlichen Entwickelung*, p. 2 (1913).
[3] That such a religious unity did not exist in earlier days in Israel is shown clearly enough by the Prophets.

approach and deal with the subject in a spirit of greater detachment than, from the nature of the case, is possible when dealing with that which is one's own.

Complicated as the Jewish Liturgy is in its present form, it is far less so now than it was in days gone by; while in its first beginnings it was simple in form, various circumstances contributed to its development, and during the Middle Ages this development increased to an enormous extent, so much so that it is no exaggeration to say that it became altogether overloaded with extraneous matter, much of which was not worthy of a place in this venerable liturgy. It was, however, not until the beginning of the nineteenth century that a thoroughgoing reform of the Jewish Liturgy was initiated.

The first cause of development was the outcome of a natural desire to put into the prayers and thanksgivings a fuller expression of thought and aspiration; then there grew up a tendency to incorporate in the Liturgy the devotions which had been framed by outstanding religious leaders; historical occurrences of national interest also offered material which was incorporated in the prayers, and, these becoming stereotyped, continued to be used even when the original cause to which they owed their form was forgotten. But the most pronounced period of development of the Jewish Liturgy commenced in the sixth to the seventh century, approximately, with the incorporation of *Piyyutim* (a corrupt form from the Greek word for "poet," see p. 272); these were poetical compositions of very varying quality and of great number which by degrees found a place in the Liturgy and increased its bulk to a very appreciable extent. Most of these poems have now been eliminated; the few that remain are the most choice and are fully worthy of their place; they will be referred to later on.

In the course of the centuries various liturgical "Uses," technically called *Minhagim*, have come into existence, differing more or less from each other, though the original groundwork is to be discerned in each. Two main groups, the Palestinian and the Babylonian, are recognised; the foremost representatives of either group are the Ashkenazic and Sephardic Rites respectively;[1] there are subdivisions of less importance, which need not, however, concern us. The Rite to which, in the main, we shall direct our attention is the Ashkenazic; this has been published in a most convenient form in Hebrew and English.[2] The Sephardic Rite is much more elaborate, containing as it does a great deal of the material which grew up in the Middle Ages.[3]

One of the first things which will strike even a cursory reader of the Jewish Liturgy is its Scriptural atmosphere; the incorporation of Biblical phrases and passages in the synagogue prayers is one of their marked characteristics. The Psalms are especially drawn upon here, and, of course, the books of the Law are utilised largely for this purpose. But, in addition to this, long passages from Scripture (*e.g.* Exod. xv.) and a copious use of Psalms constitute a considerable part of all the services. The important place which from the earliest times was accorded to the interpretation and explanation of the Old Testament[4] further emphasises the desire felt for making the Scriptures the foundation of the liturgical structure, and illustrates what has always been one of the great principles of Jewish religious practice, viz. that

[1] But see Gaster, *The Book of Prayer and Order of Service*, p. xiv (1901), who maintains that the Sephardic Rite represents the Palestinian tradition.

[2] *The Annotated Edition of the Authorised Daily Prayer Book*, with historical and explanatory notes, and additional matter, compiled in accordance with the plans of the Rev. S. Singer, by Israel Abrahams (1914).

[3] These forms are printed in *Forms of Prayer* by De Sola (5 vols.); new edition by Dr. Gasker, 1901–6.

[4] Hence the rise of the Targums.

L

instruction in the Word of God is an indispensable part of worship.

The influence which, especially, the Pentateuch and the Psalms have had upon both the language and the thought of the Jewish Liturgy can be paralleled by the like influence which the Epistle to the Hebrews and the Apocalypse have had upon the early liturgies of the Church.

In the Jewish Liturgy the general term for prayer is *Berakhah,* the root of which, in its original signific....

cation, means "to kneel down"; but the noun came to mean that for which a man knelt down, *i.e. prayer.* Further, the act of kneeling in prayer to God implied the recognition of His Blessedness, *i.e.* of His power and mercy and goodness; hence *Berakhah* also connotes *praise*; and finally, since every act of praise involves *thanksgiving,* this, too, is an essential part of the meaning of *Berakhah.* The word has, therefore, come to have a very wide connotation, and is usually translated "Benediction," which is intended to embrace the ideas of prayer, praise, and thanksgiving. Moreover, this word is the more appropriate since the fixed form which, in course of time, the *Berakhah* tended to assume began with "Blessed is He . . ." or "Blessed art Thou . . ."; this is not necessarily always so now, though these words do occur *somewhere* in every Benediction, properly so called. A notable example of this is the Benediction with which the actual service (apart from its introductory portion) for the daily Morning Prayer opens; this contains a ninefold "Blessed be He," and concludes with: "Blessed art Thou, O Lord, a King extolled with praises." The classical example, however, is the great prayer called the *Shemoneh 'Esreh* ("Eighteen Benedictions"), of which we shall have much to say later on. Benedictions are also used for the purpose of forming a framework in which some of the more important and ancient portions of the service are set;

we shall see this illustrated when we come to examine the service for Morning Prayer.

Originally the prayers of the synagogue were variable; they were not written down until about the fourth or fifth century. An old Jewish sage used to say that "he who writes down prayers sins as though he burned the Torah."[1] The subject-matter of the prayers was fixed, but the form of words in which the prayer was offered up was left to the individual leader in prayer. All the prayers were originally quite short; the essence of the prayer-leader's task lay in guiding the congregation in regard to the *subject* of prayer; it was then left to each individual to elaborate this for himself in silent prayer and meditation. It is a point worth emphasising that provision was thus officially made for silent prayer and meditation during public worship; we shall have to return to the subject later on. The extempore character of the prayers in the early synagogue seems to have been followed in the worship of the early Church, judging by the testimony of Justin Martyr (*Dialogue with Trypho*, c. 67).

A further characteristic of the synagogue prayers is their national note; it is not only the individual congregation which prays, but the congregation as an integral part of the Jewish nation. In the Christian Church this feeling of national unity is further enlarged and enhanced by that of the Catholic Church, which transcends national limitations.

A word must be said regarding the part originally taken by the laity in the worship of the synagogue. Just as the priests and Levites were divided into twenty-four courses or classes, which in turn undertook the duties of the daily services in the Temple, and relieved each other week by week, so the Jewish

---

[1] The idea underlying this objection to the writing down of prayers was that of fear lest the holy words should fall into the hands of the profane.

L 2

laity was also, in like manner, represented by twenty-four classes. These classes, or courses, were collectively called *Mishmaroth* ("watches");[1] the particular individual class was called a *Ma'amad* ("standing"); it was so called because these representatives of the people "stood" before God during the offering of the daily services.[2] But there was this difference between the priestly and Levitical and the lay classes, that, whereas in the case of the former the *entire* class went up to the Temple when its turn came, in the case of the latter only a few representatives went up, and the remainder assembled in their local synagogue, where they offered up daily prayers and read the Scriptures.[3] When this duty of offering prayer in what may be called an official capacity by the laity began cannot be stated with certainty; but it is reasonable to suppose that it arose, in some form or other, soon after the return from the Exile, when the beginnings of so much that belongs to the later Judaism are to be sought. The custom is important both because it witnesses to the official recognition of the laity taking their part in public divine worship, and because it witnesses to the emphasis laid on prayer as distinct from sacrifices even while the Temple with its full sacrificial system was in existence.

The present Jewish Liturgy is the product of many centuries of development. The beginning of a Jewish Prayer Book in the modern sense is to be sought in the middle of the second century A.D. approximately, and, as a compilation, was originally

---

[1] מִשְׁמָרוֹת ; the word occurs in reference to the "observances" of the House of God in Neh. xiii. 14.

[2] *cp.* Ps. cxxxiv. 1, where the word is used in this technical sense.

[3] See Mishnah, *Taanith* iv. 1–4 ; *cp. Tamid* vii.; see further Schürer, *Geschichte des jüdischen Volkes*, ii. 337 f.: Elbogen, *op. cit.* p. 237.

based on the *dictum* of Rabbi Meir, about A.D. 150, to the effect that a man should utter daily a hundred Benedictions. For a long period, of several centuries, different Prayer Books were compiled on the principle of the "Hundred Benedictions."[1]

II

SOURCES OF THE PRESENT LITURGY

Although the Jewish Liturgy belongs in its origins to a period long anterior to the beginning of the Christian era, the earliest written liturgical details belong to a much later time. This is not to be wondered at, for, as we have seen, in ancient times it was regarded as a sinful act to write down prayers. It was not until the completion of the Talmud in the sixth century that prayers began to be written down. Many liturgical notes and much information regarding the early Liturgy are, however, to be found scattered about in the Mishnah, Talmud, and Midrashic works. But obviously a fixed Liturgy must have been long in existence, since it is referred to as so well known in these writings.

The earliest source which gives a connected and detailed account of the Liturgy is the tractate *Sopherim*, belonging to about A.D. 600 (see p. 130). It is the latter part of this tractate, chaps. xvi. xxi., in which many liturgical details are preserved. It is Palestinian in origin, like all the smaller treatises. There are, besides this, various collections of liturgical prayers which have been made from time to time, and other early writings dealing specifically with the Liturgy, which are invaluable since they contain a mass of traditional matter regarding the content, order, and ceremonial of the services of the Temple as well as of the synagogue. The earliest extant

[1] מֵאָה בְּרָכוֹת, Elbogen, *op. cit.* pp. 7 f., 358.

collection of prayers is what is called the "Hundred Benedictions" of Natronai (*circa* A.D. 860). But the first Jewish Prayer Book, so far as is at present known, is that of Amram (about A.D. 875),[1] which contains the Sephardic, or Spanish, Rite. The next in date is the *Siddur*[2] of Saadya (892–942); then follows the great *Machsor*[3] *Vitry* (*circa* 1100), compiled by Simcha ben Samuel, of Vitry; it represents the ancient French Rite, which is closely connected with the more widespread German, or Ashkenazic, Rite.[4] Among the more notable works of the Middle Ages important for the details they give concerning the early Liturgy are: the *Mishneh Torah* of Maimonides (1180), in the concluding book of which the text of the prayers is given, as well as various authoritative decisions concerning the Liturgy in other parts of the work; the *Minhag*[5] of Abraham ben Nathan ha-Jarchi, belonging to the same time as the preceding; and David Abudraham's commentary on the Prayer Book (1340).[6]

As in the Christian Church there are different Liturgies, the Roman, Gallican, Sarum, etc., so, too, in the Jewish Church; but in the latter all go back to one of two fundamental Rites, the Palestinian and the Babylonian. The former has been almost entirely superseded, and even the fragments of it to be found in the Talmud show Babylonian impress; it is, however, represented in the tractate *Sopherim*, in the *Siddur* of Saadya, and in the *Machsor Vitry*;

[1] It is published by A. Mark in *Jahrbuch der jüdischen literarischen Gesellschaft*, v. (1907); also by A. Frumkin (Jerusalem 5672).
[2] *Siddur* means the "Order" of prayers; no published edition of this exists as yet.
[3] *Machsor* also means "Order" of prayers, but one which contains more detail and explanation than a *Siddur*.
[4] It is published by Luzzato (1889).
[5] *Minhag* means ritual "custom" or "use."
[6] Elbogen, *op. cit.* p. 11.

Amram represents the Babylonian Rite. As for the two chief forms of the Liturgy in present use, the Sephardic and the Ashkenazic, the former represents the Babylonian Rite;[1] it is used in all parts of the world where the Sephardic, or Spanish, Jews have settled. The Ashkenazic Liturgy represents the Palestinian Rite ; this is used, with certain variations, mainly in England, America, Germany, Holland, Russia, Poland, and Italy.[2]

III

NON-SACRIFICIAL ELEMENTS IN THE TEMPLE WORSHIP

The present Jewish Liturgy is a greatly developed form of the early (pre-Christian) synagogue worship. But the early synagogal Liturgy, which consisted purely of spiritual worship, was derived from the worship of the Temple, with its sacrificial system. In order, therefore, to seek to trace out the origin and background of the earliest elements in the Jewish Liturgy, it is necessary to try to discover whether any elements of worship *apart* from the sacrificial system existed in the Temple Liturgy. Although in the synagogal Liturgy the counterpart of the sacrificial worship had its place,[3] direct and indirect evidence is forthcoming that there existed in the Temple worship itself certain elements distinct from the sacrificial service, and it is in these that the real origin of the synagogal Liturgy is to be found.

[1] Though, as noted above, Gaster denies this.
[2] In Italy the Sephardic Rite is also used where there are Sephardic Jews.
[3] It is insisted upon again and again in the Talmud that the prayers of the synagogal Liturgy were instituted to correspond with the sacrifices, *e.g. Berakhoth* 24*b*, referred to by Blau in *JE* viii. 132*b*.

Important evidence on this point may be gathered from Is. i. 12–15. Although the prophet is here inveighing against the hollowness and insincerity of the people's worship of God, his words show, none the less, that there existed in the Temple forms of worship apart from the sacrificial system; for, in addition to the multitudes of sacrifices, oblations, and incense, he speaks not only of the observance of new moons and sabbaths, but also of the "spreading forth of hands" and "many prayers." The last two phrases, which both point to the same thing, bear witness to the existence of a service of prayer distinct from sacrifices. Further, another example of divine worship during which prayer instead of sacrifice was the most prominent feature was the gathering together of the people on fast-days. These gatherings were in existence in pre-Exilic days, and they were not necessarily held in the proximity of the altar; indeed, it seems clear that sometimes there was no sacrifice at all, and that the worship consisted solely of prayers together with informal confession of sins. These assemblies for prayer on fast-days "exercised a great influence in moulding the form of the later worship of the synagogue. The description of the accustomed ceremonial at these gatherings on fast-days which we possess belongs, it is true, to later times; the Mishnah depicts this ceremonial as it existed in the Tannaitic period (*i.e.* roughly A.D. 1–200), but most of the forms then in use—and just the more important ones—agree with what we read in the Old Testament and Apocryphal books regarding this; so that there can be little doubt as to the antiquity of the ceremonies described in the Mishnah as taking place on the fast-days." [1] But, as Elbogen goes on to say, these gatherings were in no sense of regular occurrence, they were spasmodic and rare, and they formed no pattern of

[1] Elbogen, *op. cit.* p. 235.

daily worship such as belongs to the synagogue. Most authorities are agreed that the beginnings of the *regular* daily gatherings of the synagogue are to be sought during the Babylonian Exile ; not that the non-sacrificial elements in the Temple worship were without influence on the character of these gatherings—quite the contrary ; but during the Exile the only thing that could take the place of the daily sacrificial services of the Temple was the meeting together of the people for prayer, etc., at the corresponding times, morning and evening, at which the Temple services had been held. During the Exile the national consciousness, the nation's ideals, aspirations, and hopes, were conserved and fostered by the daily assembling of the people in order that they might worship and pray to the God of their fathers, and confess before Him the national sins and shortcomings for which they were being justly punished, and that they might hear the reading and explanation of their Law which had been handed down, in one form or another, for so many generations. It is in these daily gatherings during the Exile that we must see the pattern which was followed as, by degrees, the settled institution of the synagogue came into being. The chief elements contained in that pattern were prayer, confession, the reading of the Scriptures, and the explanation of the latter. On the return from the Captivity these elements constituted an important part in the worship of the people even after the rebuilding of the Temple ; the books of Deutero-Isaiah, Ezra-Nehemiah, Haggai, and Zechariah show this clearly enough, and we have also the evidence of the Mishnah. In this latter we learn that the offering up of the daily morning sacrifice was suspended while the ministering priests went in a body to the " Hall of hewn stone " (*Lishkath ha-gazith*) for a service of prayer (*Tamid* v. 1–3). We learn also that the important element of reading the Scriptures centred in portions from the Pentateuch, and, above all, in the reading of the *Shema*ʿ and the Ten Commandments; indeed, so important was this part of the Liturgy considered to be that it soon came to be introduced by a formal thanksgiving for the divine revelation, of which it constituted a part; it was also followed by a declaration of the hope that the revelation which had been accorded to the nation's forefathers might be continued to the congregation of Israel. This was followed by a prayer that God would accept the sacrifice of the altar; then came the priestly blessing.[1] This is all part of the Temple Liturgy and shows how important the non-sacrificial elements had become. The Mishnic tractate *Megillah*, which, like *Tàmid*, reflects the conditions as they were, at any rate, before the beginning of the Christian era, gives as the main parts of the synagogue Liturgy: prayer (the *Shemoneh ʿEsreh*), the *Shema*ʿ, the Torah lesson, the lesson from the Prophets, explanation of Scripture, and the priestly blessing (*Megillah* iv.); this, with slightly more detail, corresponds closely with the evidence of *Tamid*. In addition to this, we know from various sources about the use of Psalms both in the Temple and in the synagogue;[2] this constituted the praise portion of the service.

While, then, it is not possible to trace out in detail the development of these elements of worship, we may regard it as certain that, even before the Maccabæan era, the Temple worship included, apart from the sacrifices: prayer, confession, reading and explanation of Scripture, the *Shema* and the Ten Commandments being accorded special prominence, and Psalms. These are the elements, belonging to the non-sacrificial part of the Temple worship and prac-

---

[1] *cp.* Elbogen, *op. cit.* p. 236.
[2] *e.g. Tamid* vii. 4. See for further details, Oesterley, *The Psalms in the Jewish Church*, pp. 110–128 (1910).

tised daily, which constitute the foundation of the daily worship of the synagogue ; out of them and around them many developments have arisen in the course of ages, but, as we shall see in the next section, they stand out (with one exception) as clearly as ever in the Jewish Liturgy of the present day.

IV

THE STRUCTURE OF THE DAILY MORNING SERVICE

The daily morning service, called *Shacharith*, contains the groundwork of the regular services of the synagogue ; there are certain variations in the afternoon (*Minchah*) and evening (*Ma'arib*) services, as well as the additions on those for Sabbaths, New Moons, and festivals ; but *Shacharith* may be regarded as the basis. Its main divisions are as follows : (1) Introductory, or preparatory portion ; (2) the *Zemiroth* (" Psalms ") ; (3) the *Shema'* (" Hear [O Israel]") ; (4) the *Shemoneh 'Esreh* (" Eighteen [Benedictions]") ; (5) the *Tachanunim* (" Supplications ") ; (6) *Kĕriath ha-Torah* (" The Reading of the Law") ; (7) concluding portion. A general outline-analysis of the contents of each of these divisions will be the best means of giving a bird's-eye view of the structure of the whole service.

(1) INTRODUCTORY, OR PREPARATORY PORTION. (*a*) Prayer on entering the synagogue. (*b*) The canticles *Yigdal* and *'Adon 'Olam*. (*c*) The Morning Benedictions. (*d*) Supplications. (*e*) Scriptural and Rabbinical passages dealing with the subject of sacrifices. (*f*) The putting on of the *Tallith* and *Tephillin*.

(2) PRAISE PORTION. (*a*) Songs of praise : (i) Opening Benediction, *Baruk shĕāmar* ; (ii) 1 Chron. xvi. 8–36 (= Ps. cv.), Ps. xcvi. ; (iii) Hymn

of praise composed of extracts from the Psalms. (*b*) Psalm c. (*c*) Hymn of praise composed of Scriptural extracts. (*d*) Pss. cxlv.–cl. (*e*) Passages of praise : (i) 1 Chron. xxix. 10–13 ; (ii) Neh. ix. 6–11 ; (iii) Ex. xiv. 30–xv. 18 ; (iv) concluding Benediction, *Yishtabbach Shiměka.* Half of the *Kaddish.*

(3) THE SHEMA'. (*a*) Introductory Benedictions : (i) *Yotzer* ; (ii) *'Ahabah.* (*b*) The *Shema'.* (*c*) Concluding Benediction : *Geullah.*

(4) THE SHEMONEH 'ESREH : The Eighteen (Nineteen) Benedictions.

(5) THE TACHANUN. (*a*) Psalm vi. (*b*) *Vehu Rachum* and "Lord God of Israel" (said only on Mondays and Thursdays). (*c*) "O Guardian of Israel."

(6) THE READING OF THE LAW (on Mondays and Thursdays). (*a*) The opening of the Ark and taking out of the Scroll of the Law. (*b*) The calling out of three persons for the reading of the Law. (*c*) The reading of the Law. (*d*) The elevation of the Scroll. (*e*) The Scroll is returned to the Ark. (*f*) Pss. xxiv., cxlv., xx. (*g*) "And a redeemer shall come to Zion," followed by *Kedushah* and two prayers. *Kaddish,* followed by the *'Alenu* Prayer.

(7) CONCLUDING PORTION. (*a*) Hymn of Glory. (*b*) The Psalm for the day. (*c*) The Prayer for Sustenance. (*d*) The Ten Commandments. (*e*) The "Thirteen Principles" of Faith. (*f*) The *'Akedah* (Gen. xxii. 1–19) and "the Manna" (Ex. xvi. 4–36).

Of these seven divisions the last is not an essential part of the service ; a few words of comment on them may be offered here, but the contents of the other divisions will be dealt with a little more fully in separate sections.

THE INTRODUCTORY PORTION. The whole of this portion was originally in the nature of a private devotional preparation for the service which was to follow ; only by degrees did it become incorporated into the service itself. Though some parts of it are

ancient, excepting for the Biblical passages it contains
no pre-Christian material. The canticle *Yigdal*, so
called from its opening word, "*Magnified* be the
living God, and praised," is quite late; it belongs to
the thirteenth or fourteenth century; its contents are
based on what is called the Creed of Maimonides, or
the Thirteen Principles of Faith (see below, pp. 160,
288). The other canticle, '*Adon 'Olam* (" Lord of
the world "), is a sacred poem belonging to the
eleventh century; it deals specifically with the
doctrine of God; originally it was evidently an
evening prayer, as is suggested by the words: " Into
His hand I commend my spirit, when I sleep and
when I wake." The Morning Benedictions which
follow are five in number, and conclude with the
words of the priestly Benediction (Num. vi. 24–26);
in them the worshipper blesses God for His commandment concerning the washing of hands, for the
creation of man by divine wisdom, for the Law, for
the teaching of the Law, and for the choice of Israel,
the people of the Law, from among the nations of the
world. These are followed by a number of quite
short Benedictions which begin with: " Blessed art
Thou, O Lord our God, King of the Universe."
Among the Supplications, which come next, one has
a particular interest because it corresponds in content,
and in part verbally, with the three first sentences of
the Lord's Prayer; it runs thus:

" Our Father, which art in Heaven,[1] show mercy towards us
for Thy great Name's sake whereby we are called;[2] and
fulfil unto us, O Lord our God, that which hath been written,
At that time will I bring you in, and at that time will I gather
you . . . "

---

[1] *cp. Pirke Aboth*, v. 23 : " Be strong as a lion to do the will
of thy Father which is in Heaven."

[2] *lit.* " Thy great Name which is called over us "; the
phrase comes from Deut. xxviii. 10; according to the Old
Testament idea, the people belonged to him whose name was
called over them.

This last sentence refers to the coming of the Kingdom, and the second sentence is an implicit hallowing of God's Name;[1] so that one can say with truth that the content of the first three clauses of the Lord's Prayer is contained in this supplication.[2] In the first two supplications also there are phrases strongly reminiscent of other clauses in the Lord's Prayer, viz. : "O lead us not into the power of sin, or of transgression or iniquity, or of temptation, or of scorn." And again : "May it be Thy will, O Lord my God, and God of my fathers, to deliver me this day, and every day, from arrogant men and from arrogance . . . and from any mishap, and from the adversary that destroyeth."

The Scriptural (Num. xxviii. 1-8 ; Lev. i. 11 ; on Sabbaths Num. xxviii. 9, 10 is also added) and Rabbinical passages which now follow refer to the sacrifices ; they are intended to emphasise the truth that the prayers of the synagogue are *spiritual sacrifices* and correspond to the sacrificial system of the Temple. Finally, the putting on of the *Tephillin*, or Phylacteries, is done in accordance with the commands given in Ex. xiii. 1-10 ; 11-16 ; Deut. vi. 4-9 ; xi. 13-21.[3]

THE CONCLUDING PORTION. This portion is not, strictly speaking, part of the service ;[4] and it varies considerably in different Rites. Some elements of this part of the service are, however, very ancient. Of special interest is the Psalm for the day ; this is a

---

[1] In the preceding supplication occur the words : " Sanctify Thy Name upon them that sanctify it, yea, sanctify Thy Name throughout Thy world."

[2] *cp.* also the words in one of the Benedictions in the evening service : " Our God, which art in Heaven, assert the unity of Thy Name, and establish Thy Kingdom continually, and reign over us for ever and ever."

[3] On the wearing of the *Tephillin* see *R WS*, pp. 447 ff.

[4] It is left to the devout to use part or all privately, according to the desire of the individual worshipper.

pre-Christian element.   In the Mishnah (*Tamid* vii. 4),
quoted in the Prayer Book, it is said : "These were
the Psalms which the Levites used to recite in the
Temple : on the first day of the week they used to
recite *The earth is the Lord's* (Ps. xxiv.) ; on the
second day *Great is the Lord* (Ps. xlviii.) ; on the
third day *God standeth in the congregation of the
mighty* (Ps. lxxxii.) ; on the fourth day *God of
vengeance* (Ps. xciv.) ; on the fifth day *Exult aloud unto
God our strength* (Ps. lxxxi.) ; on the sixth day *The
Lord reigneth* (Ps. xciii.) ; on the Sabbath *A Psalm, a
song for the Sabbath day* (Ps. xcii.).   It is the Psalm
and song also for the hereafter, for the day which will
be wholly a Sabbath and a rest for life everlasting."
As is well known, in the Septuagint five of these
chosen Psalms have inscriptions referring them to the
days of the week ; this is, however, not the case with
the Psalms for the third and fifth days.   Another
very ancient element in this part of the service is the
recitation of the Ten Commandments, for, according
to *Tamid* v. 1, these were read daily in the Temple.

There follow then some responses and the " Prayer
for Sustenance," which is based upon Scriptural
texts.   The presence of the Ten Commandments, after
this prayer, is interesting.   As we have just seen, the
Decalogue was used daily in the Temple Liturgy,
where it was read before the *Shema'* (Mishnah,
Tamid v. 1 ; Bab. Talm. *Berakhoth* 11*b*, 12*a*) ; but it
was excluded from the service on account of the
attitude adopted by certain sectaries who maintained
that only the Decalogue, not the rest of the Law, had
been revealed by God to Moses.   When this exclusion
took place is not absolutely certain, but in all
probability it was during the first century A.D.
Though printed in the Daily Prayer Book,[1] the

[1] Some twenty years ago the late Chief Rabbi H. Adler
allowed the Decalogue to be read in English on Sabbaths
in the synagogues under his jurisdiction.

Decalogue is not now part of the official service, and is only used privately by those who care to do so.

The Decalogue is followed by " The Thirteen Principles of Faith," of which the canticle *Yigdal*, as we have seen, is a poetical version. These " Principles" were compiled from Maimonides'[1] commentary on the Mishnah ; they are also known as the "Creed of Maimonides." They form the nearest approach to a formal creed which the Jews possess, but are not binding on the Jews, nor are they universally accepted. "Maimonides must indeed have filled up a great gap in Jewish theology, a gap, moreover, the existence of which was very generally perceived. A century had hardly elapsed before the Thirteen Articles had become a theme for the poets of the synagogue. And almost every country where Jews lived can show a poem or prayer founded on these articles."[2] The final conclusion of the service then follows with the reading of the *'Akedah*, or " Binding" of Isaac (Gen. xxii. 1–19), and the passage about the giving of the Manna (Ex. xvi. 4–36). Dr. Abrahams explains the *raison d'être* of these passages here thus: " The *'Akedah* is not merely an eternal plea to man for readiness to undergo all trials to which he may be subjected, but it also established a human plea for divine mercy. The obedience of Abraham was from two sides an inspiration to his descendants ; it inspired self-sacrifice and self-confidence. . . . The recital of the chapter on the *Manna* implies firm belief in the providential care of the Father. . . . When the daily round of work is begun in a spirit of faith, there will be no lack of sustenance."[3]

[1] He lived 1135–1204. (See pp. 34 ff.)
[2] Schechter, *Studies in Judaism* (First Series), pp. 199f. (1896).
[3] *op. cit.* p. cii.

V

THE ZEMIROTH

It is a Jewish liturgical principle that the making of petitions to Almighty God must be preceded by offering Him praise. Hence the praises at the opening of the service proper. *Zemiroth* is the Hebrew for "Psalms."[1] We have plenty of evidence as to the use of Psalms in the Temple Liturgy ; a number of them were sung by the Levites during the offering of the sacrifices ; we are specifically told also that every morning, immediately after the sacrifices had been offered, the Levites sang Ps. cv. 1–15,[2] and every evening Ps. xcvi. In the synagogue these are joined together and said every morning as an introduction to the praise portion of the service. But, as so often occurs in the Jewish Liturgy, important parts of the service are enclosed within a framework of Benedictions ; this is so, too, in the present case ; a Benediction is said before and after the recitation of the Psalms. The opening one is called, from the words with which it begins, *Baruk shĕāmar* ("Blessed be He who spake") ; this is a composite piece, the second part of which leads over to the Psalms of praise : " Blessed art Thou, O Lord our God . . . praised by the mouth of Thy people. . . ." The closing Benediction, also called after its opening words, is known as *Yishtabbach Shimĕka*, "Praised be Thy Name." It is after the former Benediction that Pss. cv. 1–15 and xcvi. are said ; these are followed by a number of extracts from the Bible, mainly from the Psalms, strung into two

---

[1] *cp.* the titles of many of the Psalms, *Mizmor le-David*, a Psalm of David ; the word *Mizmor* is from the same root. *Zemiroth* is also a technical term for religious poems, usually sung ; *e.g.* the *Zemiroth* sung at table on the Sabbath.

[2] This occurs also, with slight variations, in 1 Chron. xvi. 8–36, which is the form adopted in the Liturgy.

M

hymns of praise, with Ps. c. in the centre. The second of these hymns of praise is composed wholly of verses containing the Name of God. Ps. c. is in all probability a remnant here of the old Temple Liturgy.

Now the opening Benediction, Pss. cv. 1–15, xcvi., and the hymns of praise with Ps. c. in the centre, all form part of the framework around the real centre of the praise portion of the service; the kernel of the whole is formed by Pss. cxlv.–cl.;[1] these are the real *Zemiroth.* The first actual mention of these Psalms as being part of the daily service of the Liturgy is by Rabbi Jose ben Chalaphta, who lived in the middle of the second century A.D.;[2] but it is very probable that they formed part of the Temple Liturgy. In the ancient Prayer Books these Psalms are immediately followed by the concluding Benediction, *Yishtabbach Shiměka,* but in course of time the three Biblical passages, I Chron. xxix. 10–13 (David's Song of Thanksgiving); Neh. ix. 6–11 (A Song of Praise); and Ex. xiv. 30–xv. 18 (The Song of Moses), came to be inserted. These three passages and the final Benediction form the rest of the framework around the *Zemiroth* proper.

At the end of this part of the service half of the *Kaddish* is said; on this see below, § IX.

VI

THE SHEMA‘

We have already seen (p. 154) that this part of the service, concentrating the mind as it does upon the cardinal tenet of the Jewish faith—belief in one God—was considered so important that in the worship of the Temple it was introduced by a formal thanksgiving

---

[1] Strictly speaking, it begins at Ps. cxlv. 15.
[2] Tractate *Sopherim* xvii. 11 (Elbogen, *op. cit.* p. 82).

for the divine revelation, and followed by the prayer that this revelation should be continued to Israel. Something similar finds its place up to the present day in the Jewish Liturgy. The *Shema'* is introduced by various Benedictions or prayers, the two central ones being known respectively as *Yotzer* ("Creator") and *Ahabah* ("Love") from the most important of their opening words. It is followed by a Benediction called *Geullah* ("Redemption"), because it refers to the Almighty as the Redeemer of Israel. It is probable that, in some form, all these three existed in the Temple Liturgy. This is certainly true of the *Ahabah*, without doubt one of the most beautiful prayers in any Liturgy ; it is as follows :

"With abounding love hast Thou loved us, O Lord our God. With great and overflowing pity hast Thou had pity upon us. O our Father, our King, for our fathers' sake who trusted in Thee, and whom Thou didst teach the statutes of life, be gracious also unto us, and teach us. O our Father, merciful Father, ever compassionate, have mercy upon us, and put into our hearts to discern and to understand ; to hear, to learn, and to teach ; to observe and do and fulfil in love all the words of instruction in Thy Law. Enlighten our eyes in Thy Law, and let our hearts cleave to Thy commandments ; and unite our hearts to love and to fear Thy Name, that we may never be put to shame. For in Thy holy, great, and revered Name have we trusted ; so shall we rejoice and be glad in Thy salvation. O bring us in peace from the four corners of the earth, and make us go upright to our land ; for Thou, O God, dost work salvation. And us hast Thou chosen from all peoples and tongues, and hast brought us near to Thy great Name for ever in faithfulness, that we might in love give thanks to Thee, and proclaim Thy unity. Blessed art Thou, O Lord, who in love dost choose Thy people Israel."

The actual *Shema'*, which receives its name from the opening word "Hear," consists of the three Biblical passages, Deut. vi. 4–9, beginning: "Hear, O Israel ; the Lord our God, the Lord is One" ; Deut. xi. 13–21 ; and Num. xv. 37–41. This was part of the Temple service which, as the Mishnah (*Tamid* v. 1) tells us, was taken over by the

M 2

synagogue. It is interesting to note that the words which immediately follow after the saying of the *Shema*—"Blessed be His Name, whose glorious Kingdom is for ever and ever"—were always said in the Temple when the Holy Name, Jehovah, was uttered.

VII

THE SHEMONEH 'ESREH

We come now to what is the most interesting and, in many respects, the most important part of the Jewish Liturgy. But before coming to speak in some detail about this venerable prayer it will be well to say a word or two as to its date ; not that this can be fixed with certainty, but there are some indications which point to a high antiquity, at any rate, of parts of it, though in its present form it belongs to about A.D. 100. Nowhere in the canonical Scriptures, it is true, is there any sign that it was known to any of the writers. But in the *Wisdom of Ben-Sira* there is a passage which demands some attention, namely, the Psalm which, in the Hebrew Version, comes after li. 12. The parallelisms between this passage and the *Shemoneh 'Esreh* are partly to be found in identity of expression, and partly in similarity of thought. These are as follows ; identical expressions in the Hebrew of each are printed in italics :

BEN-SIRA	SHEM. 'ES.
Verse	Section
2. Give thanks unto the God of praises.	3. Holy ones praise Thee every day.
5. Give thanks unto *the Redeemer of Israel*.	7. Blessed art Thou, O Lord, *the Redeemer of Israel*.
6. Give thanks unto Him *that gathereth the outcasts of Israel*.	10. Blessed art Thou, O Lord, *that gatherest the outcasts of* Thy people *Israel*.

BEN-SIRA	SHEM. 'ES.
Verse	Section
7. Give thanks unto Him *that buildeth His City* and His Sanctuary.	14. Do Thou dwell in the midst of Jerusalem *Thy City.* . . . And *build* it an everlasting building speedily in our days. Blessed art Thou, O Lord, *that buildest* Jerusalem.
8. Give thanks unto Him *that causeth a horn to flourish for* the house of *David.*	15. *Do Thou cause* the branch of *David* speedily *to flourish,* And do Thou exalt his *horn* by Thy salvation.
10. Give thanks unto *the Shield of Abraham.*	1. Blessed art Thou, O Lord, *the Shield of Abraham.*
11. Give thanks unto the *Rock* of Isaac.	18. . . . the *Rock* of our lives.
12. Give thanks unto the *Mighty One of Jacob.*	1. . . . the *God of Jacob,* the great God, *mighty* and revered.
13. Give thanks unto Him that hath chosen *Zion.*	17. May our eyes behold Thy return to *Zion.* . . . Blessed art Thou, O Lord, that restorest Thy Shekinah to *Zion.*
14. Give thanks unto the *King* of the kings of kings.	11. Reign Thou over us. . . . Blessed art Thou, O Lord and *King.*

The title of " King " is applied to God four times in addition to this one. Identical expressions grouped together in this way in the *Shemoneh 'Esreh* and in this Psalm can scarcely be fortuitous. It must be remembered that the Psalm is quite short, and though the order in which these expressions occur differs in the two pieces, yet when they are respectively found within a restricted compass the supposition of a connexion of some sort between the two is justified. The *Wisdom of Ben-Sira* belongs approximately to the year 175 B.C., so that if we could trace a real relationship between the *Shemonch 'Esreh* and this

Psalm, there would presumably be some grounds for dating the origin of the former somewhere about the beginning of the second pre-Christian century. The subject is, however, complicated by the following considerations : (*a*) Some authorities hold this Psalm to be later than the rest of Ben-Sira's book. (*b*) The conditions presupposed in the *Shemoneh 'Esreh* (*i.e.* Pharisaic) are inadmissible in 175 B.C. (*c*) With one exception, the identical expressions referred to above occur in the admittedly later Benedictions of the *Shemoneh 'Esreh* (viz. 7, 10, 14, 15). These objections are weighty, though not insuperable. In some form or other the prayer was certainly existing in 175 B.C. and doubtless for some time before this date.

Two recensions of this prayer are in existence : the Babylonian and the Palestinian ; from these we are enabled to see that it was originally shorter than it appears in its present form in the Jewish Liturgy.

The following is an English version of the *Shemoneh 'Esreh* translated from the Babylonian recension published by Dalman.[1] This is the longer form, and therefore includes the later additions, but it is the form as now found in the Jewish Liturgy. Dalman believes that this recension is originally Palestinian, but that Babylon was the centre from which later on it spread and became the universally accepted form. There is every reason to believe that originally this prayer was composed on the pattern of early Hebrew poetry, *i.e.* each paragraph consisted of two lines in rhythmic measure ; then came the Benediction.

The *Shemoneh 'Esreh* is introduced by the words from Ps. li. 15 (E.V.) :

"O Lord, open Thou my lips,
And my mouth shall show forth Thy praise."

[1] *Die Worte Jesu*, pp. 301–304 (1898).

BENEDICTION I [1]

Blessed art Thou, O Lord our God, and the God of our fathers,

The God of Abraham, the God of Isaac, and the God of Jacob.

[2][God the Great One, the Mighty One, and the Revered One], *God Most High,* [Who dost grant loving [3] mercies], *and dost possess all things,* [Who dost remember the pious deeds of the fathers, and showest compassion upon their children, and wilt bring a redeemer to their children's children for His Name's sake, in love ; Merciful King, Saviour, Helper, and Shield].

Blessed art Thou, O Lord, the Shield of Abraham.

BENEDICTION II

Thou art mighty for ever, O Lord,

[O Thou that quickenest the dead, Thou art mighty to save], *That causest the wind to blow, and the rain to descend.*

Thou sustainest the living [with mercy], *Thou quickenest the dead.*

[With great mercies Thou dost heal the sick, dost help the weak, dost support the fallen, dost loose the bound, and dost keep faith with them that sleep in the dust. And who is like unto Thee, Master of mighty acts? And who resembleth Thee, that killest and makest alive, and causest salvation to spring forth, that art faithful in quickening the dead ?]

Blessed art Thou, O Lord, that quickenest the dead.

---

[1] When used in the public service this prayer is said first by the worshippers silently ; it is then recited aloud by the Precentor or Reader.

[2] Words in square brackets are those portions which are probably later additions, according to Dalman ; we are not able to agree with him in every case.

[3] טובים.

BENEDICTION III

Thou art holy, and holy is Thy Name,
And holy ones praise Thee every day.
Blessed art Thou, O Lord, the Holy God.

After this Benediction follows what is called the *Kedushah* ("Sanctification")[1]; this is not an original part of the *Shemoneh 'Esreh,* and when it first came to be inserted is quite unknown; but it is mentioned in very early writings,[2] and its presence in the Jewish Liturgy is in any case pre-Christian. We shall have to say a word about it presently, when it will be seen to be of peculiar interest from the Christian liturgical point of view.

BENEDICTION IV

Thou dost favourably grant knowledge unto men,
And dost teach discernment unto men;
Grant us from Thee knowledge, and understanding,
and discernment.
Blessed art Thou who dost graciously grant knowledge.

BENEDICTION V

Cause us to return, our Father, unto Thy Law;
And draw us near, our King, unto Thy service;
And bring us back in perfect repentance to Thy
presence.
Blessed art Thou, O Lord, that delightest in repentance.

BENEDICTION VI

Forgive us, our Father, for we have sinned;
Pardon us, our King, for we have transgressed.
For Thou art the God of goodness, Thou dost forgive.
Blessed art Thou, O Lord, [Who art gracious], *Who*
dost abundantly forgive.

[1] The earliest direct quotation of it is *circa* A.D. 350; see Elbogen, *op. cit.* p. 62.
[2] See Zunz, *Die gottesdienstlichen Vorträge der Juden,* pp. 382, 395 (1892).

BENEDICTION VII

*Look upon our affliction, and plead our cause, and
    haste to redeem us ;*
For thou art God, [King], *Mighty Redeemer.*
Blessed art Thou, O Lord, the Redeemer of Israel.

BENEDICTION VIII

Heal us, O Lord our God, and we shall be healed ;
[Save us, and we shall be saved], *Vouchsafe* [perfect]
    healing to all our wounds,
For Thou, O God, art a merciful Healer.
Blessed art Thou, O Lord, that healest [the sicknesses
    of His people] *Israel.*

BENEDICTION IX

*Bless us, O Lord our God, in all the work of our
    hands,*
And bless our years, [and give dew and rain upon the
    face of the earth], *and satisfy the world and its
    fullness with Thy goodness,* [and give plenty
    upon the face of the earth through the richness
    of the gifts of Thy hands, and preserve and
    prosper, O Lord our God, this year with every
    kind of produce, (keeping) from it every kind of
    destruction and want ; and grant to it issue, and
    hope, and plenty, and peace, and blessing, as in
    other good years].
Blessed art Thou, O Lord, that blessest the years.

BENEDICTION X

Sound the great horn for our freedom,
*And lift up the ensign to gather all our exiles from
    the four corners of the earth to our own land.*
Blessed art Thou, O Lord, that gatherest [the outcast of
    Thy people] *Israel.*

BENEDICTION XI

Restore our judges as in former times, and our counsellors as in the beginning,
[And put away from us grief and sighing], *and do Thou alone reign over us* [in mercy, in righteousness, and in judgement].
Blessed art Thou, O Lord, [and King], *that lovest* [righteousness and] *judgement.*

BENEDICTION XII

And for slanderers [1] *let there be no hope,*
And let all the Minim [2] *be destroyed as in a moment;*
And the kingdom of arrogance do Thou uproot and crush [speedily in our days].
Blessed art Thou, O Lord, [that crushest the enemies, and] *that humblest the arrogant.*

BENEDICTION XIII

Upon the righteous, [and upon the pious], *and upon the proselytes of righteousness*
[And upon the remnant of Thy people, even all the house of Israel] *let Thy mercies be stirred, O Lord our God;*
And grant a good reward unto all that trust in Thy name [in truth; and set our portion with them for ever; let us not be ashamed, for in Thy Name have we trusted, and we have relied upon Thy salvation].
Blessed art Thou, O Lord, [the Stay and] *the Trust of the righteous.*

[1] מַלְשִׁינִים; but in the marg. and in two MSS. מְשׁוּמָּדִים "religious renegade," or the like.
[2] "Heretics"; the reference is possibly to Christians; but some eminent Jewish scholars hold that the term refers to Gnostics and not to Christians; see Joël, *Blicke* . . ., i. 26, 29.

BENEDICTION XIV

Do Thou dwell in the midst of Jerusalem, Thy city
  [according as Thou hast said],
And build it an everlasting building speedily in our
  days.
Blessed art Thou, O Lord, that buildest Jerusalem.

BENEDICTION XV

Do Thou cause the branch of David speedily to flourish,
And do Thou exalt his horn by Thy salvation.
Blessed art Thou, O Lord, that causest [the horn of]
  salvation to flourish.

BENEDICTION XVI

Hear our voice, O Lord our God, [spare us] *and have*
  mercy upon us,
And accept our prayer in mercy [and favour].
[From Thy presence, O our King, turn us not away
  empty], *for Thou hearest the prayer of every*
  mouth.
Blessed art Thou that hearkenest unto prayer.

BENEDICTION XVII

Accept, O Lord our God, Thy people Israel [and thei
  prayer],
And restore the service to the oracle of Thy House.
[And the fire-offerings of Israel and their prayer and
  their service do Thou speedily accept in love
  with favour ; and may the service of Thy people
  Israel be ever acceptable],
And may our eyes behold Thy return to Zion [in mercy,
  as of yore].
Blessed art Thou, O Lord, that restorest [speedily] *Thy*
  Shekhinah unto Zion.

BENEDICTION XVIII

We give thanks unto Thee [for Thou art He], *O Lord our God, and the God of our fathers ;*
[The Rock of our lives, and the Shield of our salvation art Thou from generation to generation. We will give thanks unto Thee, and declare Thy praise,] *for our lives which are committed into Thy hand, and for our souls which are in Thy charge ;*
For Thy miracles, and for Thy wonders, and for Thy benefits at all times, [at evening, and morning, and mid-day. Thou art good, for Thy loving-kindnesses fail not ; Thou art merciful, for Thy mercies cease not. For all the living praise Thy great Name ; for Thou art good, Thou Good God].
Blessed art Thou, O Lord ; good [and beautiful] *it is to praise Thee* [and Thy name continually].

BENEDICTION XIX

Give [goodly] *peace and blessing* [grace, and mercy, and loving-kindnesses] *unto us, even unto Israel Thy people.*
Bless us altogether, O Lord our God, [in the light of Thy countenance; for in the light of Thy countenance Thou hast given us, O Lord our God, the Law, and life, love and mercy, righteousness and peace, blessing and loving-kindnesses] ; *yea, it is good in Thine eyes to bless Thy people Israel* [with abundance of strength and peace].
Blessed art Thou, O Lord, that blessest [Thy people Israel] *with peace. Amen.*

As already pointed out, after the people have said the *Shemoneh 'Esreh* privately the reader repeats it aloud ; during this repetition in ancient days men belonging to priestly families uttered the Blessing of the Priests before the nineteenth Benediction;[1] this was done daily, but for many centuries its daily use has ceased, and it is only said on festivals, as well as on the Day of Atonement, but not when it falls on the Sabbath. The Blessing of the Priests (Num. vi. 24–26) was an important ceremony in the Temple Liturgy ; it was uttered by the priests every morning and evening over the worshippers at the bringing of the whole burnt-offering. This is, therefore, another element which the synagogue has taken over from the Temple Liturgy. This Blessing is not now necessarily said by priests ; on ordinary occasions the officiating reader utters it. It is not said if a congregation consists of less than ten males, aged thirteen years or over.[2]

The name *Shemoneh 'Esreh* (= Eighteen [Benedictions]), referring especially as it does to the *Berakhoth* or "Blessings" with which each sentence concludes, dates, then, in its present form from about the year A.D. 100. Before that time it consisted of only seventeen Benedictions.[3] The addition of the eighteenth was due to Gamaliel II. (see below). In its present form, however, the prayer consists of nineteen Benedictions ; this is because in the Jewish Liturgy the Babylonian recension has been adopted, and in this recension what in the Palestinian recension appears as a single Benediction is in the Babylonian recension divided into two, namely, the fourteenth and fifteenth. Another name which is very often given to this prayer is *Tephillah* (= " prayer "), because it is *par excellence* the prayer of the Jewish Liturgy. Yet another name by which it is commonly known is *'Amidah* (= . "standing "), because during

[1] In the Mishnah (*Sota* vii. 1) this Benediction is called *Birkath Cohanim* (= " The Blessing of the Priests ").

[2] Mishnah, *Megilla* iv. 4.

[3] Earlier still it consisted of only twelve, in all probability while there is reason to believe that in its earliest form it was made up of only six Benedictions ; see below.

its recitation the congregation stands, whereas they sit during most of the preceding part of the service.

Originally, when this prayer was offered up in the synagogue, one came forth from the congregation and recited it. He was called the *Sheliach Zibbur*, "the messenger of the congregation." This was done in order to emphasise that the prayer was offered by the congregation. The *Sheliach Zibbur* was the mouthpiece of the congregation; he was not their representative; he did not occupy a position analogous to that of a priest; it was simply that his voice was the voice of the people. Jewish worship was essentially congregational. And while as a rule (until much later times, and for convenience' sake) the congregation had their mouthpiece, they did with their own voice collectively utter certain responses belonging to this prayer; the most important of these was the *Amen* at the end. This response came originally from the Psalms, and its utterance by the congregation was essential. We are reminded of St. Paul's words in 1 Cor. xiv. 16: "Else if thou bless with the spirit, how shall he that filleth the place of the unlearned say the Amen at thy *giving of thanks* . . . ?" Regarding these last words, it is worth noticing, as an illustration of the fact that the Liturgy of the early Church was, in some of its main principles, founded on the pattern of the Jewish, that in this prayer the "Amen" follows the *giving of thanks*; of this thanksgiving we shall speak presently. The importance attached to the congregation's "Amen"[1] is well illustrated by the fact that in the large synagogue at Alexandria, where there was a difficulty for all the members of the congregation to hear when the end of the prayer was reached, an official stood up on the platform in the centre of the synagogue and waved a flag as a sign to the congregation to say the "Amen."[2]

[1] *cp.* the conclusion of Ps. cvi.   [2] Elbogen, *op. cit.* p. 435.

Regarding the structure of the *Shemoneh 'Esreh*, in its present form there is an important point to which attention must be drawn. The paragraphs, or Benedictions, fall into *three* distinct groups ; the first three are ascriptions of *Praise* : God, the Most High, Possessor of all things ; God, the Mighty One, Sustainer of the living and quickener of the dead ; God, the Holy One, who is praised every day. All the intermediate ones are *Petitions*. The three last are offerings of *Thanksgiving*. This last point is not immediately apparent in all of the three ; but a very little examination shows that thanksgiving is the underlying thought even where not directly expressed. Thus, in the last but two (it is called *'Abodah*, " service ") the prayer is made that God would accept His people Israel and restore the service in the Temple at Jerusalem ; but the service in the Temple, *i.e.* the sacrificial offerings, was, among other things, an expression of thanksgiving ; so that in its essence this Benediction is rightly regarded as coming under the head of thanksgiving. In the eighteenth Benediction the note of thanksgiving is quite clear : " We give thanks unto Thee . . . O Lord our God, and the God of our fathers. . . . We will give thanks unto Thee, and declare Thy praise, for our lives which are committed into Thy hand, and for our souls which are in Thy charge, for Thy miracles, and for Thy wonders, and for Thy benefits at all times." Then, as to the final Benediction, the note of thanksgiving is to be discerned in the words : " It is good in Thine eyes to bless Thy people Israel," where the recognition of the divine blessing accorded to the people is essentially a form of genuine thanksgiving. So that, although at first sight these last three paragraphs of the prayer do not, excepting in the case of the last but one, seem to come under the head of thanksgiving, they *do* so in their essence, and have always been regarded as expressions of thanksgiving in the Jewish Church. The *Shemoneh 'Esreh* seems, therefore, to present us with the earliest pattern of what the subject-sequence of divine worship should be, viz. first *Praise* to God, then *Petition*, then *Thanksgiving*.

The next point of interest regarding our prayer is this : the *Shemoneh 'Esreh* is the earliest example of a fixed framework of praise and thanksgiving enclosing variable matter according to the sacred seasons. We have just seen that the Benedictions are divided into three distinct groups : the first three, the last three, and the intervening Benedictions. The first three and the last three occupy, and have always occupied, a very special position ; for these six are used on every day of the year without exception. The other thirteen are used only on ordinary week-days, whereas on Sabbaths, feasts, and the Day of Atonement they give place to special petitions. The first three and the last three Benedictions form, therefore, a fixed framework. So that on a feast-day, for example, the *Shemoneh 'Esreh* consists of the first three Benedictions of Praise ; then there follow, not the ordinary thirteen Petitions as quoted just now, but special petitions (variable in number) proper to the festival or fast ; then come the three concluding Benedictions of Thanksgiving. This liturgical principle of a fixed framework of praise and thanksgiving enclosing variable matter is thus seen to be extremely ancient ; and we find it in our Communion Office—though here the praise and thanksgiving portions have changed places—for the Proper Prefaces, variable according to the season, are enclosed by the constant paragraphs of thanksgiving and praise, thus: " It is very meet, right, and our bounden duty that we should at all times and in all places give thanks unto Thee, O Lord . . ."; then at festivals comes the Proper Preface, of variable content according to the season ; and this is followed by the unchanging offering of praise: "Therefore with angels and archangels and with all the company of Heaven, we laud and magnify Thy glorious name, evermore praising Thee . . ."

It is, of course, only the liturgical principle to which attention is drawn, and which the Christian Church in all probability adopted from the Jewish; the details naturally differ.

Then we come to another interesting point in which the question of congregational responses is also involved. It has already been pointed out that after the third Benediction comes what is called the *Kedushah* ("Sanctification"), so called because of its content, to which we shall come in a moment; this *Kedushah* is now, and has been for a great many centuries, regarded as an integral part of the *Shemoneh 'Esreh*; it was certainly not so originally, as it does not figure in either the Palestinian or Babylonian texts of the prayer; nevertheless, it had already been incorporated, as an integral part of the prayer, before the Christian era, and that is the important point for us. The *Kedushah* consists of responses uttered by the reader and the people, and is as follows:

"*Reader.* We will sanctify Thy name in the world even as they sanctify it in the highest heavens, as it is written by the hand of the prophet: And they called to one another and said:

People. Holy, holy, holy is the Lord of Hosts; the earth is full of His glory.

Reader. Those over against them say, Blessed—

People. Blessed be the glory of the Lord from His place.

Reader. And in Thy holy words it is written, saying:

People. The Lord shall reign for ever, Thy God, O Zion, unto all generations. Praise ye the Lord [*i.e.* Hallelujah].

Reader. Unto all generations we will declare Thy greatness, and to all eternity we will proclaim Thy holiness; and Thy praise, O our God, shall not depart from our mouth for ever, for Thou art a great and holy God and King. Blessed art Thou, O Lord, the Holy God."

In all probability this present form of the *Kedushah* is an amplification of its primitive form; and it is

N

difficult not to believe that the form which the first Christians used was the parent of the *Sanctus* in the Church's Communion Office.

But if this is so (and it can hardly be doubted), it makes all the sadder another fact, namely, that this prayer acted as one of the means whereby the complete separation between Jews and Jewish-Christians was brought about. We have already seen that about the year A.D. 100 Gamaliel II. added a Benediction to the *Shemoneh 'Esreh*; he did this with the object of excluding Heretics or Gnostics, among whom must be reckoned Christians, from the synagogue. The Benediction he added was what is now the twelfth:

" And for slanderers let there be no hope,
    And let all the Minim be destroyed as in a moment ;
    And the kingdom of arrogance do Thou uproot and crush.
    Blessed art Thou, O Lord, that crushest the enemies, and
        that humblest the arrogant."

The jarring note of bitterness and hatred sounded in this paragraph of the prayer is wholly alien to the spirit of the rest of it. In this paragraph two types of men, hateful to the Jews, are referred to. The first, now designated "slanderers," were not originally so called ; in this paragraph in its original form the word was *Meshummadim, i.e.* renegades. So that the opening line of this paragraph ran originally :

" And for renegades [to their religion] let there be no hope."

As to the *Minim* spoken of in the second line of the paragraph, by this term was meant those who differed from the orthodox belief of the Jews, including Sadducees, Samaritans, Christians and Gnostics, and heretics generally. But the use of the word in this prayer was intended to be directed against Christians, according to Elbogen. It seems pretty evident that Justin Martyr refers to this in saying that the Jews

cursed the Christians three times daily in their synagogues ; so, too, Epiphanius, who refers to the prayer
more pointedly in saying that the Jews pray to God
that He will destroy the Nazarenes. Elbogen believes
that the word "Nazarenes" stood in the prayer at
one time.[1]

After the *Shemoneh 'Esreh* had been said it was
customary in ancient days to spend a short time in
silent prayer and supplication. During the Middle
Ages, however, this gradually became replaced by a
set form of *Selichoth* ("Petitions," or, more exactly,
"Penitential prayers"), since the word comes from
the root meaning "to forgive." These *Selichoth* (see
further § XI. on the Day of Atonement) were an
outcome of the assemblies on fast-days to which
reference has already been made (pp.152 ff.). Though
originally instituted for the Day of Atonement and
fast-days only, they were gradually extended and
used at other services as well. One of the oldest is
that beginning: "And He, being merciful, forgiveth
iniquity and destroyeth not . . ."; this is known,
from the Hebrew of the opening words, as *Vehu
Rachum* ; it contains references to many Biblical
passages, which is characteristic of all the *Selichoth*.
On ordinary occasions, instead of *Vehu Rachum*, the
Shemoneh 'Esreh is immediately followed by two sentences in which are sounded the notes of penitence,
i.e. the *Selichah* note, and that of supplication, *i.e.*
the *Tachanun* note, thus leading over to the next
part of the service, the *Tachanunim*. These two
sentences are as follows :

"And David said unto Gad, I am troubled exceedingly ; let
us fall, I pray thee, into the hand of the Lord, for His mercies
are many, but let me not fall into the hand of man" (2 Sam.
xxiv. 14).

---

[1] *op. cit.* p. 36. On the other hand, Abrahams, in his edition
of the Prayer Book, p. lxiv f., holds strongly that the reference
throughout the Benediction is to sectarian Jews.

" O Thou who art merciful and gracious, I have sinned before Thee.

O Lord, full of mercy, have mercy upon me and receive my supplications " (*Tachanunai*).

VIII

THE TACHANUNIM

The word *Tachanunim* means " Petitions for grace " ; the origin of these is very interesting. In the Temple worship during the service on the Day of Atonement the whole congregation twice prostrated itself upon the ground : first when the Levites sounded with their trumpets and the high-priest gave the blessing, and again when the high-priest pronounced the absolution.[1] On these occasions of prostration the people, according to the Mishnah, offered up private prayer.[2] The custom was continued in the synagogue worship ; and these private prayers, instead of being offered up at the close of the public sacrifice, were said at the close of the congregational prayers—that is, at the end of public worship ; opportunity was then given to the individual worshipper to pour out his heart to God.[3] " By this means," as Elbogen says, " the most difficult problem of congregational worship was solved ; it gave the due adjustment between the demands of the congregation, for which united prayer was indispensable, and the reasonable craving of the individual for personal communion with God. The demand of the congregation receives prior recognition, but, this having been satisfied, opportunity is given to the individual worshipper to pour forth without restraint the inner yearnings of his heart." [4]

---

[1] *cp*. Ecclus. l. 16–21.

[2] See Elbogen, *op. cit.* p. 73.

[3] *cp*. the Psalmist's words : " Commune with your own heart . . . and be still " (Ps. iv. 4 [5 in Hebr.]).

[4] *op. cit.* p. 74.

In later times the place for private prayer was transferred to the conclusion of the *Shemoneh 'Esreh*. The point to be emphasised is that opportunity for private prayer during public worship was thus *officially provided for*. In course of time the duration of private prayers was regulated; it was laid down that "they who utter words[1] after the Tephillah"[2] might make their prayer as long as they wished, but it must not be longer than the longest prayer known[3]—that is, the prayer of the Day of Atonement. In later centuries this admirable provision for private prayers during public worship largely fell into disuse, though not wholly; and by degrees its place was taken by what are now known as the *Tachanunim, i.e.* "Petitions for grace." These have now become an integral part of the official prayers of the synagogue. What is known as the *Tachanun* is based, as we have seen, on the words of David in 2 Sam. xxiv. 14: "Let us now fall into the hand of the Lord, for His mercies are great; and let me not fall into the hand of man." It will be noticed that the *Tachanun* comes immediately after the *Shemoneh 'Esreh*, according to the old usage.

It is necessary to add that the words of Dan. ix. 3 ff. came to be brought into connexion with the *Tachanunim*; the prayer in that passage, it will be noticed, goes over into a confession of sin. This element has entered into all the *Tachanunim*, and they have thus come to be very largely, like the *Selichoth*, penitential prayers. This transformation of private prayers into public penitential prayers is a fact full of human interest.

---

[1] To "utter words" is an early technical term for private prayer.

[2] Another name, as we have seen, for the *Shemoneh 'Esreh*.

[3] *Tos. Berakhoth* iii. 6, quoted by Elbogen.

IX

THE READING OF THE LAW

One of the main objects of public worship was *instruction in the Law,* and for this purpose various sections from the Pentateuch and other parts of the Bible were introduced into the regular prayers. But besides these were readings from the *Scroll.* The Pentateuch is now, in most synagogues, read through on Sabbaths once a year; this custom comes down to us from Babylonian usage. In Palestine the Pentateuch was read through once in three years, this being what is known as the *Triennial Cycle.*[1]

The Scrolls of the Law are kept in the Ark, which is placed at the east end of the synagogue. When the Ark is opened and when the Scroll of the Law is taken out various sentences based on Scriptural passages are said. On Mondays, Thursdays, Sabbath afternoons, and on Fast-days three persons are called to the reading of the Law: a priest,[2] a Levite,[2] and an Israelite; these in days gone by read the Pentateuch passages themselves; now, however, this is done by the officiating reader. Benedictions are said before and after the reading of the Law; these embody passages from Scripture. Then come Pss. cxlv. and xx., followed by a passage beginning with a citation from Is. lix. 20, 21: "And a Redeemer shall come to Zion . . .", which leads over to the concluding portion of the service. This we have already considered.[3]

---

[1] Abrahams, *Annotated Prayer Book,* p. lxxviii.

[2] *i.e.* one descended from a priestly family, or a Levitical family, respectively.

[3] The daily afternoon service is a shortened form of morning service; the daily evening service is also based upon it, but modified in some respects and adapted to evening time; it is not regarded as obligatory.

X

KADDISH

Kaddish means "Sanctification"; it was in its origin a doxology uttered by a teacher at the close of his discourse, and had nothing to do with the worship of the synagogue; but in course of time it was incorporated in the Liturgy to mark the close of parts of the service. In the first form in which it occurs in the service it is abbreviated, and is known as *Half-Kaddish*. *Full Kaddish* is said at the conclusion of the service proper, *i.e.* after the *Shemoneh* ·*'Esreh*; in this form it is known as *Kaddish tithkabbal*, from the opening word of one of the sections, "*May there be accepted* the prayers and supplications of all Israel by their Father which is in Heaven; and say ye, Amen." A third form of *Kaddish* was said at the close of reading extracts from Rabbinical writings; hence it is called Rabbinical *Kaddish*. But the two most interesting forms of *Kaddish* are "Mourner's *Kaddish*" and the "*Kaddish* of Renewal." The former of these was "originally recited at the close of the seven days' mourning, with the religious discourses and benedictions associated with it, but (*Sopherim* xix. 12) only at the death of a scholar; afterwards, in order not to put others to shame, it was recited after every burial."[1] The "Mourner's *Kaddish*" is recited by mourners in the synagogue during the first eleven months after the death of a parent, and on anniversaries afterwards. This constitutes a *memorial* of the departed, though it is not a prayer for the departed. It seems, however, possible that "Mourner's *Kaddish*" represents a faint echo of, or substitute for, something that was originally a definite prayer for the departed. Elbogen points out that, according to

[1] Kohler in *JE* vii. 401.

Shabbath 119*b*, there was a mystic idea of the miraculous efficacy which the recitation of this *Kaddish* had both for the living and the dead. The following story,[1] told of Rabbi Akiba, who lived in the early part of the second century A.D., throws an interesting sidelight on the point: Rabbi Akiba was once walking through a forest when he met a man rushing along carrying a great burden ; the Rabbi accosted him, asking him why he was thus hurrying along with that burden on his back. The man replied that he was condemned to do so throughout the centuries because of the sins he had committed when he had lived as a mortal on earth. Rabbi Akiba asked him if he had had no son. The man replied that he could not say, for he had died before his wife had borne him a child ; one might have been born after he had died, but he did not know. Then the man continued his endless journey. Rabbi Akiba thereupon bestirred himself to seek out the man's widow. After much toil he found her, and learned that she had given birth to a son after her husband's death. Then the Rabbi told her to teach her son to say the " Mourner's *Kaddish*," and to bid him recite it in the synagogue. She did so ; and the boy recited the " Mourner's *Kaddish*" in the synagogue. Soon after the man appeared to Rabbi Akiba in a night-vision, and thanked him for what he had done, telling him that his punishment had ceased, and that he was now resting in Paradise in peace.

The story clearly suggests that at one time the " Mourner's *Kaddish*" partook of the character of a prayer said for the benefit of the departed ; this is made the more probable by the fact that what is called " Renewal *Kaddish*" is said at the close of the

[1] It is only the substance of the story which is given ; it was told to the writer by a well-known Jewish minister ; it is from an ancient Midrashic source.

service for the burial of the dead. The "Renewal" here refers to the new world hereafter. Though "Mourner's *Kaddish*" is not directly a prayer for the departed, that does not mean to say that the Jewish Liturgy does not contain such prayers (see pp. 201 ff.).

The following is a translation of *Kaddish*[1] in its full form :

"And now, I pray Thee, let the power of the Lord be great, according as Thou hast spoken. Remember, O Lord, Thy tender mercies and Thy loving-kindnesses ; for they have been ever of old. (This is not said aloud on any occasion during the service.)

Magnified and sanctified[2] be His great Name in the world which He hath created according to His will. May He establish His Kingdom during your life and during your days, and during the life of all the house of Israel, even speedily and at a near time, and say ye, Amen.

Reader and People. Let His great Name be blessed for ever and to all eternity.

Reader. Blessed, praised and glorified, exalted, extolled and honoured, magnified and lauded be the Name of the Holy One.

Reader and People. Blessed be He !

Reader. Though He be high above all the blessings and hymns, praises and consolations, which are uttered in the world ; and say ye, Amen.

People. Accept our prayer in mercy and in favour (said privately).

Reader. May the prayers and supplications of all Israel be accepted by their Father which is in heaven ; and say ye, Amen.

People. Let the name of the Lord be blessed from this time forth for evermore (said privately).

Reader. May there be abundant peace from Heaven, and life for us and for all Israel ; and say ye, Amen.

People. My help is from the Lord, who hath made heaven and earth (said privately).

Reader. He who maketh peace in His high places, may He make peace for us and for all Israel ; and say ye, Amen."

---

[1] Its original language is Aramaic, not Hebrew.
[2] It is this word which gives the name to this prayer.

When Half-*Kaddish* is said it begins at "Magnified and sanctified be His great Name," and ends with the sentence said by the Reader: "Blessed, praised and glorified." Rabbinical *Kaddish* differs from the ordinary form in that it inserts after the Reader's words "Blessed, praised and glorified . . ." the following sentence: "Unto Israel, and unto the Rabbis, and unto their disciples, and unto all the disciples of their disciples, and unto all who engage in the study of the Law, in this or in any other place, unto them and unto you be abundant peace, grace, loving-kindness, mercy, long life, ample sustenance, and salvation from the Father which is in Heaven, and say ye, Amen." Then it goes on at "Let the Name of the Lord be blessed" to the end. Mourner's *Kaddish* is the same as ordinary *Kaddish* up to the end of "Blessed, praised and glorified"; the two sentences which follow this are omitted; the place of the Reader is taken by the mourner, who says all the versicles, while the people make the usual responses. Renewal *Kaddish*, so called because of the reference to the new creation hereafter, belongs to the Burial Service; it is said by children after the burial of a parent, the responses being uttered by the people present; it is as follows:

Mourners. "May His great Name be magnified and sanctified in the world that is to be created anew, where He will quicken the dead, and raise them up unto life eternal; will rebuild the city of Jerusalem, and establish His temple in the midst thereof; and will uproot all alien worship from the earth, and restore the worship of the true God. O may the Holy One—Blessed be He—reign in His sovereignty and glory during your life and during your days, and during the life of all the house of Israel, even speedily and at a near time; and say ye, Amen."

It then continues at "Let His great Name be blessed for ever and to all eternity," and the rest is the same as in ordinary *Kaddish*; but the Reader takes no part in Renewal *Kaddish*.

The reference to the rebuilding of Jerusalem and the re-establishment of the Temple points to this form of *Kaddish* as belonging to a date subsequent to the destruction of Jerusalem in A.D. 70.

This is, then, the order of the daily Morning Prayer in the synagogue, the central elements of which were originally: Confession, the *Shema‘* and the Ten Commandments, the *Shemoneh ‘Esreh*, the Reading of the Law and its Interpretation, Psalms, and the Priestly Blessing (not necessarily in this order). Around these, in course of ages, large developments have grown up, as well as modifica-- tions in the order of the different elements in the service. While Confession, the reciting of the Ten Commandments, and the Reading of the Law (this latter taking place only on Mondays and Thursdays, and of course on Sabbaths) do not occupy quite the same prominent position as in the early centuries of our era, the *Shema‘* and the *Shemoneh ‘Esreh* form, as ever, the most outstanding features of the worship of the synagogue.

XI

THE SERVICES FOR THE SABBATH

The very special sanctity with which the Sabbath is, and always has been, regarded by the Jews finds expression in various striking ways both in the arrangement of the services as well as in the services, and in the celebration of special rites peculiar to the Sabbath. There are six services held in celebration of the Sabbath. A short account of each of these will give some insight into the character of this very important weekly festival.

(i) *Inauguration of the Sabbath*

Originally, and, as far as can be gathered, long before the beginning of the Christian era, this was a home service, and continued so for many centuries. It is still a home service; but during the Amoraic [1] period there was instituted, first in Babylonia and later in Palestine, a synagogue service as well as a home service for the inauguration of the Sabbath, on Friday nights.

The home service begins with the lighting of the Sabbath lights. It is the special duty of the woman of the house to kindle these two candles,[2] the lights being the symbol of joy at the coming festival which it is the woman's privilege to proclaim. Then follows the *Kiddush, i.e.* "Sanctification" of the day, said by the head of the house. This is a Benediction uttered over bread and wine. The contents of the *Kiddush* are as follows:

Gen. i. 31–ii. 3.

The Blessing over the wine: "Blessed art Thou, O Lord our God, King of the universe, who createst the fruit of the vine."

A Benediction is joined to this in the words: "Blessed art Thou, O Lord our God, King of the universe, who hast sanctified us by Thy commandments and hast taken pleasure in us, and in love and favour hast given us Thy holy Sabbath as an inheritance, a memorial of the creation, that day being also the first of the holy convocations,[3] in remembrance of the departure from Egypt.[4] For Thou hast chosen us and sanctified us above all nations,[5] and in love and favour hast given us Thy holy Sabbath as an inheritance. Blessed art Thou, O Lord, who hallowest the Sabbath." [6]

---

[1] See pp. 22 ff., 116 ff.

[2] In the Mishnah, *Shabbath* ii. 6, it is said: "Because of three transgressions women die in child-birth: because they do not pay due regard to . . . and to the (Sabbath) lights."

[3] Lev. xxiii. 1 ff.   [4] Deut. v. 15.

[5] Deut. vii. 6, 7.   [6] Gen. ii. 3; Ex. xx. 11.

The Blessing over the bread : " Blessed art Thou, O Lord our
God, King of the Universe, who bringest forth bread from
the earth.' [1]

Then follows the ordinary Sabbath meal.[2]   The text
of *Kiddush* is practically the same in all the various
Rituals—" a proof," as Elbogen says, " that it rests on
good ancient tradition." [3]

A very much later custom is the *synagogue* service
of the Inauguration of the Sabbath.   This dates from
the end of the sixteenth century.   As in the home
service, the Sabbath lights are kindled (not, of course,
by a woman in this case) ; and, moreover, a shortened
form of *Kiddush* is said (the Genesis passage being
omitted), but this comes now during the first Sabbath
service proper.   Mr. Abrahams points out that the
saying of *Kiddush* in the synagogue " arose from the
custom of entertaining and lodging wayfarers in the
synagogue precincts, and thus the rite was part of
the meal provided for the communal guests.   The
public *Kiddush*, however, as an act of sanctification,
was retained long after it ceased to be customary
to associate the guest-house with the place of
worship." [4]

The Service for the Inauguration of the Sabbath,
which varies in the different Rituals, begins with the
kindling of the Sabbath lights, during which is said :
" Blessed art Thou, O Lord our God, King of the
universe, who hast sanctified us by Thy commandments, and commanded us to kindle the Sabbath
light."   This command is not based upon any Biblical
ordinance, but upon tradition which is also regarded
as divine.   Then Ps. xcv. (the " Venite ") is said,
together with Pss. xcvi.–xcix. and xxix.   These are
followed by a beautiful hymn, called *Lekah Dodi*

---

[1] Ps. civ. 14.
[2] It is important to note that originally *Kiddush* took place
after the festal meal ; *cp*. Elbogen, *op. cit*. p. 107.
[3] *op. cit*. p. 112.   [4] *op. cit*. p. cxl.

190 RABBINICAL AND MEDIÆVAL JUDAISM

("*Come, my friend,* to meet the bride "); it was composed by Alkabetz (Solomon the Levite, *cp.* p. 289) in the first half of the sixteenth century, and is spoken of by Schechter as "perhaps one of the finest pieces of religious poetry in existence." [1] In it the Sabbath is personified as a bride, and every worshipper is called upon to go forth and meet her. The poem consists of nine stanzas, after each of which the refrain is sung : " Come, my friend, to meet the bride ; let us welcome the presence of the Sabbath." *Lekah Dodi* is found in all the Rituals. Then come Pss. xcii. (the Psalm for the Sabbath day) and xciii. This ends the Inauguration Service in the synagogue.

(ii) *Service for Sabbath Eve (Maarib)*

This follows immediately after the foregoing, and is in its structure the same as the ordinary week-day evening service, though there are naturally some variations and additions in details. [2] The reading of the Mishnah treatise *Shabbath,* chap. ii., after the *Shemoneh 'Esreh* is one of these additions ; this passage is chosen because it gives directions regarding the Sabbath lights. It is followed by a passage from the Talmudic tractate *Berakhoth* which speaks of the peace which is to be the lot of those who love the Law. At this point of the service *Kiddush* is said (see above). The rest of the service concludes as on ordinary days, excepting that *Yigdal* is sung at the end of the service.

It is the custom on the eve of the Sabbath and on holy-days at the conclusion of this service for parents to pronounce a formal blessing upon their children, whether young or grown-up. This is a home rite ;

---

[1] *Studies in Judaism* (second series), p. 228.
[2] Regarding the saying of the *Shemoneh 'Esreh* on Sabbaths and festivals, see above, pp. 175 ff. It consists here of only seven Benedictions.

but it is sometimes done in the synagogue by the Rabbis, only, of course, as regards boys. When done at home the father, or the mother, places both hands on the head of each child ; to boys is said : " God make thee as Ephraim and Manasseh " ; to girls : " God make thee as Sarah, Rebekah, Rachel, and Leah." Then follows the blessing proper upon all : " The Lord bless thee, and keep thee ; the Lord make His face to shine upon thee, and be gracious unto thee ; the Lord turn His face unto thee, and give thee peace." Finally, Prov. xxxi. 10–31 is read. This custom is ancient, for, although not incorporated into the Liturgy until the sixteenth century, it is already referred to in the tractate *Sopherim* xviii. 5, which embodies a mass of ancient material.

(iii) *Service for Sabbath Morning*

The structure of this very important service is to a large extent identical with that for week-days ; but, as one would naturally expect, there are some variations and some notable additions. Up to the end of the Praise portion (*Zemiroth* ; see above, § V.) there are the following differences : The addition of Num. xxviii. 9, 10 to the " sacrificial passages " ; the meditation and benedictions for the *Tephillin* are not said ;[1] instead of Ps. c. (see p. 156), there are said Pss. xix., xxxiv., xc., xci., cxxxv., cxxxvi., xxxiii., xcii., and xciii. ; and after Ex. xiv. 30–xv. 18[2] (see p. 156) four ascriptions of praise are uttered before the concluding Benediction of praise, *Yishtabbach Shiměka.* Of these four additions a few words must be said. By far the most important of them, called *Nishmath*, from the opening word (" The *breath* of every living being shall bless Thy name "),

[1] The *Tephillin* are not worn on Sabbaths.
[2] Originally this probably belonged exclusively to the Sabbath *Zemiroth*, also called *Pesuḳê de Zimra.*

is a beautiful hymn of praise, and ancient. It is found in a more or less identical form in all the Rituals, and is referred to as well known by Rabbi Jochanan (first century A.D.). A strange thing about *Nishma'h* is that in the Middle Ages it was widely held to have been written by the Apostle Peter; how this curious belief arose seems to be quite unknown. *Nishmath* is a long hymn of praise, and full of Scriptural phraseology. The other three are quite short, the second being from Is. lvii. 15; all breathe forth an intense spirit of praise.

The service then continues as on week-days; the introductory and concluding Benedictions to the *Shema'* are, however, fuller. The *Shemoneh 'Esreh* on Sabbath mornings consists of only seven Benedictions; the three first and the three last are the same as on week-days, though the *Kedushah* (see pp. 177 ff.) is somewhat amplified on Sabbaths. It is the fourth which is the distinctive feature of the *Shemoneh 'Esreh* on the Sabbath; it runs thus:

Moses rejoiced in the gift of his portion, for Thou didst call him a faithful servant; a diadem of glory didst Thou place upon his head, when he stood before Thee on Mount Sinai; and in his hand he brought down the two tables of stone, upon which the observance of the Sabbath was prescribed, and thus it is written in Thy Law.

Then follows Ex. xxxi. 16, 17, the points being, as Mr. Abrahams says, that "the observance of the Sabbath is ordained in the Decalogue, but *also* it is written elsewhere in the Law. The Sabbath is referred to in ten passages over and above the fourth commandment." [1] The service then continues as on weekdays; but the ceremony of the Reading of the Law is more elaborate on Sabbaths. In addition to the Reading of the Law, there is, on Sabbaths, also the Reading from the Prophets. This is called the *Haphtarah*, which means "dismissal," or perhaps

[1] *op. cit.* p. cxlviii.

"conclusion," for it comes at the end of the service. The reading of the *Haphtarah* was introduced long before the beginning of the Christian era.[1]

Another ceremony, also very ancient, in connexion with the Sabbath may be mentioned, viz. the announcing of the new month. This is done on the Sabbath preceding new moon. " In ancient times it was the duty of the Sanhedrin to declare the beginning of the new month, which was originally fixed by actual observation, and not only by astronomical calculation. The declaration was accompanied by blessings and praises (*Sopherim* xix. 9). The synagogue announcement is a survival of this ancient rite." [2] The prayer said in the synagogue on this occasion dates from the third century A.D., though it is not incorporated in the older Rituals ; it runs as follows :

" May it be Thy will, O Lord our God, and God of our fathers, to renew unto us this coming month for good and for blessing. O grant us long life, a life of peace, of good, of blessing, of sustenance, of bodily vigour, a life marked by the fear of Heaven and a dread of sin, a life free from shame and reproach, a life of prosperity and honour, a life in which the love of the Law and the fear of Heaven shall cleave to us, a life in which the desires of our heart shall be fulfilled for good. Amen."

(iv) *Additional Service for the Sabbath*

This service, called *Musaph* (" Addition "), corresponds to the additional sacrifices in the Temple worship on Sabbaths, new moons, and festivals, commanded in Num. xxviii., xxix. It opens with the *Shemoneh 'Esreh,* consisting of seven Benedictions, of which, as usual, the three first and three last are as on ordinary days ; the central Benediction appropriately makes mention of the additional sacrifices offered in the Temple on Sabbaths. The *Kedushah*

---

[1] *cp.* Luke iv. 16 ff.   [2] Abrahams, *op. cit.* p. clxi.

for *Musaph* differs from the usual one in its reference to the vision of Isaiah and the declaration of the Unity of God. It is known as the "Great Kedushah." Then follows *Kaddish*. The next part of the service opens with the canticle *'En Kelohenu* ("There is none like our God") and extracts from the Talmud and the Mishnah. The *'Alenu* Prayer ("For us it is the duty to praise the Lord"), which is then said, belongs specially to the *Musaph* of New Year, though it has been transferred to the daily morning service as well. It is a very ancient prayer, in all probability pre-Christian, and deals specially with the divine Kingship. While in the first half a somewhat particularistic note is struck, the second half is thoroughly universalistic, as the following extract will show:

> "Let all the inhabitants of the world perceive and know that unto Thee every knee must bow, every tongue must swear. Before Thee, O Lord our God, let them bow and fall; and unto Thy glorious name let them give honour; let them all accept the yoke of Thy kingdom, and do Thou reign over them speedily, and for ever and ever. For Thine is the kingdom, and to all eternity shalt Thou reign in glory."

Then comes Mourner's *Kaddish* (see p. 184) and *'Adon 'Olam* (see p. 157). The "Unity Hymn for the Sabbath Day" is then said; this is a late composition, belonging to the end of the eleventh century. The service concludes with the *Hymn of Glory*, Ps. xcii., and Mourner's *Kaddish* is repeated if mourners are present.

(v) *Service for Sabbath Afternoon*

This service is called *Minchah* (see p. 155). After some introductory sentences and Ps. cxlv., and "And a Redeemer shall come to Zion . . . ," *Kaddish* is said; then the first section (*Parashah*) of the Lesson (*Sidra*) from the Pentateuch of the *following Sabbath* is read. The *Shemoneh 'Esreh*, which follows, has again seven

Benedictions, of which the intermediate one (the fourth) is proper to this service ; its special notes are the Unity of God and the Sabbath rest. *Kaddish* again concludes this first part of the service. Then come the Psalms, viz. civ. and the fifteen Songs of Ascent (cxx.–cxxxiv.).[1] From Passover to New Year one chapter of *Pirke Aboth* is read every week ; during the rest of the year the Psalms mentioned are all read every Sabbath ; this is followed by the *'Alenu* Prayer and Mourner's *Kaddish*.

(vi) *Service for the Conclusion of the Sabbath*

This service is largely the same as that for the ordinary weekday evening service ; but it opens with Pss. cxliv., lxvii., and then continues as usual, viz. *Vehu Rachum* (see p. 179), *Shema', Shemoneh 'Esreh, Kaddish*, Ps. xci., "And a redeemer shall come" (see p. 156), *Kaddish*. Then follows a long passage, peculiar to this service, made up of numerous passages from the Old Testament, and the service concludes with Ps. cxxviii.

The *Habdalah*. This is primarily a home service, and is always said at the Conclusion of the Sabbath, which from very early times, long before the beginning of the Christian era, was celebrated by a special meal, just as in the case of the Inauguration of the Sabbath. The word *Habdalah* means "Separation," *i.e.* between the holy Sabbath and the ordinary weekdays. The ceremony marking this celebration is interesting. The head of the house takes a cup of wine in his right hand and utters a Benediction over it beginning with the words : " Behold, God is my salvation " ; it is made up from other citations from the Psalms and Isaiah, and concludes with the words : " Blessed art Thou, O Lord our God, King of the universe, who createst the fruit of the vine."

[1] These Psalms and the reading from *Pirke Aboth* are not the same all the year round.

O 2

Then he takes spices, and says over them: "Blessed art Thou, O Lord our God, King of the universe, who createst divers kinds of spices." Then he spreads his hands towards the lights, saying: "Blessed art Thou, O Lord our God, King of the universe, who createst the light of the fire." Finally, he takes the cup once again in his right hand and says: "Blessed art Thou, O Lord our God, King of the universe, who makest a distinction (lit. *who separatest*, from the same root as *Habdalah*) between holy and profane, between light and darkness, between Israel and other nations, between the seventh day and the six working days. Blessed art Thou, O Lord, who makest a distinction between holy and profane." After this a concluding hymn is said: "May He who maketh a distinction between holy and profane pardon our sins." This hymn, belonging probably to the eleventh century, is of a strongly penitential character, and is maintained by some to have been originally written for the concluding service of the Day of Atonement.

The *Habdalah* is also celebrated in the synagogue as part of the service.

XII

THE FESTIVAL SERVICES

The three great Jewish festivals, Passover (*Pesach*), Pentecost (*Shevuoth*), and Tabernacles (*Succoth*), are known as the "Pilgrim Festivals," called in Hebrew *Regalim* (plural of the word for "foot"), because the pilgrims went up to Jerusalem on foot to celebrate them.[1]

[1] According to Ibn Ezra (A.D. 1092–1167). "The Rabbinic rule was that every pilgrim should walk on foot at least the final stage of the journey up from the city of Jerusalem to the Temple, deriving the rule from the word *Regalim* (Mishnah, *Chagigah* i. 1)" (Abrahams, *op. cit.* p. cxci).

On the eve of festivals the service is a somewhat shortened form of that said on Friday afternoon preparatory to the Sabbath. The other festival services are as on the Sabbath, but with two distinguishing marks. The first of these is the festival *Shemoneh 'Esreh.* As in that for the Sabbath, this, too, consists of seven Benedictions, of which the fourth is proper to the festival; the latter runs as follows (the italicised words denote the beginnings of the different paragraphs):

" *Thou hast chosen us from all peoples* ; Thou hast loved us and taken pleasure in us, and hast exalted us above all tongues ; Thou hast sanctified us by Thy commandments, and brought us near unto Thy service, O our King, and hast called us by Thy great and holy Name.

And Thou hast given us in love, O Lord our God, appointed times for gladness, festivals and seasons for joy ; this day of [*at Passover*] the Feast of Unleavened Bread, the season of our freedom ; [*at Pentecost*] the Feast of Weeks, the season of the giving of our Law ; [1] [*at Tabernacles*] the Feast of Tabernacles, the season of our gladness.

Our God, and God of our fathers, may our remembrance rise and come and be accepted before Thee, with the remembrance of our Fathers, of Messiah the son of David, Thy servant, of Jerusalem Thy holy city, and of all Thy people the house of Israel, bringing deliverance and well-being, grace, loving-kindness and mercy, life and peace on this day of [*according to the festival*]. Remember us, O Lord our God, thereon for our well-being ; be mindful of us for blessing, and save us unto life. By Thy promise of salvation and mercy, spare us and be gracious unto us ; have mercy upon us and save us ; for our eyes are bent upon Thee, because Thou art a gracious and merciful God and King.

O Lord our God, bestow upon us the blessing of Thy appointed times for life and peace, for joy and gladness, even as Thou hast been pleased to promise that Thou wouldst bless us Sanctify us by Thy commandments, and grant our portion in Thy law ; satisfy us with Thy goodness, and gladden us with Thy salvation ; purify our hearts to serve Thee in truth ; and

---

[1] " The revelation on Sinai, according to traditional computation, occurred on the sixth or seventh of Sivan, *i.e.* on the Feast of Weeks " (Abrahams, *op. cit.* p. cxcii).

let us inherit, O Lord our God, with joy and gladness Thy holy appointed times ; and may Israel, who hallow Thy name, rejoice in Thee. Blessed art Thou, O Lord, who hallowest Israel and the seasons."

These four paragraphs are all ancient ; they have undergone some unimportant verbal changes, but in substance they belong at least to the early centuries of the Christian era. They did not find a place in the Liturgy all at the same time, and they are not cited in the Talmud as forming one connected whole ; each was originally an independent piece. Elbogen (*op. cit.* p. 133) points out that where they are cited in the Talmud the source is Babylonian, but that traces of a Palestinian recension are to be discerned in the tractate *Sopherim.* This would indicate a still greater antiquity for them.

Secondly, there is a special *Kiddush* for festivals, in order that a specific reference to the festival being celebrated might be made in this indispensable Benediction.

While there are various other differences according to the particular festival observed, the *general structure* of all the festival services is similar to that of the daily Morning Prayer. The same applies to the New Moon and New Year festivals, also the Day of Atonement and *Chanukkah* (" Dedication ") and *Purim* (" Lots ").

XIII

THE DAY OF ATONEMENT AND OTHER FAST-DAYS

The former is by far the most important of the fast-days of the synagogue. Fast-days in the Jewish Church come historically under two categories : fasts which were inaugurated as some special occasion required (see, *e.g.*, 1 Kings xxi. 9 ; Joel i. 14 ; ii. 15), and those which were held in commemoration of some tragic event in the nation's history. It is only the latter which were regularly observed ; and of these the four

Biblical ones mentioned in Zech. viii. 19 are still observed, viz. " the fast of the fourth month (= Tammuz), of the fifth month (= Ab), of the seventh (= Tishri), and of the tenth month (= Tebeth) "; these were inaugurated during the Exile in memory of events connected with the destruction of the Temple and Jerusalem in 586 B.C.; other minor fasts are also still observed. The most important fast-days, however, are those included in the penitential season of ten days with which the Jewish New Year opens, and which culminate in the Day of Atonement. On this day the *Shemoneh 'Esreh* has special Benedictions proper to the season; these are too long to quote here, but a short passage may be cited in order to show how the special subject of the season is brought in: " . . . And Thou hast given us in love, O Lord our God, this Day of Atonement for pardon, forgiveness, and atonement, that we may obtain pardon thereon for all our iniquities; an holy convocation, as a memorial of the departure from Egypt." Confession of sin and penitential prayers follow; these comprise the alphabetical confessions *'Ashamnu* (" We have trespassed ") and *'Al Chêṭ* (" For the sin [which we have committed] "). These are both ancient, especially the latter, parts of which " point to a period during which sacrificial rites were still performed in the Temple, or shortly after their cessation. That, however, alphabetical confessions were in use much more anciently than we have them liturgically recorded is clear from the *Didaché*, a work which belongs to the first century and bears distinct traces of such a confession, as Rendel Harris has shown. The forms in our Liturgy, though in one sense dating from the Geonic age, may go back to a very much earlier date."[1]   The hymn *Abinu Malkenu* is said on the ten days (Sabbath excepted) of penitence.

[1] Abrahams, *op. cit.* p. cci.

At the close of the Day of Atonement the special prayer called *Ne'ilah* is said. This word means "shutting," in reference to the Temple gates, which were closed at the approach of sunset; at this time the priests pronounced their Blessing upon the people in ancient days. The prayer received its name from this, as it was said at the same time, viz. at the close of the service, which lasts all day.

Belonging to a later period is the opening service of the Day of Atonement, held on the preceding evening, called *Kol Nidre* (= "All vows"); the name comes from the formula of remission of vows which is said immediately before the service. In spite of the fact that the Babylonian *Geonim* raised great objections to *Kol Nidre*, it has been incorporated in the Liturgy since the ninth century. Originally the remission of vows referred only to the past year; but in the twelfth century it was made to refer to the coming year. The abuses which this might easily bring in its train will be obvious; but, as a matter of fact, the remission refers only to obligations in reference to a person individually, not in reference to a second person; and these are only in respect of ritual duties, and have nothing to do with the affairs of ordinary life.

One other special ritual act on this day is the blowing of the *Shophar* ("ram's horn"), which is sounded to mark the close of the solemn fast-day; this is a very ancient custom; it used also to be blown, according to Josephus (*Bell.* IV. ix. 12), on the termination of the Sabbath, and, according to the Mishnah, it was also blown to announce the coming of the Sabbath. The *Shophar* is also sounded on New Year's Day.

We have only drawn attention to specific points proper to the services for the Day of Atonement; the rest of the services follow the lines of the ordinary daily services.

XIV

THE BURIAL SERVICE; PRAYERS FOR THE DEPARTED

The study of the mourning customs among the Israelites and later Jews leads to the conviction that the *majority* of them were practised for the sake of the living, not for the benefit of the departed. Some of these customs are to be explained as protective measures against what was believed to be the danger of hostile action of the spirits of the departed towards the living. But this cannot be said of all those customs; such an act, for example, as that described in 2 Macc. xii. 43–45 (to be quoted presently) is obviously intended to be for the benefit of the departed. It must be acknowledged—and it is acknowledged by some at least of the leading authorities on the subject [1]—that some of these customs do not, even in their oldest known form, presuppose the slightest fear of hostile action on the part of the dead. As long as the old *Sheol* belief existed anything in the shape of prayers for the departed was impossible, for two reasons: first, there was not, according to that belief, anybody to pray *for*, so that the idea could not have entered into people's heads; and, secondly, there was nobody to pray *to*, for, according to the old *Sheol* belief, God was only concerned with men while living.

With the rise of a belief in the resurrection it is obvious that men's thoughts on the subject must have undergone a change, likewise in two directions. While they could not be expected to take much interest in a more or less impersonal shade, it was very different if a departed loved one were firmly believed to be living after death, and living in a fuller sense

[1] *e.g.* Marti, Torge, and others; *cp.* also Stade, *Biblische Theologie des alten Testamentes*, i. pp. 138 ff.

than ever before; the realisation that he was still living necessitated continued interest in him; if that realisation is in any sense real, then a person's interest in a loved one cannot cease merely because his life is now unbounded, while before it was restricted. Belief in the resurrection, then, necessitated interest in the departed. Concurrently with this it was also inevitable that with a belief in the resurrection an enhanced doctrine of God must have arisen; for while, according to the old *Sheol* belief, God's interest in man was restricted to his life here on earth, when the life of man was believed to continue hereafter God's interest in him could no longer be restricted to what was, comparatively speaking, a moment of his existence. In effect, Christ refers to this in saying: "God is not a God of the dead, but of the living"; that closed the mouth of His adversaries, for it was their belief, too, though they failed to realise its implications. These parallel thoughts, then, concerning God and man in what we call the Hereafter led to prayers for the departed among the Jews. One of the earliest notices, perhaps the earliest known one, is found in 2 Macc. xii. 43–45, where it is said that Judas Maccabæus offered sacrifices and prayers for the departed: " And he made a collection, man by man, to the sum of two thousand drachmas of silver; and he sent this to Jerusalem for a sin-offering, acting therein well and honourably, for he was bearing in mind the resurrection. For if he were not expecting that the fallen would rise again, it would have been superfluous and senseless to pray for the dead. And if, doing this, he was looking for the splendour of the gracious reward laid up for them that have fallen asleep in godliness, holy and pious was the thought." Though this is, doubtless, unhistorical, it none the less reflects the tendency of thought and practice at the time when the book was written, probably just before the beginning of the Christian era, as there are distinct indications that Philo was acquainted with it.

The study of the history of the Jewish Liturgy shows that, while the principle of development in external form has throughout the ages been acted upon, the essential original elements have been maintained. This is true of both the Sephardic and Ashkenazic forms of the Liturgy. In both of these prayers for the departed are used ; the *form* of these has undoubtedly been subjected to modification, but the *principle* of offering them has certainly been acted upon ever since belief in the resurrection of the dead became a dogma of Judaism ; and this took place long before the beginning of the Christian era. We have already referred to " Mourner's *Kaddish* " and " Renewal *Kaddish* " (see pp. 184 f. above) and their significance in the present connexion. We turn now to the Jewish Burial Service, where this short prayer is uttered when the coffin is being lowered into the grave : " May he [or she] come to his [or her] place in peace " ; but more striking is the prayer which is offered up in the house of the mourners ; one or two extracts from this may be given : " O Lord and King, who art full of compassion . . . receive, we beseech Thee, in Thy great loving-kindness the soul of [the name of the departed is then mentioned], who hath been gathered unto his [or her] people. Have mercy upon him, pardon all his transgressions.[1] . . . O shelter his soul in the shadow of Thy wings. Make known to him the path of life ; in Thy presence is fullness of joy ; at Thy right hand are pleasures for evermore. Vouchsafe unto him of the abounding happiness that is treasured up for the righteous. . . ."

---

[1] *cp. Pirke de Rabbi Eliezer*, xxxix. (end), where Isaac prays for the dead Esau thus ; " Sovereign of all the universe, let mercy be shown to this wicked one, for he had not learnt all the precepts of the Torah " (Gerald Friedlander's edition, p. 310 [1916]).

That is taken from the Liturgy of the Ashkenazic Jews; the other division of the Jews, the Sephardim, has its own Liturgy, in which much is retained which finds no place in the Ashkenazic Ritual. It will be worth while, in conclusion, to turn to this other Liturgy, for the Sephardic Jews have in their Liturgy elaborate, and in some cases beautiful, prayers for the departed. " In substance many of them are believed to date back to the time of Hillel—*circa* 30 B.C.–A.D. 10— and they contain passages of great beauty. They are also of interest as representing at least the type of prayer for the dead which must have been familiar to the earliest circles of Jewish Christians." [1] The following are a few examples taken from the Sephardic Ritual in present use : " Have mercy upon him, we beseech Thee, O Lord, Thou living God and King of the universe; for with Thee is the fountain of life. And continually may he walk in the land of life, and may his soul rest in the bond of life." Again : " May the Gracious One, in the abundance of His mercy, forgive his transgressions ; may his good deeds be before His eyes, and may he be near unto God with all His faithful ones and walk before Thee in the land of life. And continually may he walk in the land of life, and may his soul rest in the bond of life." These are two of seven sentences which are chanted during a procession round the bier ; each ends with the refrain : " And continually may he walk in the land of life, and may his soul rest in the bond of life." The two just quoted are addressed to God ; others are the expression of prayer, but they are addressed to the departed, thus : " The gates of heaven mayest thou find opened, and the city of peace mayest thou see, and the dwellings of confidence and angels of peace to meet thee with joy ; and may the high-priest stand to receive thee ; and thou, go thou to the end, for thou shalt rest and rise up again. And continually may he

[1] Miss Dampier in *Church and Synagogue*, xi. 77.

walk in the land of life, and may his soul rest in the bond ('bundle'; see 1 Sam. xxv. 29) of life." But the fullest and most beautiful prayer, which is well worth quoting in full, is that which is offered up after the committal; this prayer is called the *Hashkabah* (from the root meaning "to lie down"), and it is said in what is the Jewish equivalent of our cemetery chapel. This prayer is as follows:

"May the repose which is prepared in the celestial abode, under the wings of the Divine presence (*i.e.* the Shekinah) in the high place of the holy and pure—who shine and are resplendent as the bright light of the firmament—with a renewal of strength, a forgiveness of trespasses, a removal of transgressions, an approach of salvation, compassion and favour from Him that sitteth enthroned on high, and also a goodly portion in the life to come, be the lot, dwelling, and the resting-place of the soul of our departed brother (to whom may God grant peace in Paradise), who departed from this world according to the will of God, the Lord of heaven and earth. May the supreme King of Kings, through His infinite mercy, have mercy, pity, and compassion upon him. May the supreme King of Kings, through His infinite mercy, hide him under the shadow of His wings, and under the protection of His tent; to behold the fair beauty of the Lord, and to wait in His temple; may He raise him at the end of the days, and cause him to drink of the stream of His delights. May He cause his soul to be bound up in the bond of life, and his rest to be glorious. May the Lord be his inheritance, and grant him peace; and may his repose be in peace, as it is written: 'He shall come in peace; they shall rest in their beds; everyone walking in his uprightness.' May he, and all the people of Israel, who slumber in the dust, be included in mercy and forgiveness. May this be His will, and let us say, Amen."

This *Hashkabah* prayer is repeated every evening during the week of mourning, and also, like the "Mourner's *Kaddish*" in the Ashkenazic Liturgy, on the anniversary of the death.

A high authority on Jewish belief and practice, the late Rabbi Singer, writes as follows on this subject: "Unless we are prepared to maintain that at his death the fate of man is fixed irretrievably and for ever, that therefore the sinner who rejected much of God's love during a brief lifetime has lost all of it eternally, prayer for the peace and salvation of the departed soul commends itself as one of the highest religious obligations." [1]

Many interesting subjects in connexion with the Jewish Liturgy have not been mentioned ; our object has, however, been to deal only with the most central and important parts.

[1] *Lectures and Addresses*, p. 72.

PART IV
THE MEDIÆVAL LITERATURE

PART IV

THE MEDIÆVAL LITERATURE

[LITERATURE : The following works of a general and comprehensive nature may here be mentioned : J. W. Etheridge, *Jerusalem and Tiberias, Sura and Cordova : A Survey of the Religious and Scholastic Literature of the Jews* (London, 1856) ; M. Steinschneider, *Jewish Literature* (London, 1857) ; Winter und Wünsche, *Die Jüdische Literatur seit Abschluss des Kanons*, 3 vols. (Berlin, 1897) ; Zunz, *Die gottesdienstlichen Vorträge der Juden*, 2nd ed. 1892 ; Israel Abrahams, *A Short History of Jewish Literature* (London, 1906). See also *JE* under the names cited. A useful bibliographical conspectus is contained in Strack and Siegfried's *Lehrbuch der neu-hebräischen Sprache*, pp. 93–132 (*Abriss* by Strack) : 1884.]

I

INTRODUCTORY

THE transitional period which connects the earlier Talmudic with the mediæval literature is marked by the era of the Geonim. The title *Gaon* (plur. *Geonim*),[1] which means *Excellency*, was given to the heads of the two Babylonian Academies of Sura and Pumbeditha, who presided over the schools which had completed the work of fixing the text of the Talmud in its final form. The period of the Geonim dates, according to Bacher, from the year A.D. 589, when Mar Rab Chanan of Iskiya became Gaon of Pumbeditha. The last Gaon of Sura (Samuel b. Chophni) died in 1034 ; the last Gaon of Pumbeditha (Hai) died in 1038. Thus "the activity of the Geonim covers a period of nearly 450 years." During this

[1] Probably derived from Ps. xlvii. 5 (E.V. 4), *gě'on Ya'akob*, "The excellency of Jacob."

period the centres of Jewish learning were in Babylonia and Persia.

The Jewish communities in these regions enjoyed
a large measure of independence, during the Geonic
period, under their own political head known as the
"Exiliarch." Though the Geonim of both Academies
went every year to pay formal homage to the
Exiliarch, and though the latter was associated with
them in the formal promulgation of specially important decrees, the Geonim seem to have occupied a
position of practically complete independence. The
Gaon of Sura ranked above the Gaon of Pumbeditha.
This apparently was due to the fact that, during the
period of the Amoraim, Sura had been the principal
seat of Jewish learning, first under its founder Rab
and his pupil Huna (third century), and later under
Ashi (died 427). During the Geonic period, too,
Sura was most prominent, the most famous of the
Geonim, Saadya (tenth century), having presided
over the Academy of Sura.

"The importance of the Geonim in Jewish history," says
Bacher, "is due, in the first place, to the fact that for a number
of centuries they occupied a unique position as the heads
of their respective schools, and as the recognised authorities of
Judaism. Their influence probably extended chiefly to the
Mohammedan countries, especially Northern Africa and Spain;
but in the course of time the Jews of Christian Europe also
came under the influence of the Babylonian schools. It was
for this reason that the Babylonian Talmud came to be
recognised as the basis for religio-legal decisions throughout
Jewry and as the principal object of study. Even the facilities
offered for such study to the Diaspora were due to the Geonim,
since the Geonic exposition of the Talmud, with regard to both
text and contents, was, directly or indirectly, the chief aid in
comprehending the Talmud. The importance of the period of
the Geonim for the history of Judaism is further enhanced by
the fact that the new Jewish science, which steadily developed
side by side with Talmudic studies, was created by a Gaon, and
that the same Gaon, Saadya, effectively opposed the dis-
integrating influence of Karaism."[1]

---

[1] Article "Gaon" in *JE* v. 570.

Of their literary work a considerable portion has not survived. They had much to do with the adaptation of the principles of the Talmud to the changing social conditions of the Jews of their time ; they improved educational methods, and deeply influenced the Liturgy.

One of the earliest literary works of the Geonic period that has come down to us is the *Sheiltoth* (= "Questiones") of Achai, composed about the middle of the eighth century, and containing about two hundred homilies on the Pentateuch. About 870 the Gaon Amram compiled a *Siddur*, or prayer book, which is one of the principal sources for our knowledge of the Jewish Liturgy. The famous Saadya will come before us as a grammarian and exegete. The last of the Geonim, Samuel b. Chophni and Hai, were also authors of many works on Bible and Talmud, and Hai was a poet.

The most characteristic branch of their literary activity, however, is to be seen in their *responsa*, or letters. The advice and guidance of these famous teachers were sought from all parts of the Jewish world on a variety of subjects, religious and literary.

"Amid the growing complications of ritual law, a desire was felt for terse prescriptions, clear-cut decisions, and rules of conduct. The imperfections of study outside of Persia, again, made it essential to apply to the Geonim for authoritative expositions of difficult passages in the Bible and the Talmud. To all such inquiries the Geonim sent responses in the form of letters, sometimes addressed to individual correspondents, sometimes to communities, or groups of communities." [1]

These letters were later collected into volumes and treatises, though many were never included in such collections. Numerous examples have come to light (some not yet published) in the collection of Genizah fragments now in Cambridge.

[1] I. Abrahams, *Short History of Jewish Literature*, p. 40.

The *responsa* form a vast literature of many thousands of documents. The beginnings of this literature date from a much earlier time than the Geonic epoch. An active correspondence, in the form of letters and replies to questions, was carried on between Palestine and Babylonia at the end of the third century A.D. But the Geonic *responsa* mark a definite development in literary form and contents. In these *responsa* the Geonim used at first Aramaic (the language of the Gemara), but later Hebrew and Arabic. After the period of the Geonim the *responsa* literature underwent further development and became widely diffused (the Spanish, French, German, and Italian schools). This literature has gone on in unbroken continuity down to the present time. The technical designation of it is *She'ēloth u-Teshuboth* ("Questions and Answers") An interesting survey of the whole literature is given in *JE* in the article " *She'eloth u-Teshuboth*," xi. 240–250.

In the following pages it will be convenient to group our survey of the mediæval literature under the following heads : *Grammar and Exegesis* (II) ; *The Mystical Literature* (III) ; *Philosophy and Ethics* (IV) ; *The Mediæval Poetry* (V) ; *Some other Forms of Literature* (VI).

II

GRAMMAR AND EXEGESIS

[See Bacher, *Die hebräische Sprachwissenschaft* and *Die Bibel-exegese* in Winter und Wünsche, *op. cit.* ii. 135–342 ; the art. *Grammar* (Hebrew) in *JE* ; numerous specimens of mediæval Jewish exegesis are given in Neubauer and Driver, *The LIIIrd Chapter of Isaiah according to Jewish Interpreters* (2 vols. text and transl. 1871).]

The rise of a sound and scientific exegesis of the Hebrew Scriptures was determined, as will be seen, by the growth and development of philological studies. The two branches of learning are intimately connected, and in the result an important exegetical literature was developed, which is a characteristic product of mediæval Judaism. But before this can be traced something must be said about the earlier type of exegesis which preceded it.

The earliest form of Scriptural exegesis is the *Midrashic*.[1]   The whole of this vast literature embodies an immense wealth of exegetic material, largely of a traditional character, which has grown up in the course of centuries.

In this connexion the development of the Halakic Midrash exercised an important influence on Scriptural exegesis.   Owing to the fact that the Rabbinical teachers found it necessary to supply a Scriptural basis for the expanding Halakah, there was developed comparatively early (in the time of the elder Hillel) a system of hermeneutic rules, seven in number— later expanded into thirteen—under the influence of which a highly artificial type of Scriptural exegesis was developed.   It was Aķiba who pressed the view that every detail of the sacred text, even the minutest, was of incomparable importance.   Nothing was to be regarded as insignificant or without special meaning; hence everything in the text was to become the subject of interpretation.[2]   Aķiba successfully founded a school of exegesis, based on these principles, which was influential in the post-Hadrianic epoch.   One of his pupils, Eliezer the son of the Galilean Rabbi Jose, formulated thirty-two rules for Haggadic exegesis.

It was the latter type of exegesis that was dominant in the Midrashic literature.   Here the Haggadic exegesis had full scope.   It dealt with the text of the Bible with great freedom, often interpreting it in a way that seems remote from the simple and natural meaning of the original words.   Not that the plain and strict meaning of the text is always ignored.

---

[1] For the meaning of the term *Midrash*, and the Midrashic literature, see pp. 57 ff. above.

[2] It should not be forgotten that it was an eminent Halakist, R. Ishmael (second century A.D.), who maintained the view (against Aķiba), which was to have an important influence on later Jewish exegesis, that the language of Scripture is to be interpreted by the standards of human speech, and not to be unduly and artificially pressed.

The "Peshaṭ," as it is termed,[1] *i.e.* the literal meaning
of the text, is often referred to and discussed, and in
many cases with fine insight and sound linguistic
knowledge. But this is entirely overbalanced by
the mass of purely Haggadic exposition. "In the
Halakic as well as in the Haggadic exegesis the
expounder endeavoured not so much to seek the
original meaning of the text as to find authority in
some Biblical passage for the concepts and ideas, the
rules of conduct and teachings, for which he wished
to have a Biblical foundation. To this were added,
on the one hand, the belief that the words of
the Bible had many meanings, and, on the other,
the importance attached to the smallest portion, the
slightest peculiarity of the text ; hence the exegesis
of the Midrash strayed further and further away from
a natural and common-sense interpretation."[2]

It must also be remembered that the Midrash is
essentially homiletical in tendency. It aims at
religious edification rather than scientific investigation of the meaning of the text. As such it was
necessarily one-sided, and sooner or later a reaction
was bound to set in against its almost exclusive
predominance. The elements for this already existed
in the distinction drawn between the "Peshaṭ" and
the "Derash," and also in the attitude of opposition
taken up by R. Ishmael and his followers against
the school of Aḳiba. It will be remembered that
Ishmael insisted that the language of Scripture is to
be interpreted naturally, in accordance with the standards that apply to human speech, and ought not to
be pressed unduly and artificially in detail. Ishmael is
even reputed to have exclaimed once, in rejecting an
exposition of Eliezer ben Hyrḳanos : " Truly you say

---

[1] It should be noticed that the "Peshaṭ" is carefully and
deliberately distinguished from the "Derash" (דרש), *i.e.* the free
Haggadic exposition, especially by the Babylonian teachers.
[2] *JE* iii. 164 (*s.v.* "Bible Exegesis").

to Scripture : Be silent, while I am expounding."[1] It
was the Babylonian Amoraim who first used the expression "Peshat" to designate the primary sense in
contradistinction to "Derash," the Midrashic exegesis.
It was in Babylonia also that the important principle was laid down that the Haggadic exegesis could
not annul the primary sense. These distinctions
were later destined to exercise a determining influence in the development of Jewish exegesis. Another
factor that helped to prepare the way for a closer and
more literal exposition of the Biblical text was the
labours of the Masoretic scholars. Though great
care had always been lavished on preserving a correct
Hebrew text of the Old Testament Scriptures by
the Scribes, this branch of learning received a great
impetus in the seventh century, when vowel-signs
were introduced. Henceforward Masoretic studies
steadily developed, and the body of Masoretic
tradition—all concerned with the exact determination
and preservation of the Biblical text—steadily grew
for centuries.[2] Such activities must obviously have
contributed largely to the more exact exegesis of the
Bible which gradually grew up. Perhaps the most
important part in bringing this about must be
assigned to the Karaites—themselves keen grammarians and textual scholars—who boldly challenged
the claims of the current exegetical tradition, and,
indeed, the authority of Rabbinical tradition generally, and insisted that the sole fount of authority for
the religious life was to be found in the plain text of
Scripture. Founded in the eighth century by Anan,
this sect, which has lasted to the present day, has
remained only a comparatively small and heretical
branch of Judaism ; but it has, by reaction, exercised
a permanent influence on the development of exegesis in the main body of orthodox Judaism. A

[1] Cited from the *Sifra* on Lev. xiii. 49 in *JE, ibid.*
[2] The Masora was printed for the first time in 1525.

century and a half after the rise of the sect the great
Jewish exegete Saadya (892–942) inaugurated a new
epoch—"the period of the Peshat"—in the interpretation of the Hebrew Bible. Engaged in controversy with the Karaites, he was yet profoundly
influenced by them. A great scholar, and the creator
of Hebrew philology, Saadya also occupied the most
authoritative position of his time in Jewry as the
Gaon of Sura, and was able, in virtue of his unique
opportunities as well as of his own great personal
qualifications, to bring the large majority of orthodox
Jews, who still held to tradition, into new paths in
the matter of Bible study. Saadya, in fact, put
Jewish Biblical exegesis on a new line of development. His most important work, the Arabic translation of the Scriptures, aims at giving, not a bare
reproduction of the original text, but a rational
exegesis embodied in a free translation. He wrote
a number of other important works, some of which
have come down to us only in fragmentary form.
The principles which he applied to the interpretation
of the Bible, and which exercised a profound influence
on the later exegesis, may be summarised as follows :

(1) His fundamental postulate is that reason is the
true basis of all exegesis, and in accordance with this
principle "the exposition of the text must contain
nothing that is obscure or that contradicts logical
thought." He does not deny the divine origin or the
divine authority of the Bible ; and the miracles he
thinks serve as witnesses to the veracity of the
Prophets, and of Scripture generally. At the same
time these postulates are not irreconcilable with the
claims of reason ; anthropomorphic language about
God is regarded as figurative.

(2) Besides the authority of reason, the collateral
authority of the Scriptures themselves is recognised
as a source of sound exegesis (parallel passages and
illustrative texts).

(3) He also recognises, to some extent, the authority of tradition in his Bible exegesis, so far as this is compatible with the paramount claims of a rational exegesis.

The last of the Geonim, Hai (died 1038), who was a great Talmudist, and the author of a famous lexicon also devoted himself to Bible exegesis (he wrote a commentary on Job). He is cited by Ḳimḥi in his commentary. But Saadya's true successors, both in philological and exegetical study, are to be found in the great Jewish schools of North Africa and Spain. Kairwan, in North Tunis, became one of these centres, and was already growing in importance even during Saadya's lifetime. It was here that Dunash ibn Tamim[1] (tenth century) was one of the pioneers of the comparative study of Hebrew and Arabic as an aid to Biblical exegesis. Another North African earlier still, Judah ibn Koreish, had compiled a work in which Arabic, Aramaic, and New-Hebrew are systematically compared with Biblical Hebrew. Judah also recommended in this connexion the study of the Targum (Aramaic). It was, however, in the Spanish schools, where Hebrew philology was most fruitfully studied and developed from the middle of the tenth to the beginning of the twelfth century, that the foundations of the later mediæval exegesis were laid. "From the time of Ḥasdai ibn Shaprut to that of Samuel ibn Nagdela (second half of the tenth to the first half of the eleventh century) eminent and gifted scholars vied with one another in placing the science of Hebrew grammar on a firm basis—a basis that has not been overthrown even by the philology of the nineteenth century. They also developed Hebrew lexicography to a point far in advance of all preceding endeavours: Menaḥem ben Saruk's dictionary ; Dunash ibn Labrat's

---

[1] Not to be confounded with Dunash ben Labrat (also born in North Africa). Ben Labrat was a younger contemporary of Dunash ibn Tamim.

critical work ; Judah ben David Hayyuj's work that
came like a revelation ; Abulwalid's critical work ;
the literary controversy between him and Samuel ibn
Nagdela ; the writings of both as well as of others
belonging to their circle ; and, finally, Abulwalid's
chief work, composed of a grammatical and lexical
part—all these works mark the development of the
philologic literature in Spain. Those of Hayyuj and
Abulwalid especially furnished a firm basis for a Bible
exegesis that, on its linguistic side at least, was free
from gross errors and mere guesswork." [1] Abulwalid's
great work, which is a combination of a grammar and
a lexicon,[2] is especially rich in exegetic material. It
should be added that these scholars, though, of course,
they knew Hebrew, used as their ordinary medium
the Arabic language.

Two eminent philologists of the Spanish-Jewish
school who directed their attention to Biblical
exegesis proper were Moses ibn Giktilla of Cordova
and Judah ibn Balaam of Toledo (both flourished in
the eleventh century). The former wrote commentaries on Isaiah and the Psalms, from which Abraham
ibn Ezra frequently quotes. These commentaries
are the first comprehensive attempt to explain the
respective Biblical books historically. Ibn Giktilla's
exegesis is thoroughly rationalistic (e.g. he gives
rationalistic explanations of the Biblical miracles),
and was violently attacked by Ibn Balaam. Both
wrote in Arabic.[3]

[1] JE, ibid. 167.
[2] Abulwalid ibn Janah (Rabbi Jonah) was the greatest
Hebrew philologist of the Middle Ages. The work of his
referred to above is divided into two parts—the Luma and the
Book of Roots. The latter has been edited, in the Arabic text,
by Dr. Neubauer (Oxford, 1875). Abulwalid was born at
Cordova between the years 1085 and 1090, and died at
Saragossa in the first half of the eleventh century.
[3] Ibn Giktilla's work is important because he was the first
exegete to give purely historical explanations of the prophecies

But the Jewish-Spanish schools also brought forth new elements which were destined to influence Biblical exegesis. These were associated with the development of poetry and the philosophy of religion. In this connexion two famous names may be mentioned, representatives both of poetry and the philosophy of religion, Solomon ibn Gebirol (1021–1058)[1] and Moses ibn Ezra (1070–1138). In order to reconcile the Biblical statements with the postulates of philosophy the text was treated with considerable freedom. Allegory was also used to some extent. "In consequence the elements of a new form of Midrash found their way into Bible exegesis, made subservient to philosophic speculation. The Peshaṭ exegesis, which had been freed from the fetters of the early Midrash, contained in the traditional literature, found itself now confronted by a new enemy—the philosophic Midrash."[2]   Meanwhile, in those countries which lay outside the domain of the Arabic culture, *i.e.* the Christian countries of Europe, especially France and Italy, the old Midrashic exegesis remained paramount, and continued to develop along its own lines. Its schools produced some famous exponents of this type of exegesis, called "Darshanim," and notably Moses ha-Darshan (flourished in Narbonne middle of the eleventh century). It also came to expression in the *Yalḳut Shimeoni*, a vast Midrashic compilation (often from older sources) embracing the entire text of the Hebrew Bible, and dating perhaps from the middle of the thirteenth century.

of Isaiah and the Minor Prophets. He wrote several important works on grammar and philology, and occasionally wrote in Hebrew. David Ḳimḥi several times quotes from Ibn Giḳtilla in his Psalms commentary (*cf.* on viii. 3 ; xvi. 2 ; xxv. 1; xxxv. 20).

[1] Gebirol was one of the first to revive the study of Neoplatonism in Europe. (See above, p. 33.)

[2] *JE, ibid.* 168. Abraham ibn Ezra gives several specimens of Ibn Gebirol's philosophico-allegorical Bible interpretation.

Strangely enough, however, it was in this field (northern France) that there arose, in complete independence of the Spanish-Arabian school, a new school of Bible exegesis which endeavoured to arrive at a literal and simple interpretation of the Bible text—the Peshaṭ —and deliberately set this in contrast with the Midrashic exegesis. The founder of this school was the famous Rabbi Shelomoh Yiṣḥaḳi (Solomon ben Isaac), commonly called Rashi (died 1105). The value of Rashi's work is well known to all students of the later Hebrew literature. His commentary on the Talmud is indispensable, and is practically always printed with the text in printed editions. But his Biblical commentaries also occupy an almost unique position in Jewish exegetical literature, especially his running commentary on the Pentateuch. This work, which soon acquired the widest popularity, has a peculiarly Jewish flavour about it which marks it out among similar works. There are no graces of style, but the comments are terse and to the point. Not a word is wasted. It also combines in a remarkable manner the new with the old. The author uses the old Midrashic exegesis by a process of selection in such a way as to evolve explanations which conform to the Peshaṭ. The more fanciful and far-fetched Midrashic applications are rejected. In addition he pays constant attention to the linguistic side of the exegesis, and often gives the vernacular French equivalents of the Hebrew words. " There is," says Dr. I. Abrahams, speaking of Rashi's Pentateuch commentary,[1] " a quaintness and fascination about it which are lacking in the pedantic sobriety of [Abraham] ibn Ezra and the grammatical exactness of [David] Ḳimḥi." [2] Rashi's work was continued by his sons-in-law, and by his distinguished grandson, Samuel ben Meir (Rashbam, 1100–1160), whose commentary on

[1] For editions, see pp. 133.
[2] *Short History of Jewish Literature*, p. 73.

the Pentateuch may be regarded as, perhaps, marking the highest point reached by the exegetic school of northern France. In his work and that of Joseph Ḳara the Peshaṭ was adopted in a more thoroughgoing and independent way than in that of Rashi himself.

The schools of northern France died away in the early part of the twelfth century, owing to the tumults brought about by the Crusades. Jewish exegesis, however, in the Christian countries of Europe was destined to receive a new and fruitful impulse from a Jew who had absorbed the whole culture of Spanish Judaism at the highest point of its intellectual development. This was Abraham ibn Ezra, who was born at Toledo some time before 1100. Ibn Ezra left his home, a mature man, in 1140, and spent nearly thirty years (1140–1167) in wandering over Italy, Provence, northern France, and England, everywhere, as he himself says, "writing books and revealing the secrets of knowledge." In 1158 he visited London. His scholarship and literary activity were many-sided and astonishing. He was distinguished as a mathematician, a poet, and an exegete. His commentaries, written in Hebrew, are the most important products of his literary activity. They are distinguished in many ways—by the author's mastery over his material, by their attractive style and graceful Hebrew, and by their originality combined with profound learning and critical acumen. His Pentateuch commentary, side by side with Rashi's, has enjoyed great popularity among Jewish exegetical works. His own exegetical method is most clearly expounded in the preface to his commentary on the Pentateuch, where he criticises the various methods hitherto employed by exegetes. He clearly distinguishes between the Peshaṭ and Derash, and accords only a limited place to the new philosophical Midrash. Dr. I. Abrahams well sums up his method as follows : " In his commentaries he rejected

the current digressive and allegorical methods, and
steered a middle course between free research on
the one hand, and blind adherence to tradition on
the other. Ibn Ezra was the first to maintain that
the book of Isaiah contains the work of two
prophets—a view now almost universal. He never
for a moment doubted, however, that the Bible was
in every part inspired, and in every part the Word of
God."[1] The Kimhis were worthy coadjutors in, and
continuators of, his work.

One other name must be mentioned before we
reach the period of David Kimhi, that of Moses ben
Maimon (Maimonides), who is by common consent
to be regarded as "the greatest Jew of the Middle
Ages." Maimonides (1135–1204) was an older contemporary of David Kimhi (1160–1235), and is
constantly quoted by the latter in his commentaries.[2] Born at Cordova, and, like Ibn Ezra,
inheriting the culture of Spanish Jewry, Maimonides
also helped to disseminate this culture in other lands.
Forced to leave Spain, owing to Mohammedan persecution, he emigrated with his family in 1165 to
Palestine, and after a time settled in Egypt, in
Fostat, or old Cairo, where he ultimately died.

Maimonides wrote both in Hebrew and Arabic.
Though he contributed no set commentary on any
Biblical book, his chief philosophical work, composed
in Arabic and subsequently translated into Hebrew
by R. Samuel ibn Tibbon, and known as "The
Guide of the Perplexed" (Hebrew *Moreh Nebukim*),[3]
contains a wealth of exegetic material. His funda-

[1] *op. cit.* p. 69.

[2] Maimonides was, of course, a younger contemporary of
Abraham ibn Ezra. See pp. 34 f.

[3] Two translations of the *Guide* were made during the
author's lifetime. The original was written about 1190. It was
studied by both Mohammedans and Christians (*e.g.* Aquinas).
For best edition, see p. 265.

mental aim in this work is to reconcile the postulates of philosophy, based on the Aristotelian system as expounded by Arabian thinkers, with the data of the Bible. He recognises an exoteric and esoteric sense in the words of Scripture. "The 'secrets of the Law' hidden in the Biblical words are found by investigation into the esoteric meaning. But such secrets, as sought by Maimonides, have nothing to do with mysticism; he undertakes the investigation with absolute rationalism, as may be seen particularly in his explanation of certain Bible stories and his exposition of the reasons for the Law. He finds the teachings of the Aristotelian physics and metaphysics in the chapters on Creation (Gen. i.), and in that of the Heavenly Chariot (Ezek. i.). His rationalism, however, halts at the facts of prophecy and of the Bible miracles, though here, too, rational investigation comes into play. One of the most original and daring aids to exegesis is evolved by the doctrine concerning prophecy, namely, the theory of visions—whereby he transfers a number of Bible stories from the realm of fact into the realm of psychic experience. The principle of the exoteric and esoteric sense of Scripture leads him to allegorical exegesis . . . but his allegory remains within the bounds prescribed to it, by his rationalism on the one hand, and by his faith in tradition on the other." [1]

It was through the influence of this great work of Maimonides that the Aristotelian philosophy became firmly entrenched in Jewish thought, and also a chief factor in subsequent Bible exegesis.

A distinguished part in the diffusion of learning throughout European Jewry during the twelfth and

---

[1] *JE, ibid.* 170. "Maimonides," says Dr. Abrahams (*op. cit.* p. 84), "like Saadya, recognised a higher function for reason. He placed reason on the same level as revelation, and then demonstrated that his faith and his reason taught identical truths." .

thirteenth centuries was played by the family of Kimhi, the most famous of whom is David Kimhi. The father of David was Joseph Kimhi (RiKam), who, as grammarian, exegete, poet, and translator, took an active share in the work in which Ibn Ezra was engaged, was a contemporary of the latter, his lifetime falling within the years 1105–1170, and, like Ibn Ezra, was of Spanish birth and knew Arabic. Owing to Arab fanaticism, he was forced to leave Spain and emigrated to Narbonne, Provence, where he seems to have remained for the rest of his days, living the life of a poor scholar-student and teacher. It is probable that Ibn Ezra, who visited Narbonne in 1160, met Joseph Kimhi. He quotes the latter in his Bible commentaries. Both scholars worked along the same lines, and, though Joseph Kimhi was inferior to Ibn Ezra both in brilliance and in learning, it may yet be claimed for him that he was "the first successful transplanter of Judæo-Arabic science to the soil of Christian Europe." [1]

In the department of grammatical study, though not profoundly original—he was especially dependent upon Hayyuj and Ibn Janah—he did some important work and made some advance, more particularly in minor details. These books have been published: *Sefer Zikkaron* (ed. by Bacher, Berlin, 1888) and *Sefer ha-Galuy* (ed. by Matthews, Berlin, 1887). Both works contain interesting features. Thus the author makes a point of examining the language of the Liturgy, and in his philological discussions adduces evidence from the Talmud, Targums, and Arabic. He also wrote a number of exegetical works, not all of which have survived, while some of his work which exists in manuscript is still

---

[1] *cp.* Grätz (*History of the Jews*, iii. 404): "Joseph Kimhi's merit consists solely in the fact that he introduced the Jewish culture of Spain into South France, and completed lastingly the results of Ibn Ezra's fugitive activity."

unpublished. Of his published work mention may here be made of his commentary of Proverbs, *Sefer Hukkah* (Breslau, 1868). He usually follows the method of the Peshat, and in his exposition pays careful attention to the context. He quotes from and criticises predecessors ; he avoids reading into the text of Scripture the scientific knowledge of his time. We must here pass over the important work he accomplished as translator and poet.[1]

Joseph Kimhi died, as has been said, about 1170, leaving a younger son, David, who at this time was a boy of about ten years of age, under the care of an elder son, Moses Kimhi (ReMaK), who at this time was probably a mature man,[2] and was a scholar and commentator of mark. Commentaries of his on Proverbs and Ezra-Nehemiah are printed in the Rabbinical Bibles, where they are wrongly attributed to Ibn Ezra. He also wrote treatises on grammar, and one of these (the *Mahalak*) became widely used as a concise methodical text-book of Hebrew grammar, and in the first half of the sixteenth century was a favourite text-book with non-Jews. It was edited many times, and translated into Latin by Sebastian Münster.

It was under the care and guidance of Moses Kimhi that the young David, destined to become the most illustrious of his line, grew up. It is hardly surprising that with such connexions and under such influences David Kimhi should have become one of the most accomplished of Jewish scholars, well versed in the whole range of Hebrew literature. In later times one of the sayings from *Pirke Aboth* (iii. 21) was applied to him : "Without *Kemah* (= *fine flour*, the etymon of the name *Kimhi*) no Torah."[3] He

[1] For details see *JE* vii. 496 f.

[2] Moses Kimhi died about A.D. 1190.

[3] The name was pronounced "Kamhi" in Arabic-speaking circles. From the meaning of *Kemah* = "corn ground *small*" is to be explained the French surname "maistre petit."

is also sometimes called "Sefardi" ("Spaniard"), on account of his family's connexion with Spain.

David Ḳimḥi's work was equally notable both in the domain of grammar and philology and in that of exegesis. What may be described as his *magnum opus*, the *Miklol*, to which he constantly refers in his commentaries, is a combination of a Hebrew grammar and a dictionary of the Bible. This treatise is divided into two quite distinct parts, which were later separated, the second part being issued separately under the title *Sefer ha-Shorashim*, or "Book of Roots"; the title *Miklol* was then retained exclusively for the first or grammatical part. While not strikingly original, Ḳimḥi's work has high merit. He is no mere compiler, but marshals his material with the sure hand of a thorough scholar, who possesses in a high degree the power of lucid systematisation and popular exposition. "His grammatical material is drawn chiefly from the works of Ḥayyuj and Ibn Janaḥ and from the writings of his own father. He tries to understand the language from itself, seeking analogues in later Hebrew, less frequently in Aramaic and Arabic."[1] Ḳimḥi's *Miklol* has exercised a lasting influence not only on Jews but on Christians, and is still taken into account by scientific grammarians, *e.g.* by E. König, who, in his monumental work on Hebrew grammar, writes with constant reference to Ḳimḥi.[2]

In the field of exegesis Ḳimḥi produced commentaries on Genesis, the Prophets, Psalms, and Chronicles, and possibly on other parts of the Bible. Here, again, the qualities exhibited in his grammatical

---

[1] *JE* vii. 494.

[2] Both parts of the *Miklol* have been frequently printed, the grammar as recently as 1862 by Rittenberg at Paris, and the lexicon at Berlin in 1847 (by Biesenthal and Labrecht). A Latin translation of the second part (the "Book of Roots") was issued in 1535, and of the first part (the grammar) in 1540, by Guidacier (Paris).

and philological work, which appear in his exposition, made his commentaries exceedingly popular and influential. That on the Prophets is printed in the Rabbinical Bibles, and parts of it have been translated into Latin for Christian use.[1] The commentary on the Psalms was first printed in 1477, and again in the Rabbinical Bible of Chayim, but not in those of Buxtorf and Frankfurter.

His exegesis is based primarily upon an exact and grammatical construction of the text. As a rule, he adheres strictly to the literal meaning (the Peshat), but he notices, from time to time, the old Haggadic explanations, as well as (occasionally) the later philosophico-speculative exposition. He constantly quotes older authorities (especially Abraham ibn Ezra), and in his citations from the Targum often offers valuable data for the criticism of its text.

The effect of the important new principles introduced by Maimonides on Jewish thought generally, and on Jewish exegesis in particular, was profound and far-reaching. During the following three centuries the philosophic exegesis of Scripture, with its rationalism and its use of allegory, constantly asserted itself and was expressed in many works of an exegetical character. "Many Bible commentaries," says Professor Bacher, "were primarily concerned with finding the tenets of philosophy in Scripture." Not that this type of exegesis succeeded in ousting altogether its rivals. The old Midrashic

[1] *Isaiah* (Melanimeus, at Florence, 1774); *Joel* and *Jonah* (Leusden, Utrecht, 1656), and *Malachi* (De Muis, Paris, 1618). *Amos* was rendered into German in 1581 (by Veke), and *Zechariah* into English (by McCaul) in 1837. It should be added that Ḳimḥi's commentary on *Chronicles* is accessible also in the Rabbinical Bibles; that on *Genesis* was printed separately in 1842 (Pressburg). A critical edition of the Hebrew text of Ḳimḥi's commentary on the Psalms (Bk. I.) was edited by Dr. Schiller Szinessy (Cambridge, 1883): English translations (Psalms i.–viii.) by Dr. Greenup, 1918, and by R. G. Finch (S.P.C.K.), 1919.

tradition, as well as the Peshat, was still recognised, while a new element—the mystical Kabbalistic—also became influential. And all the time the reputation of Rashi and Ibn Ezra steadily grew. In fact, what happened was that all these factors acted and reacted on each other, and are often to be detected side by side in the same works.

It would, indeed, have been a disaster for Judaism if the tendencies represented by Maimonides' work had triumphed absolutely. From this disaster Judaism was saved by the protest of the anti-Maimonists, which took a somewhat embittered form in the controversy that broke out and continued for a considerable period after the great teacher's death. In the end, as has been well said, "the triumph of Maimonides was complete all along the line. But the opposite party gained something for which it contended. The philosophical conception of Judaism was allowed a high place in the schools, but Judaism was not merged into rationalism. This was due to the anti-Maimonists, while the mediæval Kabbalah (or mysticism) applied to the Jewish religion that touch of emotion which Maimonides so conspicuously lacked. Again, the aim of Maimonides to provide a code (the *Mishneh Torah*) which should form a final court of appeal in Jewish life was unsuccessful. Into Spain itself the French methods of studying the Talmud were introduced during the century following the death of Maimonides. So far from destroying *pilpul*—casuistical discussion—the *Code* or *Mishneh Torah* itself became the object of pilpulistic comment. This was to the advantage of Judaism. Pilpul is to law as laboratory work to science."[1] In spite of opposition the influence of Maimonides became all-powerful. Before the publication of the *Guide of the Perplexed* the students of philosophy within the ranks of Judaism had been few; but ever since

[1] *Maimonides*, by David Yellin and Israel Abrahams, p. 152 f.

they have been both numerous and powerful. The influence of Maimonides also has served as a wholesome check upon the extravagances of the Kabbalistic movement.

The books of the Bible that especially lent themselves to exegetic treatment from the philosophic point of view were the Wisdom Books (Proverbs, Ecclesiastes, and Job), and another book, which had long been subjected to allegorical treatment— Canticles. Maimonides' pupil and spiritual son, Joseph ibn Aknin, produced a commentary on it of the philosophic-allegorical type; Samuel ibn Tibbon, who translated Maimonides' Arabic into Hebrew, wrote a commentary of this kind on Ecclesiastes, and his son Moses another on Canticles. One of the most important products of this line of thought is the *Malmad ha-Talmidim* of Abba Mari ben Jacob Anatoli (son-in-law of Samuel ibn Tibbon), a collection of sermons on the perikopes of the Pentateuch. Here the allegorical exegesis is pursued in the style of Philo, even the personages and occurrences of the Pentateuch being resolved into philosophic concepts and postulates. The philosophic exegesis was pursued during the fourteenth century, its most notable representative being Levi ben Gershon (died 1344), "a strict Aristotelian who wrote commentaries on most of the Biblical books." Similar commentaries on the Pentateuch were written by Nissim ben Moses of Marseilles, at the beginning of the fourteenth century, and by Samuel Zarza of Valencia (fourteenth century). Mention may also be made here of the *Akedath Yitzhak* ("Offering of Isaac") of Isaac Arama, "the last great exegetic work written in Spain before the expulsion" (in 1492). It consists of sermons, largely of a philosophical nature. The influence of this type of thought can also be seen in the work of Don Isaac Abarbanel (or Abravanel), who was one of the victims of the expulsion. Abarbanel was born in Lisbon in 1437, and died in Venice in 1508. His career was chequered. For some years before the expulsion (1484–1492) he occupied a high position of State under Ferdinand and Isabella. Then he was driven from Spain in the general expulsion, and went in succession to Naples, Corfu, and Venice, where he died in happiness and honour. As a commentator it has been said of him that "no predecessor . . . came so near as he did to the modern ideal of a commentator on the Bible."[1] He wrote commentaries on the whole of the Hebrew Bible (except the Hagiographa), and was the first Jewish exegete to prefix introductions to works of this kind, dealing with such questions as authorship, date, etc. He also cites, without animus, the views of Christian exegetes, such as Jerome, Augustine, and Nicholas de Lyra. These excellences made Abarbanel's work highly esteemed in Christian circles, where they were closely studied and exercised a lasting influence. Abarbanel's training in high affairs of State had made him realise that to understand ancient writings the social and political environment in which they were born must be considered and envisaged. Though he was much influenced by Maimonides, and was himself an Aristotelian, Abarbanel was not fundamentally in sympathy with the root-conceptions of the philosophic school. He firmly believed in the reality of God's revelation in history, and especially in that of the history of the Chosen People. "Had Abravanel," says Dr. Ginzberg,[2] "not been misled by the *Guide* of Maimonides, for whom he shared the traditional veneration, he might have given an exposition of his views on the relations of philosophy and religion. As it is, however, these views are confused, being at one and the same time

---

[1] I. Abrahams, *Short History of Jewish Literature*, p. 139.
[2] In *JE* i. 127 f.

Maimonistic, anti-Maimonistic, and in a measure even cabalistic." His formal treatises on philosophy exhibit this mixed character. The most important of these are the *Miphaloth 'Elohim* ("Deeds of God"), which is mainly based on Maimonides, and the *Rosh 'Amanah* ("Pinnacle of Faith"), a defence of the Thirteen Articles of the Creed formulated by Maimonides. He also wrote three works in defence of the Messianic Belief (1496-98), one of which is in the form of a commentary on Daniel, whom, contrary to Jewish tradition, he reckons among the Prophets.

From the eleventh to the fourteenth century a line of French scholars, continuing the tradition of Rashi, occupied themselves with Talmudical studies. From the "additions" (*Tosaphoth*) which they compiled to Rashi's famous commentary on the Talmud these scholars acquired the name of "Tosaphists." The "Tosaphists" were essentially casuists, delighting in subtle analysis and discussion, while, on the other hand, the ideal of the Spanish school of Talmudists was simplification. The Tosaphists displayed so keen a critical insight, and attained so great a mastery over the Talmudical material, and were, moreover, so filled with the old Rabbinical spirit, that their fame and reputation spread far, even into Spain itself Their *obiter dicta* on exegetical matters were afterwards collected into different compilations ; and commentaries were written under their influence by Eliezer of Beaugency (twelfth century), who was a pupil of Samuel ben Meir, Rashi's grandson. Those on Isaiah and Hosea have been published ; others exist in MS. in libraries. Eliezer, whose work is almost entirely free from Midrashic elements, was mainly concerned with the endeavour to trace the logical connexion of verses and passages.

The most eminent of the Tosaphists was Jacob

ben Meir Tam, commonly called "Rabbenu Tam" (1100–1171), a brother of Samuel ben Meir, and, of course, a grandson of Rashi. He was not only a great Talmudist, but also did important work as a grammarian, and was, besides, a liturgical poet, but not a Biblical commentator.

The great reconciler between the French and Spanish schools was Moses ben Nachman, commonly called Nachmanides (Ramban), himself a Spaniard (1195–1270). Of the French Rabbis he says: "They are our masters in Talmud, and to them we must go for instruction."[1] Inheriting the culture of Spain, he also possessed much of the Spanish independence and breadth of view. He was also a poet, and a man of a warm and sympathetic temperament. Exiled from Spain, a victim of Christian zeal, he settled in Palestine in 1267, and died there about 1270.

He wrote some important theological works, notably "The Sacred Letter," in which he defended the divine character of man's earthly nature ("the flesh"), and "The Law of Man" (*Torath ha-Adam*), in which there is much wise reflection on suffering and death. Pain and suffering, he says, are "a service of God, leading man to ponder on his end and reflect about his destiny." His greatest work was, however, his commentary on the Pentateuch (written about 1268). There is much in this that charms and impresses the reader. It is not only scholarly, but full of original thought, based upon independent study. But its most significant quality is its mysticism, in which we can discern the first beginnings of Kabbalistic doctrine. True, this is restrained and guarded in Nachmanides' work, and is rigidly confined to a secondary place. But it is there. The underlying principle of this type of exegesis is that the words of Scripture have implicit in them a deeper esoteric meaning, apart from the plain literal sense. "This conception,

[1] I. Abrahams, *op. cit.* p. 97.

together with the assumption that all truths about God and creation, the universe and man, which are cognisable by the human mind, and which have been so cognised, must be found in Scripture,"[1] is clearly enunciated ·by Nachmanides in the preface prefixed to his Pentateuch commentary. Here it appears openly avowed for the first time, and gained much from the powerful recognition of so famous a scholar. This principle asserts itself in his typological exegesis of the Biblical narrative. Thus the six days of Creation are regarded as a prophecy of the six thousand years of the world's history, to be succeeded by the seventh, or millennial age. Jacob and Esau are prototypes of Israel and Rome, and Joshua's battle with Amalek prefigures the Messianic conflict which is imminent. These ideas and applications are not, of course, original with Nachmanides—they belong to the old apocalyptic tradition—but their recrudescence in the orthodox teaching of the Rabbis, at this time, was a novelty. Not that he was a Kabbalist in the full sense—he did not, for instance, accept the Kabbalistic tenet of the eternity of matter and the world (*Kadmuth hā-'ōlām*), and differed from them on other important points. But his mystical tendencies were marked.

Another form of mysticism, based upon the letter of Scripture, arose in Germany in the thirteenth century, represented in the writings of Elijah ben Judah of Worms (1176–1238). This consisted in the manipulation (by combination and interchange) of the letters of the Scriptural text, and by similar manipulation of their numerical values (Gematria). The Kabbalistic method of exegesis is founded upon this method, which it uses in combination with the allegorical and typological exegesis. These methods of exegesis, together with others (non-Kabbalistic), are represented in the commentary of Bachya ben Asher of Saragossa (1291) on the Pentateuch, which

[1] *JE* iii. 170.

enjoyed a wide popularity. Four methods of exegesis are mentioned in the introduction to this work as applicable to the text of Scripture: (1) The method of the Peshat; (2) that of the Midrash; (3) that of reason (*i.e.* the philosophic exegesis); (4) that of the Kabbalah. It was about this time that the great classical exposition of the Kabbalistic mysticism—the famous book *Zohar*—appeared in Spain. More will be said of this below.

The four methods of exegesis just referred to as exhibited in Bachya ben Asher's work can be traced, in various degrees of emphasis, throughout the prolific exegetical literature that was produced in the various centres of Jewry during the three centuries that followed the death of Maimonides. Some of the more prominent and important of these works have been referred to above, and must be passed over in silence here. The period that followed was one of stagnation and decline in general culture, marked by a sterile devotion to purely Talmudic studies, which was only brought to an end in the eighteenth century by the movement initiated by Moses Mendelssohn. At the same time a similar growth of Kabbalistic study, also one-sided, took place by way of reaction, which was accompanied by much superstition.

Abarbanel stands on the threshold of this epoch, but really belongs to the one that was passing away. A younger contemporary, Elias Levita (1469–1549), in Italy devoted himself to Masoretic studies, and produced his epoch-making work *Masoret ha-Masoret* (standard edition by C. D. Ginsburg, 1867). He and his contemporary, Jacob ben Chayim, also a Masoretic scholar, stimulated the study of Hebrew in Europe. (His Introduction to the Rabbinic Bible, Hebrew and English, has been edited by C. D. Ginsburg, 2nd edition, 1867). The most prolific exegete was Moses Alsheik of Safed (second half of the sixteenth century), who produced voluminous commentaries, largely homiletical and Midrashic in character, on most of the books of the Bible.

III

THE MYSTICAL LITERATURE

[LITERATURE : Dr. Philipp Bloch, *Die jüdische Mystik und Kabbala* (in Winter und Wünsche, iii. 219–286) ; J. Abelson, *Jewish Mysticism* (1913) ; articles *Cabala* (by Ginzberg in *JE* iii. 456–479), *Zohar* (by Broyde in *JE* xii. 689–693) ; Ginsburg, *The Kabbalah* (London, 1865) ; Mathers, *The Kabbalah Unveiled* (London, 1887) ; A. Franck, *La Kabbale* (2nd ed. 1889).

The whole of the *Zohar* has been translated into French by Jean de Pauly.

See also Steinschneider, *Jewish Literature*, and Schechter, *Studies in Judaism*, first series, pp. 1 ff. (on the Chassidim).]

The general name of the mystical type of thought that finds expression in Jewish literature is *Kabbalah* ("Cabala'), which means "tradition," "the received or traditional lore."[1] This is the specific term used for "the esoteric or mystic doctrine concerning God and the universe, asserted to have come down as a revelation to elect saints from a remote past and preserved only by a privileged few."[2] At first the elements embraced in the tradition were simple, but under the influence of the Neoplatonic and Neopythagorean philosophy it gradually assumed a speculative character. In the Geonic period this lore gathered round a sort of holy book entitled *Sepher Yetzirah*, or "Book of Creation," and was systematically studied by the elect called "mekubbalim" or "Ba'alê ha-Kabbalah," *i.e.* those initiated into, or possessors of, Kabbalah.[3]

---

[1] Heb. קַבָּלָה from קבל "to receive."

[2] Kohler in *JE* iii. 456.

[3] Afterwards called "maskilim" ("wise," from Daniel xii. 10). The technical term הכמה נסתרה = "hidden wisdom" also furnished a designation from its initial letters ח״ן = "grace"; the initiates were known as יודעי חן (Eccles. ix. 11) = "adepts in grace."

During the thirteenth century and onward these, studies, which had been more or less confined to small circles, received a great impetus and became widely diffused. They gave rise to an extensive literature, written in a peculiar dialect of Aramaic, and grouped around a new holy book—the *Zohar*—which suddenly made its appearance, but claimed to be a work of great antiquity, its reputed author being the famous second-century R. Simeon b. Yochai. This Kabbalistic literature grew up, to some extent, in opposition to the Talmud.

Though the *Zohar* was compiled in its present form in the Middle Ages, it embraces much older elements, and, in fact, is essentially a reshaping of old material. The Kabbalistic tradition can, indeed, be traced back to a considerable antiquity. Books containing the secret lore of the " wise " circulated within small circles, as an esoteric literature, at a comparatively early period (*cf.* Dan. xii. 9–10 ; 2 Esdras xiv. 45–46). There was, in fact, a continuous esoteric tradition, which has run on from ancient down to modern times. The name Kabbalah suggests this, and the Kabbalists were perfectly right in maintaining that the ideas to which they gave expression, and which they were constantly reshaping, were old. How old is not always realised. " A study of the few still existing apocryphal books [of the Old Testament]," says Kohler,[1] " discloses the fact, ignored by most writers on the Cabala . . . that the 'mystic lore' occasionally alluded to in the Talmudic or Midrashic literature . . . is not only much more systematically presented in these older writings, but gives ample evidence of a continuous Cabalistic tradition ; inasmuch as the mystic literature of the Geonic period is only a fragmentary reproduction of the ancient apocalyptic writings, and the saints and sages of the Tannaitic period take in the former the place occupied by the Biblical protoplasts, patriarchs, and scribes in the latter."

The Slavonic Enoch (not later than the early part of the first century A.D.) is remarkably illuminating in its realistic presentment of some of the Kabbalistic ideas—*e.g.* as to the process of creation, the constitution of the heavens, and so on ; the wonders of the Creative Wisdom can also be traced in other apocryphal and apocalyptic books (*e.g.* Ben-Sira, *Testament of*

---

[1] In *JE* iii. 457.

Abraham). In fact, the two great themes of this early mystical tradition were the cosmogony and the mysteries of the Divine Chariot or Throne. " The speculation which gave rise to the tradition starts from Ezekiel's Chariot-vision (Ezek. i.). . . . The material of which it is composed, and which is constantly reshaped, consists mainly of descriptions of the seven heavens, ' with their hosts of angels, and the various store-houses of the world, and of the divine throne above the highest heaven.' " Heaven is pictured as filled with light of inexpressible brilliance, and the Divine Chariot as surrounded by fiery angels of warlike aspect. The mystic who is allowed to enter the celestial sphere usually receives divine disclosures about the future or the spiritual world.

In order to enjoy this experience he had to prepare himself to enter the ecstatic state, and this was brought about especially by ablutions and fastings, but sometimes also by fervent invocations and by other means.   He was rewarded by " the vision of the Divine Chariot" (or *Merkabah*).[1]   The typical mystic imagined himself entering the Divine Chariot and floating through the air.   Such were called *Yôrĕdê. Merkabah, i.e.* " those who go down (*i.e.* embark) into the ship-like chariot." [2] It is in this chariot that they are supposed to ascend into the heavens, where, in the dazzling light, they are able to penetrate the secrets of the universe.   The heavenly charioteer is Metatron,[3] the angel next the Throne, whose name is like God's, who possesses all knowledge and imparts it to man. The affinities of the Ḳabbalistic literature with ancient Gnosticism have been pointed out by Kohler, and afford further evidence of the antiquity of the ideas embodied in this literature.

Two elements may be broadly distinguished here : (*a*) The mythological element, and especially the grossly anthropomorphic descriptions of the Deity, which occur in the older writings embodied in the present form of the *Zohar*, and doubtless belong to the old tradition of ancient lore ; (*b*) the speculative Ḳabbalah, which probably was derived from Alexandria in the first century or earlier, " with her strange commingling of Egyptian, Chaldæan, Judæan, and Greek culture." It was in this congenial soil that the seeds of the mystic philosophy were sown.

It is important to emphasise the fact, which has been referred to above, that the Ḳabbalistic tradition

[1] G. H. Box, Introduction to the *Apocalypse of Abraham*, p. xxix.   [2] Jellinek.

[3] According to Kohler, this name was suggested by that of Mithra.

is a continuous development from older sources. This is sometimes lost sight of when the *Zohar* is spoken of scornfully as a "forgery," clumsily put together by Moses de Leon in the thirteenth century. As a matter of fact, there is little, if anything, that is original in Moses' work, which was essentially a reshaping of old traditional material, and actually embodied older works in their original form.

A considerable Hebrew literature of the Ḳabbalistic-mystical type seems to have been current in the Geonic period. Many of these books are no longer extant, but some have survived. One of the most remarkable is that known as *Shi'ur Ḳomah*, an extraordinary treatise on the bodily dimensions of God. It exists in fragments, the largest of which is included in the Ḳabbalistic book *Sepher Raziel*. It apparently was current in the eighth and following centuries as an independent work, and in its present form may have been redacted, at the latest, in the eighth century. But in substance it is much older, having affinities with the early Gnostic systems of thought.[1]

Closely allied to this, and in its present form probably belonging to the same period, is the "Hekaloth" literature, a number of fragments treating of the heavenly "Halls" (*hēkaloth*), which, according to Hai Gaon, originated with the mystics who experienced the heavenly chariot-ride (*Yôrĕdê Merkabah*), already referred to. These, according to the same authority, "brought themselves into a state of entranced vision by fasting, asceticism, and prayer, and imagined that they saw the seven [heavenly] halls, and all that is therein, with their own eyes, while passing from one hall into another."

The most remarkable literary production of this kind, however, is the *Sepher Yetzirah* ("Book of

[1] For specimens of the contents in translation, see *JE* xi. 298 (*s.v. Shi'ur Ḳomah*).

Creation "), which, in its present form, may belong to the Geonic period. This work enjoyed so great a reputation in the ninth century that Saadya wrote a commentary on it. It forms the link between the earlier mystic literature and the later Kabbalah. The doctrine of emanations, which played so prominent a part later, as well as the mystic power of the letters of the Hebrew alphabet, are here enunciated in an early form. The ten " Sephiroth," according to this book, constitute the fundamentals of all existence, being the ten principles that mediate between God and the universe. They include the three primal emanations that proceed from the Spirit of God, viz. (1) spiritual air, (2) primal water, (3) fire. Six others consist of the three dimensions (height, length, breadth) to the left and right ; and these nine, together with the Spirit of God, form the ten " Sephiroth," which are eternal. The first three are the ideal prototypes of Creation, which became possible when infinite space, represented by the six other Sephiroth, was produced.

While the three primal elements constitute the substance of things, the twenty-two letters of the Hebrew alphabet constitute the form. The letters hover, as it were, on the boundary-line between the spiritual and the physical world ; for the real existence of things is cognisable only by means of language, *i.e.* the human capacity for conceiving thought. As the letters resolve the contrast between the substance and the form of things, they represent the solvent activity of God ; for everything that is exists by means of contrasts, which find their solution in God, as, for instance, among the three primal elements, the contrasts between fire and water are resolved into *ruach*, " air " or " spirit " (" spiritual air ").

The doctrine of emanations is, of course, really

Neoplatonic. It attempts to answer the question, how the finite can be brought into touch with the infinite, by the view that all existing things are an outflowing which ultimately proceeds from God. God embraces them all, animate and inanimate.

The *Sepher Yetzirah* prepared the way for the mediæval Kabbalah. Its doctrine of the ten Sephiroth has obvious affinities with the later representation in the *Zohar* and allied literature, though there are important points of difference.[1] Its importance is obvious, for it brings us into the heart of Jewish mysticism.

Besides the *Sepher Yetzirah*, the following are the most important books or fragments belonging to the mystic literature of the period of the Geonim that have survived : (1) "The Alphabet of R. Akiba" (two versions published in Jellinek's *Beth ha-Midrash*, vol. iii.) ; (2) " The Garden of Eden" (*Gan 'Eden*) in Jellinek, ii., iii., v. (different versions) ; (3) Tractate on "Gehinnom" (Jellinek, i.) ; (4) " The Sword of Moses" (*Harba de-Mosheh*), ed. by Gaster, 1896 ; (5) *Hibbut ha-Keber* (Jellinek, i.) ; (6) *Hekaloth* (already referred to) in several versions in Jellinek, ii., iii. (also in Wertheimer's *Jerusalem*, 1889) ; Midrash Konen (Jellinek, i., and several times printed). Fragments of this early mystical literature also exist in the *Pirke de R. Eliezer*, Midrash *Tadshe*, and *Numbers rabba*.

The revival of Kabbalistic literature that took place in the Geonic period makes it certain that many scholars belonging to the Babylonian schools cultivated the mystic lore. Some of the Geonim themselves were deeply interested in these studies, and it is not without significance that certain Kabbalistic works, even though they may have been compiled at a later time, were ascribed to the authorship of particular Geonim.

Another remarkable fact is that the German Kabbalah owes its origin to Babylonia. It was a Babylonian, Aaron ben Samuel ha-Nasi, who, emi-

[1] For a discussion of these, see Abelson, *Jewish Mysticism* chap. v.

grating to Italy in the first half of the ninth century, carried with him these teachings, and imparted them to the Kalonymides, who carried them to Germany about 917. They were not published till nearly three centuries later, when Judah the Pious (died 1217), himself a member of the family, commissioned his pupil, Eleazar of Worms, to introduce the oral and written Kabbalistic doctrine into larger circles. This explains the strange fact that the German Kabbalah is a direct continuation of the Geonic type of mysticism. In Italy and Germany it had remained untouched by foreign influences.

On the other hand, in Arabic-speaking countries the Græco-Arabic philosophy reacted upon the Kabbalistic tradition; and, in particular, the influence of the philosophical doctrines of Solomon ibn Gebirol (1021–58), the great exponent of Neoplatonism, was marked. Thus the three sources from which the Kabbalah of the thirteenth century was derived were the esoteric tradition of the Talmud, the Geonic mysticism, and the Arabic Neoplatonic philosophy.

The essential doctrines of the German school of Kabbalists, whose principal literary exponent was Eleazar of Worms (died 1237),[1] are as follows :

God is exalted beyond mortal comprehension. In order to make Himself visible to inferior beings (both angels and men), He created out of the divine fire His *kabod* ("glory," "majesty"),[2] which has both size and shape, and sits on a throne, as God's visible presence, in the east. This "glory" is veiled by a curtain (*pargod*) on the east, north, and south from the world of angels, but is open to the illumination of the divine light from the west. All the anthropomorphic statements of Scripture are referred to this "glory." The German Kabbalah also assumes the existence of different worlds, viz. (1) the world of the "glory" (*kabod*); (2) that of

---

[1] R. Eleazar ben Jehudah, called "Rokeach," was probably born in Mainz. He lived and died at Worms.

[2] *cp.* the Rabbinical "Shekhinah."

angels ; (3) that of the animal soul ; (4) that of the intellectual soul. The lack of the late philosophical element here is obvious, and clearly reflects the ancient type of mystical thought which goes back to the Talmudic period. It responded to the needs of religious feeling in revolt against a dry and intellectual legalism.

"While study of the law was to the Talmudists the very acme of piety, the mystics accorded the first place to prayer, which was considered as a mystical progress towards God, demanding a state of ecstasy. It was the chief task of the practical Cabala to produce this ecstatic mysticism, already met with among the Merkabah-travellers[1] of the time of the Talmud and Geonim ; hence this mental state was especially favoured and fostered by the Germans. Alphabetical and numerical mysticism constitutes the greater part of Eleazar's works, and is to be regarded simply as means to an end, namely, to reach a state of ecstasy by the proper employment of the names of God and of the angels, 'a state in which every wall is removed from the spiritual eye.'"[2]

The origins of the Kabbalistic tradition in southern France (Provence) and Spain are more difficult to trace. The transmission, according to the Kabbalists themselves, can be traced to Jacob ha-Nazir (beginning of the twelfth century), who initiated Abraham ben David of Posquières. The son of the latter, Isaac the Blind, is reputed to have been the teacher of Azriel (born about 1160), who played an important part in the formulation of the speculative Kabbalah.

A rudimentary form of the speculative Kabbalah appears in the treatise known as *Masseket Aziluth*, which contains the doctrine of the four graduated worlds. The book emphatically enjoins that the doctrine must be kept secret, and insists that the learners must be of proved piety. These injunctions suggest an early date. The idea of the Sephiroth is presented simply and unphilosophically, and the angelology and representation of Metatron harmonise with the views on these subjects prevalent in the Geonic period. The rudiments of the speculative system are here, but undeveloped. Possibly, as Ginzberg suggests, it may be a product of the later Geonic period.

---

[1] *i.e.* the mystics who travelled through the heavens in the divine chariot (*Merkabah*). [2] Ginzberg in *JE* iii. 465.

A book of fundamental importance for the development of the speculative Kabbalah is the work known as *Bahir* ("Brilliancy"), which apparently was compiled in the thirteenth century in the school of Isaac the Blind. In the style of a Midrash on the first chapters of Genesis, it adopts the method of a dialogue between master and disciples. It develops the doctrine of the Sephiroth of the *Sepher Yetzirah*, only here the ten Sephiroth are different. They are divided into three primary ones—primal light, wisdom, and reason—and seven secondary ones. Here for the first time the doctrine of emanation is clearly enunciated.

The world, according to this book, is not the result of an act of creation *ex nihilo*. "Like God, it existed from all eternity, not only in potentiality but in actuality ; and the Creation consisted merely in the appearance of that which was latent in the first 'Sephirah'[1] . . . which emanated from God. This Sephirah gave birth to 'Hokhmah' ('Wisdom'), from which emanated Binah ('Intelligence'). From these three, which are the superior 'Sephiroth' . . . and form the primary principles of the universe, emanated, one after another, the seven inferior Sephiroth, from which all material things are formed.[2] . . . The ten Sephiroth are the energy of God, the forms in which His being manifests itself."[3]

Other interesting points about the book are its insistence on the doctrine of metempsychosis (by means of which the problem of the suffering righteous is solved), and its enunciation of the doctrine of a celestial trinity There are many parables in the book.

The most important teacher of speculative Kabbalah was a Spaniard, Azriel (1160–1238), who had been trained in philosophy, and was prepared to expound Kabbalistic doctrine in a manner that would appeal to philosophers.

[1] *i.e.* the primal light (אור הגנוז "the hidden light ").
[2] *cp. Pirke de R. Eliezer*, iii., end ("By ten *ma'amaroth* (= Sephiroth) was the world created, which are reduced to three," etc.). [3] *JE* ii. 443.

" Starting from the doctrine of the merely negative attributes of God, as taught by the Jewish philosophy of the time, Azriel calls God the 'En-Soph' (אין־סוף = 'Endless One'), the absolutely Infinite, that can be comprehended only as the negation of all negation. From this definition of the En-Soph, Azriel deduces the potential eternity of the world—the world with all its manifold manifestations was potentially contained within the En-Soph ; and this potentially existing universe became a reality in the act of creation. The transition from the potential to the actual is a free act of God ; but it cannot be called creation, since a 'creatio ex nihilo' is logically unthinkable, and nothing out of which the world could be formed exists outside of God, the En-Soph. Hence it is not correct to say that God creates, but that He irradiates ; for, as the sun irradiates warmth and light without diminishing its bulk, so the En-Soph irradiates the elements of the universe without diminishing His power. These elements of the universe are the Sephiroth, which Azriel tries to define in their relation to the En-Soph as well as to one another."

According to the Kabbalists, Nachmanides was a pupil of Azriel, and, if so, certainly his most important pupil. But this is difficult to accept. For though Nachmanides had pronounced mystical tendencies, as we have seen, yet in his commentary on the Pentateuch he contradicts some of the most fundamental tenets of Azriel's system. Thus he emphasises creation "ex nihilo," and insists that attributes can be assigned to God—a view which is totally irreconcilable with the doctrine of the En-Soph. Yet it is true to say that Nachmanides played an important part in extending the influence of Kabbalistic doctrine. His own tendency towards such doctrine was marked, as was also the case with his most important pupil and successor, Solomon b. Abraham ibn Adret (RaSHBa) (1235–1310), the great Talmudist. A distinguished pupil of Ibn Adret was the famous exegete, Bachya ben Asher of Saragossa (died 1340), whose commentary on the Pentateuch did much to spread Kabbalistic doctrine. Here the method of the Kabbalah (termed by him *the path of light*) is followed (together with that of the Peshat, Midrash, and, to some extent, philosophical exegesis), and occupies a large space. By means of it Bachya sought to penetrate into the deep (esoteric) meaning of Scripture, and to bring hidden truths to light. This work, frequently reprinted, has enjoyed a wide popularity, and many super-commentaries have been written upon it.

Azriel's system was worked out completely in a number of Kabbalistic works of the second half of the thirteenth century which have survived in fragmentary form. Their aim was to systematise the doctrines of the Bahir and of Azriel. One of the most important is a small book known as *Sepher ha-Temunah* ("Book of Form"). Here the attempt is made to illustrate the principle of emanation by means of the forms of the letters of the Hebrew alphabet. The doctrine of the Sephiroth is systematised. They are regarded as powers inhering in the En-Soph, like the limbs in the human body, the entire complex forming one indivisible whole. They are thus penetrated by, and are the organs of, one common will. In this way the problem, which had occupied the Kabbalistic thinkers, as to how the divine will was transmitted to the different Sephiroth, is solved. This book also enunciates, for the first time, the doctrine of double emanation, which becomes henceforth an integral part of the Kabbalistic system, and represents the attempt of the Kabbalists to solve the problem of evil, without falling into the dangers of pantheism. The doctrine imputes a double aspect to the Sephiroth, a positive and a negative. The positive aspect represents the active divine element, which produces all that is good —the energy that is constantly striving for perfection ; while the negative (or passive) aspect corresponds to the finite, and represents the imperfect and limited. Evil is therefore regarded as essentially imperfection, a negative rather than a positive element in the universe.

Another important work belonging to this category is the *Ma'areketh hā-'Elohuth*. Here Azriel's system is presented in its most complete form.

While this speculative mysticism, which was concerned with strictly metaphysical problems—the nature of God and His relation to the world—was being developed (from the end of the twelfth century to the beginning of the fourteenth), another school was working out a system from a different point of view, the religio-ethical, laying all the stress upon the practical side of religion. Both systems were striving to realise the union of the soul with God. The speculative thinkers endeavoured to attain this by constructing a theory of God and the universe essentially monistic in character, while the other school strove to make the union possible and practicable for everyday life.

Two important names may be mentioned in this connexion : Todros Abulafia (1234-1304) and Abraham Abulafia (1240–1291). The former of these, a wealthy and influential Spanish Jew, liberally supported Ḳabbalistic scholars and himself wrote two Ḳabbalistic works, viz. *Sha'ar ha-Razim* ("The Gate of Secrets"), a commentary on Psalm xix., and an important book entitled *'Otzar ha-Kabod* ("The Treasury of Glory"), in which the Haggadoth of the Talmud are interpreted for the first time in a Ḳabbalistic sense. Here quotations from the *Zohar* occur for the first time. More important still was Abraham Abulafia, also of Spanish birth, who at the age of twenty began a life of ceaseless wandering. He went to Palestine, then to Italy, and returned to Spain, where he became subject to visions, and took up the study of the *Sepher Yetzirah* and its numerous commentaries. This study and the influence of Eleazar of Worms greatly affected him. He devoted himself to the mystical study of the letters of the alphabet, numerals, vowel-points and accents, and especially to the letters of the Divine Name (the Tetragrammaton). With the aid of these symbols, combined with the practice of ascetic rites, men could, he declared, attain the heights of the mystical life. He produced a book called *Sepher ha-Yashar* ("Book of the Righteous"), and wrote other works. At one time he gave himself out as a prophet and Messiah, and created much excitement among the Jewish masses. He abandoned speculative Ḳabbalah for " prophetical," maintaining that the former was an inferior degree of knowledge. "The highest goal is prophetism, assuring men a certain degree of community with God," and the means are the close study of the names of God, especially of the Tetragrammaton. He also employed in different ways for mystical purposes letter-symbolism. He introduced into Jewish Ḳabbalah a Trinitarian doctrine and desired, apparently, to win Christians to the Ḳabbalistic faith.

The two movements converged in the *Zohar*, the most important literary production of Jewish mysticism, which became the holy book of the Jewish Ḳabbalists. The name *Zohar*, which means " Brightness," is derived from Daniel xii. 3: *And they that be wise shall shine brightly as the brightness (yazhîru kĕzōhar) of the firmament.* Written partly in Aramaic and partly in Hebrew, it is in form a commentary on the Pentateuch, but in reality is a compendium of Ḳabbalistic theosophy. It belongs to the large class of pseudepigraphic writings purporting to be the record of a divine revelation made to R. Simeon b. Yochai (second century A.D.), who is represented as imparting this in a series of utterances to his disciples. In reality it is a composite work, drawn from many sources (some old), and was published in practically its present shape by Moses ben Shem Tob de Leon (1250 1305).

Moses de Leon lived in various parts of Spain. The question as to how far he was responsible for the present form of the *Zohar* has been much debated. That he "forged" the work cannot be proved, but that he had a considerable share in reducing it to its present shape is probable. In doing this he worked on older materials, and, like other pseudepigraphic writers, he may have regarded himself simply as an instrument for reducing to written form what had long been transmitted as a series of traditions.

This estimate is borne out by the character of the work, which is heterogeneous and can hardly be the production, in any valid sense, of a single author.

Distinct writings, too, are referred to in the work, and actually quoted. These are (*a*) *'Idra rabba* ; (*b*) *'Idra ẓuta* ; (*c*) *Matnitin* ; (*d*) *Midrash ha-ne'elam* ; (*e*) *Ra'aya Mehemna* ; (*f*) *Saba* ; (*g*) *Raze de-Razin* ; (*h*) *Sepher Hekaloth* ; (*i*) *Sifra de-Zenicutha* ; (*j*) *Sitre Torah* ; (*k*) *Tosephta* ; (*l*) *Yanuḳa*.[1]

Dr. Broyde,[2] commenting on these features, says : " The contents of the Zohar clearly indicate that the work is the production, not of a single author or of a single period, but of many authors, periods, and civilisations ; for it contains the most puzzling incongruities and irreconcilable contradictions, with lofty ideas and conceptions . . . and also mystic teachings of the Talmudic period with those of the Geonim and later Cabala." He calls attention to a passage (*Zohar* iii. 9*b*) which says :

" In the book of Hamnuna the elder we learn through some extended explanations that the earth turns upon itself in the form of a circle ; that some are on top, the others below ; that the creatures change in aspect, following the manner of each place, but keeping in the same position. But there are some countries on the earth which are lighted, while others are in darkness ; and there are others in which there is constantly day, or in which at least the night continues only some instants. . . . These secrets were made known to the men of the secret science, but not to the geographers."

Dr. Broyde points out that till the time of Copernicus the theory that the earth revolves on its own axis and is a sphere was only known to ancient Hindu philosophy, and later, outside the place of its origin, in Persia in the eighth century, where under its influence many mystic sects, including that of the Sufis, were founded. This movement undoubtedly influenced the Jews of Persia, among whom were some curious sects, and he suggests that the secret writings preserved among these sects " probably formed the nucleus of the *Zohar*. . . . In

---

[1] See further below, p. 251.
[2] Art. "Zohar" in *JE* xii. 691.

its peregrinations from Persia to Spain the Zohar probably received many additions and interpolations, among which may have been the various names of the Tannaim and Amoraim, as well as the allusions to historical events." Whatever truth there may or may not be in this theory, Persia doubtless offered a congenial home for Kabbalistic ideas. To this day Simeon b. Yochai is the greatest figure among the Rabbis to the Jews of Persia.

The Zohar, as has been remarked already, sums up the Kabbalistic ideas that had been developed up to the time of its appearance. It became not only the text-book of Kabbalistic doctrine, but the canonical book of the Kabbalists. To expound its doctrines, which do not form a coherent system, but are a blending of ideas which do not always harmonise, would require a treatise by itself.[1] It will only be possible here to glance at one or two important points in passing. The doctrine of the ten Sephiroth is throughout assumed as axiomatic As in all mystical thought, the soul occupies a dominant place in the theology of the *Zohar*, and the ideas concerning it (*e.g.* its constitution as a trinity) reflect the influence of the Platonic psychology. The doctrine of soul-transmigration also is taught.

"In the minds of the Kabbalists, transmigration is a necessity not alone on the grounds of their particular theology —the soul must reach the highest stage of its evolution before it can be received again into the eternal home—but on moral grounds as well. It is a vindication of divine justice to mankind."[2]

The doctrine of the four worlds also plays an important part in the Zoharistic system. These are (*a*) the 'Azilutic world (or world of emanation), which contains the Sephiroth; (*b*) the Beriatic world (or

[1] See an excellent summary by Ginzberg in *JE* iii. 471–479.
[2] Abelson, *Jewish Mysticism*, p. 164 f.

world of creative ideas), which contains the souls of the pious, the divine throne, and the divine halls ; (*c*) the Yeẓiratic world (or the world of creative formations), which is the abode of the ten classes of angels with their chiefs, presided over by Metatron, who was changed into fire ; (*d*) the 'Asiyyatic world (or world of creative matter), in which are the Ophannim, the angels that receive the prayers and control the actions of men, and wage war against Sammael, the embodiment of evil. There seems to be no doubt that these worlds were at first conceived realistically, but were later interpreted in an idealistic sense.

On its ethical side the Ḳabbalah teaches that love is the highest relation of the soul to God, transcending knowledge and will. Ethics is, indeed, part of religion to the Ḳabbalists.

·" The connexion between the real and ideal world is brought about by man, whose soul belongs to heaven, while his body is earthy. Man connects the two worlds by means of his love to God, which . . . unites him with God. The knowledge of the law in its ethical as well as religious aspects is also a means towards influencing the higher regions ; for the study of the law means the union of man with the divine wisdom. . . . The ritual also has a deeper mystical meaning, as it serves to preserve the universe and to secure blessings for it." [1]

It should be added that the *Zohar* has certain appendices which are attributed to its reputed author, or to some of his immediate disciples, and without which it would be incomplete.

These are (*a*) *Sifra di ẓeni 'utha* (five chapters), in which are discussed questions relating to Creation, such as the transition from the infinite to the finite, etc.; (*b*) *Idra rabba*, developing and enlarging the preceding ; (*c*) *Idra zuṭa*, a *résumé* of the two preceding. In these sections the term " En-Soph " is not applied to God—a mark of early origin. To these larger appendices are added the following fragments : (*d*) *Raze de Razin*, dealing with the connexion of the soul with the body, etc.; (*e*) *Sepher Hekaloth*, treating of the seven heavenly halls,

---

[1] Ginzberg, *op. cit. ibid.*

Paradise and Hell; (*f*) *Ra'ya mehemna*, containing a conversation between Moses, Elijah, and Simeon ben Yochai on the allegorical significance of the Mosaic commandments and the Rabbinical injunctions; (*g*) *Sitre Torah*, dealing with a variety of Kabbalistic topics; (*h*) *Midrash ha-ne'elam*, giving mystical explanations of various passages of Scripture; (*i*) *Saba* (="Old Age"), containing a conversation between the prophet Elijah and Simeon ben Yochai on the doctrine of metempsychosis (transmigration of souls); (*j*) *Yanuka* (= "child"), written in the name of a child of Hamnuna Saba (hence the title), giving injunctions about the importance of ritual washing of the hands before meals; (*k*) *Tosephta* and (*l*) *Mathnithin*, sketching the doctrines connected with emanation (the Sephiroth), etc.

Besides the *Zohar* proper, there is a *Zohar Chadash* (= "New Zohar") on Canticles, and a series of *Tikkunim* in the style of the original work.

As has already been pointed out, the *Zohar* is in form a commentary on the Pentateuch. In this connexion it is interesting to note that four types of exegesis are admitted in the commentation, or, at any rate, four distinct methods of interpretation, viz. *Peshat*, *Remez* (= "allusion," typological sense, allegory), *Derash*, and *Sod* (= "secret," esoteric or mystical sense), the initials of these four terms making *Pardes* = "Paradise." It is possible that the Christian mode of exegesis, which was well known to the Spanish Jews, may have influenced the method of the *Zohar*. The Christian method interpreted Scripture in a fourfold sense, viz. the historical or literal, the tropological or moral, the allegorical, and the anagogical.[1]

The publication of the *Zohar* took place probably in the opening years of the fourteenth century. It soon gained wide recognition, though not without some opposition, and Kabbalistic study grew. A great impetus was given to the spread of the doctrine when the expulsion of the Jews from Spain took place at the end of the fifteenth century (1492). The national misfortune stimulated such studies which

[1] This method had long before been formulated, by the Venerable Bede in the eighth, and by Rhabanus Maurus in the ninth, century.

held out to their votaries the hope of discovering, by their means, a way of deliverance from the national suffering. Kabbalists were active in Palestine and Egypt and elsewhere. Solomon Alkabiz (author of the Sabbath hymn, still sung every week in the synagogues, "Come, my Beloved, to meet the Sabbath") was a well-known Kabbalist who flourished at Safed, in Palestine, in the sixteenth century. Safed, in fact, became a centre for the movement. Even Joseph Karo, the famous Talmudist and codifier of the *Shulchan Aruk*, who died at Safed in 1575, though not a Kabbalist in the strict sense, was influenced by Kabbalistic ideas. He, in conjunction with Alkabiz, gathered around him a circle which endeavoured by stringent ascetic practices to induce a state of ecstasy in which they hoped to receive heavenly revelations and to behold visions of angels. A pupil of these two leaders, Moses ben Jacob of Cordovero (1522–70), was a famous Kabbalist, and is generally regarded as the best representative of the early Kabbalah, and, next to Azriel, the most important speculative thinker produced by the school. He wrote a well-known work called "The Garden" (*ha-Pardes*).

A new and important development in Kabbalah was initiated by Isaac Luria (1533–72). Luria introduced the doctrine that all that exists is composed of substance and appearance. According to this extremely subjective view, there is no such thing as objective cognition. With the spread of the doctrines of this school a good deal of superstitious practice went hand in hand, such as the writing of amulets, conjuration of devils, the use of mystic numbers and letters for certain purposes.

Prominent among Luria's pupils were Chayim Vital and Israel Saruk, who were great propagandists of the new doctrine. As a result a considerable Kabbalistic school grew up in Italy in the sixteenth century, and traces of its influence still remain there. But it was also attacked by Italian scholars.

Vital's son, Samuel Vital Chayim, together with Abraham Azulai, did much to spread Luria's Kabbalistic doctrine. They introduced an ascetic mode of life (mystical meditations on prayer, vigils, frequent ritual bathings, and penance), which had a noble side in the emphasis laid on a pure life, philanthropy, the practice of brotherly love and kindness.

Finally, in the eighteenth century there grew up among the Jews of Poland a remarkable movement known as "Chassidism," which, though accompanied by a good deal of superstition, was essentially a religious protest against a hard and lifeless Rabbinical formalism.

The Jewish Kabbalah also exercised a considerable influence in the Christian world. Through Reuchlin (1455–1522) it helped to leaven religious movements at the time of the Reformation, and was diligently studied by Christian scholars during the sixteenth and seventeenth centuries. It is worth noting in this connexion that a remarkable approximation to the Christian tenets regarding the fall of man developed in the Kabbalistic literature that grew up after the publication of the *Zohar*. Starting from the ancient idea of Adam's original corporeal and spiritual excellence, the later Kabbalists propounded the view that originally all souls were combined in him. It was this archetypal man whose whole nature was poisoned by the venom of the serpent, and with him all Nature, which then became susceptible to the powers of evil. Human nature was darkened, and man received a corporeal body which was weakened and deprived of its original excellence. His whole nature sank to a lower plane, and, at the same time, the 'Asiyyatic world, of which man had been lord and master, was contracted and coarsened. Even the higher worlds were affected in a similar manner. In this way the Kabbalists explain the presence of physical and moral evil in the world. Here again the Kabbalists were only developing and elaborating ancient doctrine. Thus the sin of Adam, as affecting the destinies of the whole human race, is emphasised in early Jewish apocalyptic (2 Esdras), as well as in early Christian, literature.

Various judgements have been passed upon the Jewish Kabbalah doctrines and literature. Some of their most severe critics are, and have been in the past, Jewish scholars who by temperament and training were naturally antipathetic to any forms of mystical thought. The unlovely features of the whole literature have been seized upon—its weird and fantastic ideas, its irrationalism, and its super-stitious elements—in order to discredit the whole. But this, as Dr. Abelson remarks, "is really an unfair criticism, seeing that it leaves totally out of account the preponderating mass of true poetry and spirituality which inhere in all parts of Jewish mystical speculation. . . . Nowhere in Jewish literature is the idea of prayer raised to such a pitch of sublimity as it is in the lives and writings of the Jewish mystics. If it is true to say that Judaism here and there suffers from too large an element of formalism and legalism and externalism, it is equally true to say that many of these drawbacks are corrected, toned down by the contributions of mysticism."[1] Some of the most exquisite prayers and liturgical poems of the synagogue Liturgy are the productions of the Kabbalists. By their sheer beauty and devotional power they have won their way into practically universal use in the synagogue.

IV

PHILOSOPHY AND ETHICS

[LITERATURE: Dr. Philipp Bloch, *Die jüdische Religions-philosophie* (in Winter und Wünsche, ii. pp. 699–793); Isaac Husik, *A History of Mediæval Jewish Philosophy* (Jewish Publication Society of America); the article "Philosophy" (Jewish) in Hastings's *Dictionary of Religion and Ethics*, and the relevant articles, under the personal names, in *JE*; and for Judah ha-Levi's *Kitab al Khazari*, the edition (English translation, with a valuable introduction) by Dr. H. Hirschfeld

---

[1] *Jewish Mysticism*, p. 12.

(London, 1905) ; the article "Ethics" in *JE* v. 245 ff.; on Bachya, the article in *JE* ii. 446 f.; Bachya's *Duties of the Heart*, English translation by E. Collins (London, 1903) ; J. H. Hertz (now Chief Rabbi), *Bachya, The Jewish Thomas à Kempis* (1898) ; *cp.* also I. Abrahams, *Short History of Jewish Literature*, chap. xix.]

"The Jewish religion," says Dr. Hirschfeld, "is, by its nature, opposed to philosophic pursuits and metaphysical speculation in particular. Yet, in spite of this, mediæval Jewish literature has a chapter on religious philosophy which is as extensive as it is profound." [1] The causes which led to this remarkable development are to be traced, as Dr. Hirschfeld suggests, to the fact that the Jews who were living under Moslim rule were brought into contact with the movement which stimulated the scientific spirit, and resulted in the eager pursuit of such sciences as astronomy, mathematics, and medicine. A further cause was the influence of Moslim theology, which, owing to a variety of conflicting factors, had developed a metaphysical side ; and this reacted on Judaism.

The Arab philosophy became systematic only when Greek philosophical thought, represented by Plato and Aristotle, had been made accessible in Arabic to the Mohammedan theologians. "Philosophy, called to the aid of religion, produced the aid of *Kalam* (speculative theology), and a class of theologians who styled themselves *Mutakallims*. The latter found themselves compelled to supplement the teaching of the Koran by philosophic demonstrations of the existence of God, His attributes and character as Creator and Governor of the universe.'

The first to apply to Jewish theology the philosophical methods of the Arabs was Saadya (892–942), to whom reference has already been made in a former section. Brilliantly gifted, Saadya excelled

[1] Introduction to ha-Levi's *Khazari*, p. 1.
[2] Hirschfeld, *ut cit. supra.*

in culture all his Jewish contemporaries. At the age of thirty-six (in 928) this Egyptian Jew was summoned to preside as Gaon over the famous Academy of Sura, in Babylonia. He was the great protagonist for Rabbinical Judaism against its mortal foes, the Karaites. The latter appealed to the text of the Bible to justify their rejection of the Rabbinical positions. Saadya determined, therefore, to make the Bible accessible in the vernacular (Arabic), and so produced his Arabic translation of the Scriptures, adding notes. This version won immediate favour, and displaced, in the synagogues, the old Aramaic Targum, which had hitherto been read with the original Hebrew. Saadya's version, thus publicly read, became a potent factor in impregnating the Jewish spirit with Arabic culture.

Saadya may be regarded as the creator of a Jewish philosophy of religion. His great work in this department, completed in 933, was written in Arabic, *Kitab al-Amanat wal-I'tikadab* (" Book of Creeds and Doctrines ").[1]

This is the first systematic treatment on a philosophic foundation of the doctrines of Judaism. Saadya modelled his method on the Mutazillite *Kalam*. The first two sections deal with the metaphysical problems of the creation of the world (1), and the unity of the Creator (2). In the succeeding sections the following themes are treated of : The Jewish theory of revelation (3), doctrines of faith concerning the divine justice (4), and those concerned with merit and demerit (5). Then follow sections on the soul and death (6), the resurrection of the dead (7), which, according to the author, is closely connected with the theory of the Messianic redemption (8). A concluding section (9) deals with the rewards and punishments of the future life. An appendix (10) follows on the importance of moral conduct based on right belief. This last section is really a system of ethics.

---

[1] Better known under the Hebrew title ספר אמונות ודעות, the title given to the Hebrew translation by Judah ibn Tibbon. Another Hebrew version is cited at length in *The Ethical Treatises of Berachya*, ed. by H. Gollancz (1902).

Saadya also wrote an Arabic translation of, and commentary[1] on, the mystical book *Sepher Yetzirah*, which he regarded as a genuine work of the patriarch Abraham. In this work he is not influenced by the speculative theology of the *Kalam*. Here, while regarding this (as he thought) venerable work as interesting and worthy of deep study, he evidently did not look upon it as a source for the theory of Judaism. He also wrote numerous other works in Hebrew and Arabic (on philological and Halakic questions), and compiled a *Siddur* or Hebrew Prayer Book (with explanations in Arabic), and composed liturgical poems (in Hebrew).

A contemporary of Saadya, who cites him, though himself not referred to by Saadya, is the Karaite *Al-Kirkisani*, whose work (in a fragmentary condition) has recently been made available for scholars.[2] Kirkisani was apparently well versed not only in the study of the Bible and the works of the older Karaite teachers, as well as the *Kalam*, but was also acquainted with the Mishnah and Talmud and the Rabbinical Prayer Book. He was also familiar with the tenets of the Aristotelian philosophy and with the beliefs of Christians, Samaritans, and Moslims. He seems to have written a number of works (only fragments of which survive), the principal bearing the title *Book of Lights and Lighthouses*, a sort of encyclopædia with nearly 500 chapters, dealing with a variety of subjects, historical, philosophical, polemical, exegetical, ritual, and legal. He also wrote commentaries on various books of the Bible, and a treatise on the unity of God. Specimens of his philosophical treatment are given by Dr. Hirschfeld, who shows[3] that he deals

[1] Arabic title *Tafsir Kitab al Mabadi*. It has been edited with a French translation by Lambert (Paris, 1891). A Hebrew translation exists in MS.

[2] By Dr. Hirschfeld, *Qirqisani Studies* (Jews' College Publications, No. 6, London, 1918). [3] *op. cit.* p. 19.

with "the principal doctrines which one would seek in a Jewish philosophy of religion."

These are "the existence of God, His unity and eternity, the refutation of the eternity of time and matter, and the divine attributes of the Creator of the world and His omnipotence. The Biblical anthropomorphisms are discussed by the author in Mutazzilite style later on in one of the canons of exegesis. Human free-will is alluded to in a passing remark. Although all this is gained by direct deductions from Biblical passages, the author shows himself a true follower of the Mutazzilite Kalam, in which the doctrine of human free-will occupies a prominent position. His whole attitude in regarding reason as the mainspring of metaphysical as well as of physical knowledge is Mutazzilite. In his doctrine of human free-will he is entirely in accord with Saadya, and even uses the same term to express it."

Saadya had not been dead much more than a generation when there arose in the East "the greatest philosophic genius the Mohammedan world had produced," the famous Ibn Sina (Avicenna) (980–1037). His writings, which were brought to Spain about a century after their publication, exercised considerable influence over Jewish thought in the Middle Ages.

A Latin translation of his philosophical work *Al-Shefa* ("Healing") was prepared with the aid of Jewish interpreters, and frequently used by Jewish writers. Another smaller work, entitled *The Healing of the Soul*, was translated in the fourteenth century. Of his medical treatises, the chief, called *The Canon*—a colossal work—was for centuries used in its Latin form as a text-book in European universities. Avicenna was a great master of logic and metaphysics. A thorough Aristotelian, he taught that matter, "the principle of individuation, does not directly emanate from the Godhead, although it is, in its primal origin, eternal, and includes within itself all possibilities of development. . . . The first and only immediate product of God . . . is the world-soul or world-intelligence, which unwinds an endless chain of creation throughout all the celestial spheres down to the earth. The cause that produces, however, must also conserve, for cause and effect are identical; from which it follows that the world itself, like God, must be eternal." [1] His theory, however, is not completely consistent. It seems that his Neoplatonic view of evolution gradually led him to mysticism.

---

[1] *JE* ii. 351 (article "Avicenna").

Avicenna's reputation was so high that his writings were eagerly studied by Jews.

The outstanding name among the Jewish Neo-platonic philosophers is that of Solomon ibn Gebirol (1021–58 or 1070), famous also as a poet.[1] He had much to do with the diffusion of Neoplatonism in Europe, his works enjoying a wide popularity in Latin among Christians. His main philosophic work, the Arabic original of which is lost, has survived partly in a Hebrew translation with the title *Mekôr chayyim* ("Fount of Life"), but as a whole exists only in the twelfth-century Latin translation *Fons Vitæ*. The author is here styled "Avicebron," who was supposed to be a Christian scholastic till in 1848 Solomon Munk established his true identity.

In this work Gebirol treats philosophic problems without any pronounced theological preconceptions. In a similar way Isaac Israeli (died 953), a famous physician, and the first known philosophic writer of the Arab period among the Jews, treated philosophic questions apart from theology. He was also a Neoplatonist.

Though the *Fons Vitæ* influenced the Jewish Ḳabbalah, especially in its theory of emanations, it did not exercise any marked effect upon Jewish scholastic development, and, in fact, was more influential among Christian than Jewish philosophers.

A collection of moral maxims known as *The Choice of Pearls*,[2] which was a favourite ethical handbook in the Middle Ages, is also attributed to Gebirol's authorship, but this is doubtful. A more important and highly original ethical treatise, which is probably the work of Gebirol, and was written at Saragossa about the year 1045, is the treatise entitled *The Improvement of Moral Qualities* (ed. in Arabic and English by S. S. Wise, New York, 1901). On this see *JE* vi. 529.

A highly popular ethical treatise, which in its Hebrew form has gone through about fifty editions, was produced by Bachya ibn Paḳuda of Saragossa

---

[1] Gebirol was a Spanish Jew. From this time Spain was the chief seat of Arab culture among the Jews.
[2] English translation by B. H. Asher (London, 1859).

(about 1050–1100). This is known from the title of the Hebrew translation produced by Judah ibn Tibbon (1167) as *The Duties of the Heart* (*Choboth ha-Lebaboth*).[1]

Bachya is an original thinker of high rank, well acquainted with the entire philosophical and scientific literature of the Arabs, as well as that of Jewish writers. He was also a man of deep personal piety as well as a philosopher, and is moved by deep religious feeling. The influence of Neoplatonic ideas and Sufi mysticism is apparent in the book, though these elements are never allowed to cloud the clear enunciation of a pure Jewish monotheism. *The Duties of the Heart* represents an attempt "to present the Jewish faith as being essentially a great spiritual truth founded on Reason, Revelation (the written Law), and Tradition, all stress being at the same time laid on the willingness and the joyful readiness of the God-loving heart to perform life's duties."[2] Though not formally a metaphysical treatise, the work contains a compendium of religious philosophy.[3]

Neoplatonic doctrines were also diffused by the translation into Hebrew of non-Jewish writings of this school of thought. In some cases such works have survived only in the Hebrew translation.

About this time (the latter half of the eleventh century) a reaction against extreme Aristotelian teachings, which had been growing among the Mohammedans, came to a head in the writings of the great Arab philosopher and theologian Al-Ghazali (born in Khorasan 1058, died there 1111). His most important works are *The Aims of Philosophers*, *The Destruction of Philosophy*, and *The Revival of the Science of Religion*. His writings exercised considerable influence over Jews, especially in the form of Hebrew translations.[4]

[1] The original Arabic text, under the title *Al-hidâja' ilâ farâ' id al-qulûb*, has been edited, with an introduction, by A. S. Yahuda (Leyden, 1912). For an English version, *cp.* p. 255 above. [2] *JE* ii. 447 (article " Bahya ").
[3] See the full exposition of Bachya's system in *JE* ii. 447–454.
[4] These translations began to be made as early as the thirteenth century.

The famous Judah ha-Levi,[1] though most eminent as a poet, also did important work in the domain of philosophy. He occupied much the same position in Jewish religious philosophy as that occupied by Al-Ghazali in Islam. Indeed, he seems to have been influenced by the latter. His views are expounded in the well-known apologetic work, written originally in Arabic, but circulating also in the form of a Hebrew translation by Judah ibn Tibbon, the *Kitab al-Khazari.* (Best edition, Arabic original and Hebrew translation, by H. Hirschfeld, Leipzig, 1887 ; for English translation, *cp.* p. 254 above.)

This famous apology for Judaism is cast in the form of a dialogue between the pagan king of the Chazars and a Jew who had been summoned to instruct him in the tenets of the Jewish religion.

The main principle of the treatise is to show that revealed religion is superior to natural religion ; in other words, revelation, not speculative philosophy, is the only trustworthy guide to a real knowledge of God. He defends the Jewish Scriptural doctrine of Creation ("ex nihilo") against the Aristotelian view of the eternity of matter. Judah also discusses the questions relative to the attributes of God and anthropomorphism.

The apologetic character of the book is revealed in the second Arabic title, which runs : *Book of Argument and Demonstration in Aid of the Despised Faith.* It is essentially not only a defence of revealed religion against philosophy, but a defence of traditional Judaism against assailants such as the Karaites. A considerable portion of the third part is devoted to a vindication of the Talmud. It was translated into Hebrew not more than thirty years after its publication by Judah ibn Tibbon, and again later, and many commentaries have been written on it.

In the first half of the twelfth century Neoplatonic philosophy among the Jews was represented by Abraham bar Chiyya ha-Nasi ("Abraham Judæus"), often called "Savasorda." An eminent mathematician and astronomer, he also wrote on ethics and philosophy.

[1] Born at Toledo about 1085, died in the East after 1140 (*cp.* p. 34).

262 RABBINICAL AND MEDIÆVAL JUDAISM

A profoundly religious and ethical work of his (written in Hebrew) is *Meditation of the Soul* (*Hegyōn ha-nephesh*). In philosophy he followed Ibn Gebirol, maintaining the Neoplatonic view that "matter, being void of all reality, requires form to give it existence. Now the union of these two by the will of God, which brings them from a state of potentiality into one of actuality, is creation, time itself being simultaneously produced with the created things." [1]

To this school of philosophic thought belong also the poet Moses ibn Ezra of Granada (died 1139), the author of a treatise in Arabic called *The Garden* (of which only fragments have survived); his contemporary, Joseph ibn Zaddik of Cordova (died 1149), author of a Neoplatonic work which has been preserved only in a Hebrew translation called *Microcosm* (*'ôlam ḳāṭān*); and the famous Bible commentator Abraham ibn Ezra (about 1100–1167).

Strict Aristotelianism was revived in Jewish philosophy in the second half of the twelfth century by Abraham ibn Daud ha-Levi (RABaD I.) of Toledo (1110–80), who was also an astronomer and historian. His philosophical work, *The Sublime Faith*, written in Arabic, has been preserved in two Hebrew translations.

Though not an original thinker, he is important as being "the first to introduce that phase of philosophy which is generally attributed to Maimonides, and which differs from former systems of philosophy mainly in its more thorough systematic form derived from Aristotle." [2] He considered the Arabic commentators Alfarabi and Ibn Sina (Avicenna) to be the only true philosophers, and he constantly attacks Gebirol, who represented Neoplatonic views. True philosophy, according to Ibn Daud, is an aid to revealed religion—where they seem to contradict one another a mode of reconciling them can be found. He was, however, unable to reconcile the Aristotelian doctrine of the eternity of matter with the Biblical view of Creation, which implies *creatio ex nihilo*. His doctrine of

---

[1] *JE* i. 109 (*s.v.* ' Abraham bar Ḥiyya" ; see the whole article).

[2] *JE* i. 101 (*s,v.* "Abraham ibn Daud").

God is interesting. God, as being the Prime Mover of all motion, is Himself motionless, and, being infinite, must be absolutely One and Unique. He also discusses the problems of human free-will and predestination.

An important Arabian philosopher, who exercised considerable influence on Jewish philosophy, and belongs to the twelfth century, must be mentioned in this connexion. This was Averroes, or, to give him his Arabic name, Abul Walid Muhammed ibn Ahmad ibn Roshd of Cordova (1126–98). Like Avicenna, Averroes wrote an original compendium of the Aristotelian philosophy, and also the so-called " Middle Commentaries " (which follow the text), and other works. His writings were greatly admired in Jewish circles, and owe their preservation (either in Hebrew translations or Hebrew transliterations of the Arabic text) to this fact. In Mohammedan circles they were extensively condemned. His writings were familiar to Maimonides, who, however, cannot be called his disciple, though often in agreement with him. Some of his other original works also influenced Jewish writers. One on *The Relation of Faith to Knowledge* is extant in an anonymous Hebrew translation (dated 1340), and another has the title *The Book of the Revelation of the Method of Proof touching the Principles of Religion*. Both were known to Kolonymus ben Kalonymus and Simon Duran in 1423. More famous is his reply to Ghazali's attack on the philosophers. Averroes called his reply *A Confutation of the Confutation*. Kalonymus, the son of David ben Todros, translated it into Hebrew in 1328.[1] The influence of Averroes was all-powerful in the fourteenth century, but after that rapidly declined. Levi ben Gerson and Moses

---

[1] This Hebrew translation was rendered into Latin by a Neapolitan physician, also named Kalonymus (ben David), and published in Venice in 1327.

Narboni may be regarded as followers of his philosophy.

As has been pointed out, Averroes was much studied in Jewish circles ; Maimonides frequently refers to him, often to differ from his positions. Many commentaries on, and translations of, his writings were made later in Hebrew ; and a number of original writings in Hebrew were inspired by his works. The first to introduce his philosophy to Jewish literature was Samuel ibn Tibbon (the translator of Maimonides' *Guide*), who published at the beginning of the thirteenth century an *Encyclopædia of Philosophy* which mainly consists of extracts from Averroes. Translations (into Hebrew) of his works appeared in 1232, 1260, 1284, and 1298. A new series appeared in the first half of the fourteenth century, and the second half of that century, which may be regarded as "the golden age of Averroism among the Jews," witnessed the production of many original treatises, inspired by the study of Averroes, among the Jews. Levi ben Gerson (Gersonides) and Moses of Narbonne (Messer Vidal) are especially prominent in this connexion. Mention may also be made here of the ethical and rhetorical work by Jedayah Penini (1261–1321) entitled *Bechinath 'Olam* ("Examination of the World") and his *'Iggereth ha-Hithnatzeluth* ("Letter on Self-exculpation"), defending philosophy against the attack of Solomon b. Adret, and the commentaries of Joseph Caspi on Maimonides' *Guide* —all influenced by Averroes.

The greatest Jewish philosopher of the Middle Ages, Moses ben Maimun, commonly called " Maimonides " (1135–1204), was a younger contemporary both of Averroes and Abraham ibn Daud, the latter of whom he frequently follows. Maimonides, starting with the fundamental conviction that reason, being a gift of God, cannot be irreconcilable with religion, or contradict it, sought to show that the highest form of philosophy, which he identified with the teachings of Aristotle, could be harmonised with those of Judaism.

This attempt is made in his great work *The Guide of the Perplexed* (written in Arabic about 1190, and subsequently translated into Hebrew more than once). The book is divided into two parts, the first of which deals with the apparent contradictions between Aristotle and the Bible, Maimonides attempting to show that this is due only to a literal interpretation of the latter. When the anthropomorphic language is properly explained, these, he contends, disappear. In this connexion he discusses the divine attributes. " Maimonides does not admit any positive attributes in the description of God, except those referring to God's actions. God's essence can be described only negatively." [1] The first part concludes with a history of the *Kalam*, and a criticism of its methods and teachings. This is a valuable source—till recent times the main source—of knowledge of the subject.

In the second part the principal problems of philosophy— *creatio ex nihilo*, the unity and incorporeality of God—and the nature of prophecy are discussed ; while the third part is devoted to questions of a more theological nature, such as the origin of evil, the extent of divine providence, and the meaning and purpose of the divine law. " Maimonides identifies religion, as expressed in the divine precepts of the Pentateuch, with ethics and tries to show that the precepts, if properly understood, have a moral purpose." [2]

Maimonides' works were widely studied in Christian circles, and exercised great influence on the scholastic writers, especially Albertus Magnus and Aquinas.

The best edition of the *Guide* is that of Dr. M. Friedländer, in 3 vols. (London, 1881-85). A useful conspectus is given in the volume on *Maimonides* by David Yellin and Israel Abrahams (London, Macmillan, 1903).

Maimonides' disciple and "spiritual son," Joseph ben Judah ibn Aknin (1160-1226), wrote on philosophical problems, but the controversy which arose after Maimonides' death led to a decline of philosophic studies in Jewish circles during the thirteenth century.[3]

Ibn Aknin was the author of a treatise which discussed (a) the nature of the Absolute, (b) the derivation of all things from the Absolute, and (c) *creatio ex nihilo*. This was written in Arabic, but has survived only in a Hebrew translation.

Jewish writers who dealt with philosophic problems were not wanting in the thirteenth century ; but for the most part their

[1] Malter in Hastings's *Dictionary of Religion and Ethics*, vol. ix., p. 876. [2] Malter, *op. cit. ibid.*
[3] *cp.* Graetz, *History of the Jews* (E.T.), iii. 522-545 and 623 ff.

work is destitute of originality, merely repeating what had been said already, taking the form of commentaries or compendiums. Translations of foreign works into Hebrew were also made. In this connexion the following may be mentioned : Shem Tob Palquera (1225–90) ; the Italian physician Hillel ben Samuel (1220–90), the translator into Hebrew of several works, among others of the *Liber de causis* (from the Latin text) ; .Isaac Alhalag, of South France (second half of thirteenth century), who tried to harmonise the Biblical account of Creation with the Aristotelian tenet of the eternity of matter ; and Joseph ibn Caspi of Argentière (1297–1340), who was a prolific writer.

With the dawn of the fourteenth century Jewish peripatetic philosophy was revived and given its most pronounced form by the famous Levi ben Gershon (RaLBaG), commonly called "Gersonides," who is also known as "Leon de Bagnols," and, in Latin, as "Magister Leo Hebræus" (1288–1344). Gershon, who was exegete, mathematician, and physician, as well as philosopher, began to write the philosophical work which brought him so much renown—the *Milchamôth 'Adonai* ("The Battles of the Lord")—when he was not yet thirty years of age. He wrote numerous philosophic commentaries on the Bible, on the works of Averroes, and on parts of the Talmud, as well as treatises on mathematics, astronomy, and medicine.

The following important works of Gershon were finished by 1321 (when he was thirty-three) : The *Milchamoth 'Adonai* (begun 1317), commentaries on the Pentateuch, on the earlier Prophets, on Daniel, on Proverbs, on Canticles, Esther, Ecclesiastes, and Ruth, a treatise on syllogisms (*Sepher Hekkesh ha-Yashar*), and a commentary on the Middle Commentaries and *résumés* of Averroes (part of this commentary was translated into Latin by Jacob Mantino and published in the first volume of the works of Aristotle with the commentaries of Averroes).

Levi ben Gershon occupies a unique position in the history of Jewish philosophy. "Of all the Jewish peripatetics he alone dared to vindicate the Aristotelian position in its integrity, regardless of the conflict existing between some of its doctrines and the principal dogmas of Judaism. Possessed of a highly developed critical sense, Levi sometimes disagrees with Aristotle and asserts his own views in opposition to those of his master Averroes ; but when, after having weighed the *pros* and *cons* of a doctrine, he believes it to be sound, he is not afraid to profess it, even when it is directly at variance with an accepted dogma of Jewish theology. ' The Law,' he says, ' cannot prevent us from considering to be true that which our reason urges us to believe.' "[1]

In his treatment of philosophical questions Gershon adopts the method of Aristotle. Before giving his own solutions, he subjects the opinions of his predecessors to a critical review. In his *Milchamôth 'Adonai* he discusses the nature of the soul, its relation to the intellect, the question " Is prophecy possible ? " the nature of prophecy, God's omniscience, Divine Providence, astronomy, physics, and metaphysics, Creation and miracles. Some of his philosophical theories influenced Spinoza.

Another interesting name in this connexion is that of Moses ben Joshua of Narbonne (sometimes called Moses Narboni), surnamed " Maestro Vidal Blasom " (born at end of thirteenth century, died after 1362). He studied and practised medicine with great success, and was well versed in Biblical and Rabbinical literature ; but his main activities were devoted to philosophy, and especially to the works of Averroes, of whom he was an enthusiastic admirer. He wrote (in Hebrew) valuable commentaries on the latter's works, as well as on those of Avicenna, Ghazali, Ibn Tufail, and Maimonides.

The reaction against the extreme philosophical positions of Gersonides and Maimonides was marked by the appearance of a profound philosophical work

[1] Broydé in *JE* viii. 29. (See the whole article for a full discussion of Gershon's philosophy.) ,

by Chasdai ben Abraham Crescas of Barcelona (1340–1410). The title of this is *'Or 'Adonai* ("Light of the Lord"). Crescas intended this to be the first part of a larger work. The second part, which was neve written, was to be called *Ner 'Adonai* ("Lamp of the Lord"), the whole to be a complete presentment of the contents of Judaism.

The *'Or 'Adonai* is a philosophical treatment of Jewish dogma. Its avowed object "was to liberate Judaism from the bondage of Aristotelianism, which, through Maimonides, influenced by Ibn Sina (Avicenna), and Gersonides, influenced by Ibn Roshd (Averroes), threatened to blur the distinctness of the Jewish faith, reducing the doctrinal contents of Judaism to a surrogate of Aristotelian concepts."[1]

The work is divided into four parts, which deal respectively with (1) the existence of God ; (2) the fundamental doctrines of the faith ; (3) other doctrines which, without being fundamental, are binding on the adherents of Judaism ; (4) traditional doctrines which are not binding, and which are open to philosophical construction.

Crescas is important because he met the philosophical attack on religion with philosophical weapons.

It was through Albo that his ideas more directly influenced Jewish thought.

Mention can only be made in passing of a philösopher of distinction who arose among the Karaite Jews during the fourteenth century. This was Aaron ben Elijah of Nicomedia (Asia Minor), who produced a treatise (finished in 1346) which was modelled on Maimonides' *Guide*, called *The Tree of Life*. This is a work of some importance.

Another philosophic writer of the end of the fourteenth century is Profiat Duran (called "Maestre Profiat"), whose real name was Isaac ben Moses ha-Levi, the author of a synoptic commentary on Maimonides' *Guide*, which shows considerable acquaintance with the Aristotelian philosophy.[2]

---

[1] *JE* (*s.v.* "Crescas"), iv. 351.
[2] He also wrote a critical Hebrew grammar, which was much praised by both Jews and Christians, and a polemical work

More noteworthy is Simon ben Zemach Duran (RaShBaZ) (1361-1444), a man of vast learning and a prolific author of writings on Talmudic, Biblical, religious, liturgical, and philosophic subjects. He wrote a vast treatise of an encyclopædic character entitled *Magen Aboth*, in which he displays his familiarity with philosophy and with the whole range of the secular learning of the Middle Ages. He attacked Chasdai Crescas and defended Maimonides.

The best-known Jewish philosophic writer of the fifteenth century is Joseph Albo (about 1380-1444), a pupil of Chasdai Crescas, and author of the famous work '*Ikkarim* ("Principles").

Albo's '*Ikkarim* ("Book of Principles") became a popular text-book. It may, perhaps, be regarded as primarily a contribution to the apologetics of Judaism. Like his master Crescas, he criticises Maimonides and the Aristotelian philosophy. He reduces the fundamental "roots" or root-doctrines of Judaism to three, and attaches to each of these a number of '*Shirashim*, or "secondary radicals." The three fundamental root-principles are : (1) Belief in the existence of God ; (2) belief in revelation, or communication of divine instruction by God to man ; (3) belief in divine retribution (future rewards and punishments).

After Albo there flourished several Jewish philosophic writers of merit, but none of marked originality, during the rest of the fifteenth century.

The best-known names are those of Abraham Bihago of Huesca (died about 1490), who commented on Averroes, and wrote a philosophic defence of the Jewish faith (*The Path of Faith*) ; Judah Messer Leon of Mantua ; Elijah del Medigo of Crete (1450-93), a famous professor of philosophy (at the University of Padua and elsewhere), who wrote not only in Hebrew (the *Bechinath ha-Dath*, "Investigation of Religion"), but also in Latin (on the works of Aristotle and Averroes) ; Isaac Arama of Zamora (died 1494), the author of a popular philosophic and homiletical work called *The Offering of Isaac* ;

(still unpublished) criticising Christian dogmas. This was written in 1397 at the request of Chasdai Crescas, to whom it was dedicated. Its title is *Kelimmath ha-Goyim*.

and Isaac Abarbanel (1437–1508), the author of numerous Bible commentaries, who has already been referred to in that connexion, also wrote on philosophical questions.

With the expulsion of the Jews from Spain in 1492 the great centre of Jewish science and learning was destroyed. And with this event the line of "Jewish philosophy" in the strict sense came to an end. Books dealing with philosophical questions were still written, but no great contributions were made.

The line of Jewish philosophers played, perhaps, no great *rôle* in the evolution of philosophy, but they took an important part in preserving and transmitting philosophic thought through a difficult period.

Besides the purely ethical treatises already referred to, the most notable of which is Bachya's *Duties of the Heart*, mention ought to be made of some others that were important. A book of this kind that obtained wide currency in the Middle Ages is *The Book of the Pious (Sepher ha-Chasidim)*, which has been attributed to Judah Chasid, of whom very little is known. He is supposed to have lived in Regensburg at the end of the twelfth and beginning of the thirteenth century. *The Book of the Pious*, however, seems really to be the work of no single writer, but to have grown up out of various elements— mystical, ethical, ceremonial—in the Rhinelands during the thirteenth century. Parts of it display deep insight into the cravings of the human heart.

The famous Eleazar of Worms (1176–1238), who has already been referred to in other connexions, and who was a pupil of Judah Chasid, was the author of a well-known book of a similar kind entitled *Rokeach*, by which name Eleazar himself is also sometimes called.

An anonymous ethical book which emanated from the Rhine district, and was probably written some time in the fifteenth century, is known as *The Ways of the Righteous ('Orchoth Zaddikin*).[1] It has often been printed (both in Jewish-German and Hebrew).

Another favourite class of ethical works consisted of compilations of an ethical character from the Talmud and Midrash. The oldest and most highly esteemed of these was written at the beginning of the fourteenth century by Isaac Aboab, and

---

[1] Also called sometimes *Sepher ha-Middoth*.

bears the title *Lamp of Light* (*Menorath ha-Maor*). The author lived in Spain.

Another popular compilation of the same kind is Jacob ibn Chabib's '*En Ya'akob*, which was made in the sixteenth century (*cp.* p. 138 above).

Elijah de Vidas' *Reshith Chokmah* (*Beginning of Wisdom*), first published in 1578, was also widely read. It collects maxims on such topics as the love and fear of God, repentance, holiness, and humility.

A peculiarly Jewish department of this kind of literature is the ethical will, many examples of which are extant. In these documents[1] a father (or a teacher) leaves a kind of ethical testament to sons (or disciples). They were private documents, not intended for publication, which were carefully treasured within the family circle, and were often written from the thirteenth century onwards.

A well-known example of this kind, which is really a small ethical treatise, and has found its way into many prayer books under the title *Ways of Life*, is the ethical will of R. Asher ben Jechiel (1250–1327) to his son R. Jehudah ben Asher.

One of the most interesting examples of this type of literature is the ethical will of the translator Judah ibn Tibbon, in which he gives his son excellent advice on methods of study and translation.[2]

V

THE MEDIÆVAL POETRY

[LITERATURE : Professor A. Sulzbach, *Die poetische Litteratur* (in Winter und Wünsche, iii. 1–215) ; the articles " Poetry (Lyric)," " *Piyyut*," in *JE* ; the articles on the personal names in *JE* ; the articles " Literature (Jewish)," § 5, and "Hymns (Hebrew and Jewish)" in Hastings's *Dictionary of Religion and Ethics* ; Zunz, *Die synagogale Poesie des Mittelalters* (Berlin, 1855), and *Die Litteratur-geschichte der synagogalen Poesie* (Berlin, 1865) ; Franz Delitzsch, *Zur Geschichte der jüdischen Poesie* (Leipzig, 1836) ; M. Sachs, *Die religiose Poesie der Juden in Spanien* ; Thomas Chenery, *Machberoth Ithiel* (London and Edinburgh, 1872) ; Brody and Albrecht (E.T.), *The New-Hebrew School of Poets of the Spanish-Arabian Epoch* (London, 1906 ; Hebrew text, with introduction, notes, and dictionary).

English translations (in poetical form) by Mrs. Lucas (*The Jewish Year*), Nina Salamans, and others; chaps. vii., x., xii. in Abrahams' *Short History of Jewish Literature*.]

---

[1] Heb. צַוָּאוֹת. [2] See *JE* vi. 545.

(i)

The development of post-Biblical Hebrew poetry derived its first impulse from the necessities of liturgical worship. The technical term for this kind of composition is *piyyut*, and the author of a *piyyut* is called a *payyetan*.

The word is derived from the Greek term for "poet," ποιητής. In the Midrash *piyyut* is used in the general sense of "fiction," while *payyetan* has the technical sense of an author of synagogue poetry. This fact suggests that the latter term is a secondary term for the former.

The oldest *piyyutim*, in the technical sense of the term, which are anonymous, probably date from the Geonic period (seventh century). The most famous *payyetan* of the Middle Ages is Eleazar ben Kalir, whose exact date is uncertain, but may be some time in the tenth century.[1] The oldest *payyetan* whose name is known and whose work must have been known to Saadya (died A.D. 942), since the latter quotes him, is Jose ben Jose.

Another, somewhat later, is Jannai, who is reputed to have been the teacher of Eleazar ben Kalir, while the latter was the immediate predecessor of Saadya. From this time the *payyetanim* are numerous, and were flourishing in the Jewish settlements, especially in Germany, France, Spain, and Italy.

The *piyyut* is, of course, not a fixed part of the Jewish Liturgy, but represents the "occasional" element which is used on the great festivals and certain special days. In consequence the collections of *piyyutim* differ in the different rituals. Those used by the Spanish Jews, for instance, are, as a whole, different from those used by the Germans. They are written in Hebrew —Hebrew often used in a strained and artificial way, especially by Kalir, but still Hebrew ; for though Arabic replaced Hebrew as the literary language of the Jews of the Orient, and was also used by the Jews in Spain, the Liturgy was always recited in Hebrew.

---

[1] Others would place him about 750.

In Spain, where the new Hebrew poetry attained its zenith in the eleventh and twelfth centuries, the outstanding names are Solomon ibn Gebirol, Judah ha-Levi, and Moses and Abraham ibn Ezra.

The *piyyutim* fall into different classes, varying in structure and according to their theme and place in the Liturgy. One large class, which is perhaps the oldest, is the *Selichoth*, or penitential prayers.

In its simplest and oldest form the *Selichah* is represented by such pieces as the *we-hu rachum* (Singer, pp. 57–62), which in its opening clauses runs as follows :

And He, being merciful, forgiveth iniquity and destroyeth not ; Yea, many a time He turneth His anger away, and doth not stir up all His wrath.
Withhold not Thou Thy tender mercies from us, O Lord : Let Thy loving-kindness and truth continually preserve us.

This is recited on Mondays and Thursdays, and was known as early as the Geonic period. It was originally intended for fast-days, as were some of the other anonymous *Selichoth*.

The oldest poetic *Selichoth* are in the form of litanies, arranged in short sentences, and sometimes in alphabetic acrostic. From these litanies originated the rhymeless *Selichoth*, which were modelled on the Biblical alphabetic Psalms. In course of time the construction was elaborated and rhyme introduced (sometimes middle rhymes as well), and the verses, arranged in two-, three-, or four-lined strophes, have a certain well-defined rhythm.[1] A favourite theme for these compositions was the *Akedah*, or Sacrifice of Isaac, which naturally led on to the commemoration of voluntary sacrifices made for the Jewish religion (martyrdom).

A good example of the poetic *Selichah*, with two-lined strophes, the two lines rhyming, and each strophe beginning with an alphabetic letter in order, is one known as אָנָּא הַשֵּׁם for the morning service on the Day of Atonement, the author of which is unknown, and which is probably not later than the thirteenth century. It has been rendered into English verse by Mr. Zangwill, some of whose lines may here be quoted : [2]

God and the God of our fathers, honoured and terrible Name, Pardon the sin of this people, gathered Thy praise to proclaim.

---

[1] See *JE* s.v. " *Selihah*," xi. 170 ff. for further details.
[2] See *Service of the Synagogue* (*Machzor*), ed. Davis, ii. p. 84 f.

T

Tender Thine ear for Thy glory : hark to our prayer and plea,
Song of Thy suppliant servants, yearning to reach unto Thee.

Nigh to Thy Temple this morn, to render thanksgiving I drew,
Set on confessing my sins : the sins that Thy people pursue.

·The term *piyyuṭim* is applied more specifically to
the hymns for holy-days and special Sabbaths, which
are divided into distinct classes, according to their
place in the Liturgy.

Those which are inserted in the Evening Prayer (*'Arbith*) are
termed *Ma'arbiyyoth* ; a large class, which are inserted in the
first Benediction of Morning Prayer (*Yôtzēr 'ôr*),[1] are called
Yotzer, and another, inserted in the second Benediction (known
as *'Ahabah*),[2] are called *'Ahabah* ; those inserted in the
Benediction following the *Shema'* are termed *Zulath*, from a
characteristic word which occurs at the end of the second
paragraph of that Benediction ("There is no God *beside Thee*
[*zūlāthĕkā*]").[3]
Other special names are *Ophan*, applied to the *piyyuṭ* which
is inserted at that part of the morning Benediction which refers
to the "Ophannim (wheels) and holy chayyoth" giving praise
(Singer, p. 39) ; the idea of the passage is based upon Ezekiel's
vision (chap. i.), and the theme of the inserted *piyyuṭ* is that of
the heavenly host praising the Lord ; and also *Ḳeroboth*,
Shib'ata ("seven," because the *'Amidah* Prayer for Sabbaths
and holy days consists of seven Benedictions), *Tokachah*
("reproof"), a kind of penitential discourse, and *Ḳinah*
("lamentation "), used on the Fast of the 9th of Ab.

The term *Ḳeroboth* ("prayers of approach," *i.e.* to
God ; *cp.* Jer. xii. 2) in particular is applied to the
piyyuṭim which are inserted in the earlier part of the
repetition of the morning *'Amidah* on special Sabbaths, on the three festivals, and on New Year in the
Ashkenazic Liturgy. They are associated with very
ancient melodies.

[1] See Singer, p. 37 f. ("Blessed art Thou, O Lord, . . . who
createst light").
[2] *'Ahabah* = " Love " ; *cp.* Singer, p. 39 f. ("With abounding
love," etc.).
[3] *cp.* Singer, p. 43. Sometimes *Geullah* ("Redemption")
is used.

They are constructed in accordance with a fixed scheme, always opening with a *reshuth*, or prayer of the cantor for divine guidance, accompanied by a confession of unworthiness. The *reshuth* is cantillated to a melody which reappears in the concluding verses. The main body of the *piyyut* is now generally read through in an undertone. The whole is brought to an end in a long meditation bringing in the *Kedushah*, which is termed the *Silluk* (*i.e.* "cessation," *sc.* of the singing).

The following example illustrates the opening of such a *piyyut* for the morning service of the First Day of the New Year.[1] The opening clause rhymes in the Hebrew, as well as the lines that follow.[2]

From the counsel of the wise and understanding, and from knowledge gotten of the discerning, I will open my lips in prayer and supplication, to intreat and implore the presence of the King of kings and Lord of lords.

Trembling, I now pour forth my prayerful plea,
And, suppliant, seek Thee shrined in awe supreme.
I fear that worthless Thou my deeds must deem ;
Wisdom I lack, and hope forsaketh me.

Teach me my sacred portion to possess ;
Strengthen, uphold me, weak in terror's snare.
Account my whispered plaint as incense rare,
Sweeter than honey voice of my distress.

Its guileless utterance through Thy grace confirm,
And pardon's ransom to my people speed.
Melodious let my supplication plead
For these Thy suitors, humbled as the worm.

Thy promise, from the sheltering covert heard,
Renew, and hearken to the prayer I frame.
When Thou dost search my heart, mine inward flame ;
With dread of doom my stricken soul is stirred.

[1] See *Service of the Synagogue, New Year*, p. 95 f.
[2] The author is R. Jekuthiel b. Moses of Speyer (*circa* 1070). The rhymed version is by Elsie Davis.

T 2

Lest sin be paid full due, each heart doth quake ;
As streams, the fountains of mine eyelids flow.
Craving Thy charity, I wait ; bestow
Thy pardon, for the righteous fathers' sake.

My heart grows hot the while I muse and pray,
'Tis kindled as a fiery, glowing coal ;
Doubts, like a tempest, agitate my soul ;
For terror hath invaded us this day.

All this is cantillated by the Reader. Then follows
a longer passage recited by the congregation. The
compositions called *Kinoth* are designed for use on
the 9th of Ab, the solemn fast which commemorates
the various destructions of the Holy City. Various
elegiac poems of this type were produced in the
Middle Ages, the most famous being the *Sionim* of
Judah ha-Levi. To another Spanish-Jewish poet of
the twelfth century, Baruch (1077–1127), son of R.
Isaac ibn Albalia, two *Kinoth* are attributed which
are still used in the synagogue. One of these has
been rendered into English in poetical form by the
late Canon T. L. Kingsbury, from which the following
stanzas may be quoted. The elegy consists of twenty-
two short stanzas, following the alphabetic order (and
thus forming an alphabetic acrostic) ; each stanza
again is subdivided by a double refrain, *When I forth
from Egypt came,* and *When I left Jerusalem.* The
poet " contrasts the mercies and glories of the
Exodus with the awful judgements which accompanied and followed the two falls of Jerusalem," [1] but
ends on a triumphant note. An introductory stanza,
which stands outside the alphabetic scheme, describes
the emotions which moved the poet to write. We
quote this and two others of the twenty-two :

[1] See *The Holy Tears of Jesus* (London, Hodder and
Stoughton, 1892), Appendix iii.

Introductory Stanza

Fire is kindled me within,
Bright thoughts in my heart upspring,
    How I forth from Egypt came.
Lays of mourning I intone,
Memory utters groan on groan,
    How I left Jerusalem.

Aleph

Moses sang that glorious day
Song that ne'er shall pass away,
    When I forth from Egypt came.
Jeremiah pour'd his soul
Forth in lamentable dole,
    When I left Jerusalem.

Daleth

Angel-bread from highest heaven,
Rock-stored water-streams were given,
    When I forth from Egypt came.
Wormwood, gall have been my food,
And my drink of tears the flood,
    Since I left Jerusalem.

Another elaborate kind of liturgical composition
for the Day of Atonement services is termed '*Abodah*
(" Service "), its theme being a detailed description of
the service in the Temple on that day, based upon
the Mishnah tractate *Yoma*.

Other liturgical compositions of a similar general character
are '*Azharoth* (embodying the Pentateuchal commandments),
and *Hosha'anoth*, poetical pieces with a " Hosanna " refrain,
used on *Hosha'na rabba* (the seventh day of the Feast of
Tabernacles). The cycle of festival services is termed *Machzor*
(" cycle ").

(ii)

Kalir is, in many respects, the most remarkable of the *payyeṭanim*. He was a prolific writer, no less than two hundred of his compositions being still extant in various Machzorim. He is the most essentially Jewish of the liturgical poets, drawing his materials from the Talmudim and Midrashim, and using as his medium of expression Biblical Hebrew—but a Biblical Hebrew "enriched with daring innovations." He takes great liberties with the language, uses rare words, and constantly makes allusions to the Haggadah and indulges in allegorical expressions to an extent that makes him difficult to follow. In spite of these defects, which have provoked much criticism, Kalir has always had imitators, and the "Kalirian" form of *piyyuṭ* has been perpetuated down to recent times. Kalir employed the acrostic (and also *gematria*) in order to interweave his own name into his compositions, and uses rhyme.

Saadya also added hymns to the Liturgy. Some of these have all the faults of the Kalirian *piyyuṭ* without its virtues; but others are characterised by a purity and simplicity that suggest the Spanish school, of which, indeed, in some ways Saadya was the harbinger.

Under the princely physician and statesman, Chasdai ibn Shaprut (915–970 or 990), Cordova became the home of Jewish culture and letters. There Jewish grammarians, critics, poets, merchants, and courtiers assembled under his auspices, among the rest Dunash ibn Labrat, grammarian and poet. Dunash was for a time a pupil of Saadya, and it was after the death of the latter (in 942) that he went to Cordova. His importance as a poet is considerable, as he was the first to apply Arabic metrical rules to Hebrew poetry, though very few of his verses have survived.

About half a century after the death of Chasdai, Samuel ibn Nagdela (993–1055) was head of the Jewish community in Granada, and occupied a position of commanding influence. As head of the Jewish community he is termed "the Nagid" ("Prince"). He became the principal minister of the ruler of Granada. A man of extraordinary versatility, Samuel was at once Rabbi (and a profound Rabbinical scholar[1]), statesman and man of affairs, and poet. He wrote many poetical pieces— hymns in the style of the Psalms (*Ben Tehillim*) and of Proverbs (*Ben Mishle*), as well as secular pieces such as wine- and love-songs. "When Samuel the Nagid died in 1055, the golden age of (Jewish) Spanish literature was in sight."[2]

"In the days of Chasdai," says Abraham ibn Daud, "the poets began to twitter." This, of course, refers to the poets of the new Spanish-Arabian school, who may be said to begin with Dunash ibn Labrat and his opponent, Menachem ben Saruk. In Spain Jewish poetry, though largely religious, embraced also secular subjects, and was pervaded by a totally different spirit from that of the Kalirian *piyyut*. It was purer in its diction, less artificial, and more melodious and graceful. It was brought to perfection by the great masters, Solomon ibn Gebirol, the Ibn Ezras, and Judah ha-Levi.

Solomon ibn Gebirol (born in Malaga in 1021, died in 1058 or 1070) was a man of genius, and, like many other geniuses, lived, on the whole, very unhappily. His work as a philosopher has already been discussed in a previous section. As a poet he

---

[1] He wrote a well-known Introduction to the Talmud (*Mebo ha-Talmud*). It is usually included in the printed editions of the Talmud at the end of the tractate *Berakoth*. Under the title *Clavis Talmudica* it was translated into Latin by Constantin L'Empereur (Leyden, 1633).

[2] I. Abrahams, *op. cit.* p. 62.

stands with the supreme masters of the Jewish-Spanish school. It was Gebirol who was the first of the Hebrew poets to elaborate and apply the strict Arabic metrical principles introduced by Dunash ben Labrat.[1] The poems are rhymed, all the lines, whether long or short, ending with the same syllable. They are written in pure Biblical Hebrew, and all, even the secular poems, are permeated by strong religious feeling.

His finest compositions, however, are his liturgical poems. Zunz says that "the liturgic poetry of the Spanish-Arabic Jews attained its perfection with Ibn Gebirol." Here the limitations imposed by the *payyetanic* form and involved and artificial expression are almost wholly overcome. Perhaps the best example of his genius in this department is the *Kether Malkuth*, or *Royal Crown*, a philosophical and ethical poem in rhymed prose, containing a description of the universe, sphere within sphere, and forming a glowing panegyric of the glory of God as manifested both in the realm of the material and the spiritual. Extracts from this poem are given in an English version, in poetical form, by Mrs. Lucas in *JQR* viii. 239 ff. (1896). The following stanza may be quoted :

Beyond conception great
Thy power is, wherewith Thou didst create
From out Thy glory's depths a radiant flame,
Hewn from the rock of rocks and wrought
Out of eternity, with wisdom fraught,
The soul, the living soul—thus didst Thou call its name.
By Thee Omnipotent,
Formed of the spirit's fire, and sent
To guard and keep and serve awhile this earthly
frame.

[1] Ibn Ezra cites examples from Gebirol's poems in his *Sepher Zachoth* to illustrate his description of the various metres.

His contributions to liturgical poetry were very numerous, and have found a place not only in the Spanish Rite, but also in others (Rumanian, German, and even Karaitic). These consist of *piyyuṭim* and *selichoth* (more than 100) for the Sabbaths, festivals, and fast-days.

A beautiful rendering of the poetic hymn used in the *Abodah* of the Atonement Day services is given by Mrs. Lucas in her *Jewish Year* (p. 67 f.). The opening stanza runs as follows :

> *Happy he who saw of old*
> *The high-priest, with gems of gold*
> *All adorned from crown to hem,*
> *Tread thy courts Jerusalem,*
> *Till he reached the sacred place*
> *Where the Lord's especial grace*
> *Ever dwelt, the centre of the whole :*
> *Happy he whose eyes*
> *Saw at last the cloud of glory rise,*
> *But to hear of it afflicts our soul.*

Gebirol also wrote a rhymed enumeration of the 613 precepts of the Law (*Azharoth*), and a poem of 400 lines called '*Anak*. A selection of his poems (Hebrew text and English translations) is published in *Treasures of Oxford*, by Edelman and Dukes (London, 1851), and there is a selection (of Hebrew texts only) in Albrecht and Brody's *The New Hebrew School of Poets*.

Another master of the Spanish-Jewish school of poets was Moses ibn Ezra,[1] who was also distinguished as a philosopher. He was born at Granada about 1070, and died after 1138. As a poet he appealed especially to scholars and those who were able to appreciate his command over the technical devices of the art. His poetical compositions were preferred by Al-Charizi even to those of Judah ha-Levi. Nevertheless, his liturgical poems, which number some 220 pieces, have, many of them, found a place in most of the Machzorim (with the exception of the Ashkenazic). He writes in Biblical

[1] Moses ben Jacob ha-Sallach (Arabic name *Abu Harun Musa*).

Hebrew (with a certain admixture of rare forms and usages), and some of his *piyyuṭim* are of remarkable beauty.

His secular poems are contained in two works :

(*a*) The *Tarshish* (תרשיש = "topaz"), so called because it contains 1,216 lines (תרשיש = by *gematria* 1,216), is divided into ten chapters, each of which contains the letters of the alphabet in order. It is written in the manner of the Arabic "tajnis," or "punning" rhyme, which consists of the repetition of words in every stanza, but employed in a different sense at each repetition. The ten chapters consist of (1) a dedication to a certain Abraham, while the rest have for their themes (2) wine, love, and song ; (3) the charm of country life ; (4) and (5) love-sickness and the separation of lovers ; (6) unfaithful friends ; (7) old age ; (8) vicissitudes of fortune and death ; (9) confidence in God ; (10) the glory of poetry. An edition of the Hebrew text was published by David Günzberg in 1886 (Berlin, Society of the מקיצי נרדמים). Two illuminating articles by K. Albrecht on the language of the poem appeared in vol. xix. of the *Zeitschrift f. d. Alttest. Wissenschaft*, 1899 (pp. 134–155 and 310–328), entitled *Zum Lexicon und zur Grammatik d. Neuhebraischen* (with special reference to the *Tarshish*).

(*b*) The *Divan*, still extant in MS. This contains some 300 secular poems, having for their theme the praise of friends, and elegies on the death of scholars.

The following is an extract from a rendering of one of Ibn Ezra's liturgical pieces (*The Jewish Year*, p. 112 f.). It is entitled

PENITENTIAL PRAYER

Forth flies my soul upborne by hope untiring,
The land of rest, the spring of life desiring,
Unto the heavenly dwelling-place aspiring,
To seek its peace by day and night.

My spirit does God's majesty adore,
And without wings shall to His presence soar,
There to behold His glory evermore,
At dawn, at noonday, and at night.

Another Ibn Ezra, the famous scholar, philosopher, and exegete, Abraham (born at Toledo before 1100, died, perhaps, 1167), was also a poet. Yet poetry was not his principal preoccupation, and admirable and lofty as the sentiments expressed in his poems are, and excellent as they are in form, they lack the imaginative element.

He wrote a *Divan* (260 numbers) which has been edited from a unique MS. by I. Egers. This work also contains a religio-philosophical poem in rhymed prose, based upon an Arabic prose-work of Avicenna. To the Liturgy he has contributed several hymns, which breathe a spirit of resignation. Several specimens are given in English verse in Mrs. Lucas's *Jewish Year*.

The greatest of the Jewish mediæval poets, in whom the distinctive Jewish feeling most perfectly expressed itself, was Judah ha-Levi (born at Toledo in the last quarter of the eleventh century, died in the East after 1140).

The year of his birth may have been 1085, a fateful year, in which Toledo was recaptured from the Moors by the Christian king Alfonso VI. " It was a fit birthplace for the greatest Jewish poet since Bible times. East and West met in Toledo. The science of the East there found Western Christians to cultivate it. Jew, Moor, and Christian displayed there mutual toleration which existed nowhere else. In the midst of this favourable environment Judah Ha-levi grew to early maturity." [1] It is probable that Judah was sent by his father, who was a man of means, to Lucena (near Cordova) to be educated at the school of Alfasi. It was probably at Lucena that he became the friend of Baruch Albalia, also a poet. After completing his studies he returned to Toledo, and there practised as a physician for a time, afterwards removing to Cordova. But his heart was in the East, and after the completion of his *Al-Khazari* he decided to set out for Palestine. He arrived in Alexandria, and, in spite of the entreaties of friends not to proceed further, he continued his journey to the Holy Land. He visited Tyre and Damascus, and, according to tradition, arrived ultimately outside the walls of Jerusalem, where, it is said, he was ridden down and killed by a fanatical Arab, chanting as he died the most moving of all his compositions, the famous Ode to Sion.

Judah was a real poet, and displayed his gifts in this respect in his youth. He won the admiration of his friend and senior, the poet Moses ibn Ezra. A

[1] I. Abrahams, *op. cit.* p. 75.

large place in his non-liturgical poems is occupied by pieces which are poems of friendship or eulogy. In this connexion figure such personalities as Moses ibn Ezra, Samuel ha-Nagid, and Baruch Albalia, as well as many others. Sometimes he sadly commemorates the death of friends, as his teacher Isaac Alfasi, Moses ibn Ezra, and the latter's brothers Judah and Isaac, and the pathetic lamentation over the murdered Solomon ibn Farissol (May 3, 1108).

His religious poems are pervaded by deep and passionate devotion to God. Another note that recurs is his profound love of his people and sympathy with them in their sufferings. While "Edom and Ishmael riot in the Holy City," Israel is everywhere in bondage. In one poem the poet represents Israel as pleading with God for release from the harsh bondage.

" *Come, Beloved, come Thou to me,*
  In the bower of lilacs woo me :
  Slay the friends that would pursue me.

" *Harps and chimes and cups all golden*
  To the joy of old embolden,
  'Neath the radiant glory olden."

God answers :

" *Bide thou thy time—within thy soul be peace,*
  Nor ask complaining when thy pain shall cease ;
  Speak, rhyme, and sing, for victory is thine,
  Nigh thee My tent is pitched, and thou art Mine."

National feeling, patriotism, and religion blended to a remarkable degree in the spirit of mediæval Judaism. They find their perfect expression in the poems of Judah ha-Levi. Judah believed literally in the return to Sion, and this motive determined his last pilgrimage. His famous "Zionide"—the ode addressed to Sion—has found a place in the Liturgy of the 9th of Ab, among the *Kinoth*, or lamentations which commemorate the fall of the Holy City. The opening stanza is thus rendered by Mrs. Lucas (*Jewish Year*, p. 129 f.) :[1]

Art thou not, Zion, fain
To send forth greetings from thy sacred rock
Unto thy captive train,
Who greet thee as the remnants of thy flock ?
Take thou on every side,
East, west, and south and north, their greetings multi-
    plied.
Sadly he greets thee still,
The prisoner of hope who, day and night,
Sheds ceaseless tears, like dew on Hermon's hill.
Would that they fell upon thy mountain's height!

More than 300 of Judah's poems have been incorporated into the Jewish Liturgy. A number of these have been rendered into English verse by Mrs. Lucas in *The Jewish Year*. Several collections of Judah's poems have been published (original texts). The most complete edition of the *Divan* is that of Brody, published for the *Meḳitze Nirdamim* Society (Berlin, 1894 and following years) ; the *Bethulath bath Yehudah*, edited by S. D. Luzzatto (Prague, 1840) ; the same editor also issued an edition of the *Divan* ; another volume, entitled *Ṭal Aroth* (Przemysl), appeared in 1881.

Translations have been published by Sachs (with text), Zunz (*Synag. Poesie*), Geiger (*Divan*), Heller, Kämpf, Steinschneider (*Manna*), and Sulzbach.

In English in *Treasures of Oxford* (1851), Nina Davis ("Songs of Exile"), E. G. King (in *JQR*, First Series, vii. 464), J. Jacobs ("Jewish Ideals"), Mrs. Lucas (*op. cit.*), and Lady Magnus ("Jewish Portraits") ; also in French, Italian, and Russian.

Judah, though he seems to have doubted at one time their propriety to Hebrew, uses the most complicated Arabic metres in his poems.

The New-Hebrew poetry of which Judah is the best representative hardly survived him. The old inspiration dried up under the stress of persecution

[1] The whole rendering is strikingly successful and beautiful.

Al-Charizi, indeed (thirteenth century [1]), "the genial poet of macames," who, like Judah ha-Levi, lived in Spain and travelled in the Orient, was celebrated as a poet. He may be regarded as the last great representative of the ancient classical school of Spain. But his poems are very different in spirit from those of his great predecessors.

Al-Charizi was a serious student of literature as well as a poet. A master both of Hebrew and Arabic, he shone as a translator (from Arabic into Hebrew).˙ He rendered the *Maḳamat* of the Arab poet Hariri of Bozrah into Hebrew, as well as some of Maimonides' (Arabic) works (the commentary on the Mishnah, and, in part, the *Guide*). His masterpiece was a work, composed in Hebrew (1218–20), to which he gave the name of *Tachkemoni*, which is supposed to mean "the wise one." This was written in the form of the Arabic *macame* (*makama*), a curious species of rhyming prose.

The style of the *macame* may be gathered from the following reproduction of one of Charizi's sentences :

As if the word of the Lord of life—in Israel were no longer rife ; like her of old—of whom we are told—" other vineyards I protected—my own, alas ! that I neglected !" (Cant. i. 6).[2]

This citation illustrates the clever way in which Charizi interweaves Biblical quotations so as to conform to the requirements of the rhyme. The *macame* is a species of spoken drama, in which two personages are supposed to take part : the hero, who relates various episodes about himself, and the narrator, who acts as a sort of chorus, drawing out the hero by his questions. In Charizi's poem the narrator is Heman the Ezrahite and the hero Heber the Kenite. "Each episode described by the hero is the subject of a single *makama* (poem), and has no close. connexion with that which follows, but its rambling, rhyming prose is extended and diversified by the interpolation of smaller poems, in absolutely strict rhythm and rhyme, and generally of exalted strain. . . . The episodes of the 'Tachkemoni' cover a wide field of remarkable experiences, varying from a banquet given to him in an important city of Babylonia (where, as the guest of Heman, Alcharizi tells of all the noble

---

[1] Neither the date of his birth nor that of his death is known. His Hebrew name was Judah ben Solomon ben Hophni. He was surnamed "Al-Charizi."

[2] Cited from *JE* i. 3911 (*s.v.* "Al-Ḥarizi ").

poets he has known in Spain) to a battle between Arabs 'in the
tents of Kedar,' a debate between an ant and a flea, or a reproof by a village chanticleer escaped from the butcher's knife." [1]
Charizi was witty as well as accomplished, and though, as he
complains, the victim of misfortune throughout his life, he could
rise superior to thoughts of bitterness. He ranks high as a
poet, and was a supreme master of all the technical devices
of the art.

A poet of a remarkable character, who may fitly
be mentioned in this connexion, was Immanuel ben
Solomon ben Jekuthiel (1270–1330), commonly known
as "Immanuel of Rome," the contemporary, and perhaps friend, of Dante. Immanuel was a fine scholar,
well versed in Biblical and Talmudical literature,
mathematics, astronomy, medicine, and the philosophical works of Arabians and Christians. He
wrote various works on Jewish subjects (herme-
neutics and Biblical commentaries on nearly all the
books of the Bible). But his really original work
was his poetry.

He composed both in Italian and Hebrew, but only a few of
his Italian poems have survived. "The child of his time, in
sympathy with the social and intellectual life of Italy of that
period, he had acquired the then prevalent pleasing, easy,
humorous, harmlessly flippant tone, and the art of treating
questionable subjects wittily and elegantly. He was acquainted
with Dante's works, and was influenced by them. He introduced
the sonnet form into Hebrew literature, and alternate instead
of single rhyme." [2] In old age he collected his Hebrew poems
into a *Divan* which he entitled *Mechabberoth*. The poems here
collected deal with episodes of Jewish life, and comprise satires,
letters, prayers, and dirges intermingled. The Hebrew idiom
used by the poet lends an added charm to his work. "His
parodies of Biblical and Talmudic sentences, his clever allusions
and puns, his equivocations, are gems of diction, on account of
which it is almost impossible to translate his poems into
another language." [3] One poem in the collection (No. 28)
entitled *Hell and Paradise (ha-Tophet we-ha-Eden)* is a vision
clearly modelled on Dante's *Divine Comedy*. Immanuel was an
admirer of Charizi, who in some respects influenced the form of

---

[1] *JE* i. 3911.   [2] *JE* vii. 563.   [3] *JE ibid.*

his poems. By later Jewish authorities (*e.g.* Joseph Caro) his poems were censured as frivolous and immoral, and they bore an ill-repute. By one of history's ironies, however, it seems probable that the metrical form of Maimonides' Creed known as *Yigdal*, which is printed in the Jewish Prayer Books, and universally used in synagogue worship, is really a composition of Immanuel's (see Dr. H. Hirschfeld in *JQR*, New Series, v. 529 ff., April, 1915). The *Divan* was first printed at Brescia in 1491, and has been reprinted several times since.

The elaboration of the verse structure and other devices used for poetical purposes were steadily developed, especially in the Spanish school of Jewish poetry, under Arabic influence. We have already seen that rhymed prose was used as a medium, as well as verse proper. Compositions were also written in exact metre (according to a fixed scheme), while in others only the number of syllables is counted, and even this not always. The treatment of rhyme was also much elaborated; there were single and double rhymes, the catchword (refrain), the "punning" rhyme (*Tajnis*), as well as the acrostic. These and other points of a similar character can, of course, only be studied adequately in the original texts.[1] Invaluable aid is given in these directions by the authors of *The New-Hebrew School of Poets*, already referred to.

It should be added that the measure is determined neither by the quantity of the syllables nor by the accent, but depends upon the difference between a full syllable (whether marked by a long or a short vowel) and one that is not full (*i.e.* begins with a vocal *shĕwa*). The former is called *tĕnu'ah*, the latter *yāthēd* (indicated by – and ᴗ – respectively). Thus the line

ădōn 'ōlam ăsher mālak

would be marked

ᴗ – | – – | ᴗ – | – –

i.e. it consists of a *yāthēd* (ᴗ –) followed by two *tĕnu'ōth* (– –), followed by another *yāthēd* and two *tĕnu'oth.*

---

[1] To the technical terms already referred to should be added the form called "mostegab," in which a Biblical verse is used at the beginning of every stanza.

It has been impossible in this sketch to refer to the work of many of the liturgical poets of other countries than Spain. Thus in the tenth century Simon ben Isaac of Worms was a poet in the real sense of the term. In the eleventh century Germany produced Moses ben Kalonymus, Meshullam ben Kalonymus, Simon ben Isaac, and Gershon of Judah ; in the twelfth century, Jekuthiel ben Moses of Speyer, Menachem ben Machir of Ratisbon, Meir ben Isaac, Kalonymus ben Judah, Eliezer ben Nathan, Ephraim ben Isaac of Ratisbon, and Ephraim ben Jacob of Bonn ; and in the thirteenth century, Moses ben Chasdai, Eleazar ben Judah of Worms, and Eliezer ben Joel ha-Levi. In France Solomon ben Abun (twelfth century) stands out, as also does Abraham Bedaresi, surnamed " the Orator " (Abraham of Beziers, thirteenth century), who, with his son Jeda'aya (surnamed " ha-Tenini "), were meritorious *payyetanim*. Italy, where, according to some scholars, Kalir lived, produced *payyetanim* from the tenth to the eighteenth century. But after the fourteenth century the *piyyut* was not so much cultivated, and new pieces were rarely embodied in the Liturgy after that period. Among the eminent poets of the Spanish-Jewish school ought to be reckoned Joseph Abitur, one of the earliest (died 970), who composed many liturgical pieces,[1] and to this school also belong Isaac Ghayyat, Judah ben Bileam, Bachya ibn Pakuda (the author of *Th Duties of the Heart*), and Isaac ben Reuben of Barcelona. Finally, reference may here be made to the work of a late poet, Solomon al-Kabetz of Safed (sixteenth century), the author of the famous Sabbath-hymn, *Lĕkah Dôdî*, which is sung in the synagogues on Friday evening.[2] Solomon al-Kabetz represents the fine devotional element with which the

---

[1] For an English rendering of a Sabbath hymn by him see *The Jewish Year*, pp. 37 ff.   [2] See p. 190 above.

Kabbalistic mysticism enriched the Liturgy. The hymn is a poetical greeting of "the Bride of the Sabbath." The Almighty is addressed and asked to meet His bride:

> *Come forth, my friend, the bride to meet,*
> *Come, O my friend, the Sabbath greet.*

And these lines form a refrain.[1]

One of the most famous of the Kabbalistic poets, who also belongs to the sixteenth century, is Israel Najara. He lived and died in the East. His *Songs of Israel* (*Zemiroth Yisrael*) is a work of high merit. It contains a collection of poems on the marriage of God and Israel which are couched in sensuous language. He wrote many *piyyutim* (some in Aramaic), and these, with his hymns, have found a place in many Machzorim. He also composed secular poems, and evidently was well acquainted with many languages. For an illuminating discussion of the *piyyutim* in particular, and the later Hebrew poetry in general, reference may be made to Dr. I. Abrahams's review of *The Jewish Year* in *JQR*, First Series, xi. pp. 64–91.

VI

SOME OTHER FORMS OF LITERATURE

A brief reference to some other forms of literature, which were cultivated by the Jews of the mediæval period, is necessary in any account of their literary activities. The classes of literature that require some notice in this connexion are folk-tales, travel-tales, and historical works (chronicles).

(i)

A good example of the folk-tale rendered into Hebrew is Abraham ibn Chasdai's *Prince and Dervish* (*Ben ha-melek we-ha-Nazir*), which was

[1] See Mrs. Lucas's beautiful rendering in *The Jewish Year*, pp. 167 ff.

compiled in the early part of the thirteenth century. The stories embodied in this collection are really of Indian origin, and belong to the "Barlaam and Joshaphat" cycle. Chasdai translated from an Arabic version of the original Persian, and may have introduced some original features into his book.

The theme of the story is a prince's conversion to the ascetic life and the life of renunciation associated with the teachings of the Buddha.

Another collection of a similar kind was the Hebrew translation of the famous *Fables of Bidpai*, known in Hebrew as *Kalila we-Dimna*, which also belongs probably to the thirteenth century. This version is attributed to a certain Rabbi Joel, and played an important part in the diffusion of the stories throughout Europe. It was rendered into Latin by John of Capua, a converted Jew, in 1270, and this became the basis of a German version (from which later were derived Danish and Dutch versions) · as well as of a Spanish. This book, according to Dr. Joseph Jacobs, influenced Europe more than any book except the Bible.

See further the introduction to *Kalilah and Dimnah or the Fables of Bidpai*, by I. G. N. Keith-Falconer (Cambridge, 1885). The Hebrew version of Rabbi Joel was edited by Joseph Derenbourg with a French translation, and a collation with the *Directorium* (*Deux versions hébraïques du livre de Kalilah et Dimnah*, Paris, 1881).

Another important name in this connexion is that of Berachya ha-Nakdan ("the Punctuator"), an English Jew, who is chiefly known as the author of a number of "Fox Fables" (*Mishlê Shu'alim*), which belong to the Æsop-cycle.

Berachya was a versatile writer, and translated other works (see *JE* iii. 53 f.). He was the author also of some elaborate ethical treatises, which have been edited in a sumptuous edition by Prof. H. Gollancz (*The Ethical Treatises of Berachya*, London, 1902).

Another collection is contained in Joseph Zabara's *Book of Delight,* written in 1200.[1] The author, like Berachya, uses rhymed prose, which is interspersed with snatches of verse. It is a poetical romance, partly autobiographical in character, and contains among other material a collection of fables.

An account of the book is given, with a summary translation, by Dr. I. Abrahams in *JQR,* First Series, vi. 502 ff.
To the literature already adduced above should be added Joseph Jacobs's *Jewish Ideals* (" The Diffusion of Folk-Tales "), and for Abraham ibn Chasdai, J. Chotzner's *Hebrew Humour,* pp. 117 ff. (London, 1905). See also Dr. Abrahams's *Short History of Jewish Literature,* chap. xv.

(ii)

The Jews, from the circumstances attending their dispersion over the world, acquired a considerable knowledge of, and interest in, geographical matters. Many notices of places and peoples occur scattered about in the earlier literature ; interest was especially strong in the question as to the place of exile of the Ten Tribes. But books of travel were not written till the twelfth century.

A romance, however, based upon the interest that existed in the question of the Twelve Tribes was written about 880, called *The Diary of Eldad the Danite.* It tells of fabulous Israelite empires living prosperously and happily in distant parts of the earth. This romance was the source of the story about " Prester John." Eldad's fanciful narrative was accepted as true by his contemporaries.

Various versions of the story exist and have been published (Mantua, 1480; Constantinople, 1516, 1519; etc.); also by Jellinek, etc., *Beth ha-Midrash,* iii., vi. It was early translated into Latin (1584), into Arabic, and into German (1700, 1723). It is doubtful whether Eldad was a *bona-fide* traveller.

---

[1] Joseph was born and died in Barcelona.

The first real travel-book was the famous *Itinerary* of Benjamin of Tudela, a merchant who in 1160 started on a long journey, and visited a large part of Europe and Asia (including Jerusalem and Bagdad). Though not free from admixture of fabulous elements, Benjamin's book gives much valuable information about the places he visited. Another Jew who wrote a travel-book at about the same time (travelled during the years 1179–80) was Petachiah of Ratisbon, whose book contains interesting information, especially about the reputed tombs of ancient worthies. A more important contribution to geographical knowledge is the *Kaphtor wa-Pherach* of Esthori Parchi (completed 1322). He visited Palestine, and devoted seven years to the careful exploration of the country, making a special study of ancient sites. He was a remarkably accurate observer, and collected his material (including ancient and contemporary references) with the greatest care.

Jews continued to visit Palestine in the fourteenth century, and with increasing facility. Letters and narratives describing these visits are numerous. In the sixteenth century appeared the *Itinera Mundi* (*'Iggereth 'Orchôth 'Ôlăm*) of Abraham Farissol (written 1524). This treatise embodies original research, as well as work based upon the contributions of Christian and Arabian geographers.

Parchi's work was edited, with German translation, by Grunhüt, 1912.

The best edition of Benjamin of Tudela's work is that of A. Asher, *The Itinerary of Benjamin of Tudela* (with English translation, London, 1840–41); an English translation (with a critical text) is also given (with notes) in the *JQR*, First Series, vols. xvii. and xviii., by M. N. Adler (published in book form, London, 1907).

For Petachiah of Ratisbon the edition of A. Benisch's *Travels of Petachia of Ratisbon* (with English translation) is available (London, 1856).

(iii)

In the Middle Ages Jewish histories usually
assumed the form of uncritical chronicles, mixing
legend with fact. In this respect the Jewish writers
were children of their time. An early example is
The Chronicle of Achimaaz, written in 1055 in
rhymed prose.
More important is Abraham ibn Daud, the philosopher (1110–80), whose *Sepher ha-Kabbalah* ("Book
of Tradition"), written in 1161, contains much valuable information, especially concerning the period
of the Geonim and the Jews of Spain. The object
of the book was to present the chain of tradition
as unbroken from the time of Moses to Ibn Daud's
own time, against the Karaites. The work is a
valuable historical authority on many matters.

The text is given in Neubauer's *Mediæval Jewish Chronicles*,
vol. i.

One of the sources used by Ibn Daud was
"Josippon," the curious work called *Sepher Yosippon*,
which gives a history of the Jews from the destruction of Jerusalem by Nebuchadnezzar to the fall of
the city in A.D. 70. The book, which for long passed
as "the Hebrew Josephus," was really put together in
the tenth century.

Beginning with Adam, the author passes to the legendary
history of Rome and Babylon, and reviews the story of Daniel,
Zerubbabel, the Second Temple, and Cyrus, passing on to
Alexander the Great. He then proceeds to give a history of
the Jews down to the destruction of the Temple. The book is
written in Biblical Hebrew, and was much read and prized
by the Jews in the Middle Ages.
The book, which has suffered much from copyists, has often
been printed. Sebastian Münster issued an edition (Basel,
1541). Its literary problems have been the subject of much
discussion among scholars (see *JE* vii. 259 f. and the literature
there cited).

Many of the "elegies" or *selichoth* embodied in the Liturgy contain historical episodes; but for a long time after Ibn Daud no formal historical work appeared. About 1504 a "Book of Genealogies" (*Sepher Yuchasin*) saw the light. Its author was the famous astronomer Abraham Zacuto, who had been expelled in the great expulsion from Spain in 1492.

"In this work Zacuto gives an account of the Oral Law, as transmitted from Moses, through the elders, prophets, sages, and the like, and also recounts the acts and monuments of the kings of Israel, as well as of some of the surrounding nations. In like manner, space is given to the Babylonian Captivity, the events which occurred during the period of the Second Temple, the characteristics of that period, the princes of the Captivity, and the rectors of the Academies of Sura and Pumbeditha."[1]
. The work, though often uncritical, is a valuable source for Jewish history. A complete edition by Filipowski appeared in London in 1857. Many previous editions had appeared.

With the above we may fitly conclude our account of the mediæval Jewish historical literature: Later works, of a somewhat similar kind, were, it is true, produced; but these fall outside the mediæval period proper.

David Gans (1541–1613), a German Jew, who took a real interest in the study of history, produced an extremely popular history called *The Branch of David (Zemach David)*. The founder of historical criticism among the Jews, Azariah di Rossi (1514–88), wrote a history called *The Light of the Eyes (Me'or 'Enāyim)*; and Gedaliah ibn Jachya (1515–87) was the author of a highly uncritical work called *The Chain of Tradition (Shalsheleth ha-Kabbalah)*. Mention may also be made of Abraham de Porta Leone's *Shields of the Mighty (Shilte ha-Gibborim)*, which was printed in Mantua in 1612, and Leon da Modena's *Ceremonies and Customs, of the Jews* (printed in Paris, 1637).
An historical chronicle of considerable importance, which, however, belongs to a much earlier period than the mediæval,

[1] *JE* xii. 627.

is the *Seder 'Olam Rabbah,* the earliest post-Exilic chronicle preserved in the Hebrew language. It is referred to in the Babylonian Talmud, and in its present form contains thirty chapters, which give a chronological record extending from Adam to the revolt of Bar-Cochba. The work, which is of considerable interest and importance, was first printed in Mantua in 1514. It has been reprinted several times, and has been made the subject of commentaries. Recent editions are those of Ratner (with critical and explanatory notes; Wilna, 1897); A. Marx (first ten chapters with German translation and introduction; Berlin, 1903); and J. M. Leiner (containing the commentaries of Jacob Emden and Elijah Wilna, together with the editor's own notes; Warsaw, 1904).

A later work, supplementing the former, is the *Seder 'Olam Zuta.* This chronicle extends to the time of the Babylonian Exiliarchs.

[The best collection of texts for the chronicle literature is contained in Neubauer's *Mediæval Chronicles,* 2 vols. (Oxford, 1882, 1895), with a valuable introduction and chronological notes. To the literature already adduced should be added the article "Historiography" (by Dr. Joseph Jacobs) in *JE* vi. 423 ff.; and on "Josippon" an article by Neuhauer in *JQR,* First Series, xi. 355 ff.

A legendary recasting of the history of the world from the Creation to the death of Judas Maccabæus is contained in the *Chronicles of Jerahmeel,* edited in an English translation, with introduction, by Dr. M. Gaster, 1899.]

CHRONOLOGICAL TABLE
APPENDIX
AND
ADDENDA

CHRONOLOGICAL TABLE

I.—To the Maccabæan Period and the Establishment of Roman Rule in Palestine.

B.C.

587. The fall of Jerusalem (to Nebuchadnezzar).
550. Cyrus.
548 and following years. Deutero-Isaiah.
539. The fall of Babylon.
536. The beginnings of the Return.
529. Cambyses.
521. Darius I. (Hystaspis).
521–332. *The Persian period.*
520. Haggai and Zechariah.
520–516. The building of the Second Temple.
490. Battle of Marathon.
486–484. Revolt of Egypt and Persian reconquest.
485–464. Xerxes I.
464–424. Artaxerxes I. (Longimanus).
450 ?. Malachi.
448. Revolt of Megabyzus in Syria.
445. Nehemiah Tirshatha.
444. Fortification of Jerusalem.
  [Date of Ezra's Mission doubtful; if placed in the reign of Artaxerxes II., probably between 397 and 380.]
424–404. Darius II. (Nothus).
404–358. Artaxerxes II. (Mnemon).
  [? Ezra promulgates a new edition of the Mosaic Torah, containing Priestly Code, about 380.]
358–338. Artaxerxes III. (Ochus).
335–331. Darius III. (Codomanus).
  [Jaddua High Priest.]
332. Battle of Issus; Persian Empire overthrown by Alexander the Great; the Samaritan schism.
  [A Samaritan temple erected on Mount Gerizim.]
332–166. *The pre-Maccabæan Greek period.*
331. Foundation of Alexandria.

300   CHRONOLOGICAL TABLE

B.C.
323–285. Ptolemy I. Soter, king of Egypt.
    [Onias I., Simon I., High Priests.]
320. Capture of Jerusalem by Ptolemy; *Judæa passes under Egyptian rule.*
285–247. Ptolemy II. Philadelphus.
    [Eleazar and Manasseh High Priests.]
C. 250. Translation of the Pentateuch into Greek (LXX).
[? 300–250. The Chronicler (author of 1 and 2 Chronicles and Ezra-Nehemiah).]
247–222. Ptolemy III. Euergetes.
    [Onias II. High Priest.]
223–187. Antiochus III. Magnus, *king of Syria.*
    [Simon II. High Priest.]
203. Capture of Jerusalem by Antiochus; *Judæa passes under Syrian rule.*
199–198. Jerusalem captured by Scopas for the Egyptian king Ptolemy V. Epiphanes, but is defeated by Antiochus, king of Syria, at Paneas.
187–175. Seleucus IV. Philopator.
187. The sacrilege of Heliodorus.
180 ?. Composition of the Wisdom of Ben-Sira in Hebrew.
175–163. Antiochus IV. Epiphanes, king of Syria.
174. Deposition of the High Priest Onias III.; Joshua (Jason) succeeds him.
171. Jason supplanted by Menelaus.
170. Onias III. murdered.
170, 168. Massacres (by Antiochus and Apollonius) at Jerusalem.
168 (Dec.). The " abomination of desolation " set up.
167. Maccabæan revolt (headed by Mattathias) breaks out.
166. Death of Mattathias; Judas Maccabæus heads the revolt.
166–165. Judas organises his army; victory at Emmaus.
165. Victory of Jews at Beth-Zur; rededication of the Temple (December).
164. Book of Daniel (?), death of Antiochus Epiphanes.
163–162. Judas defeated at Beth-Zacharias.
162. Alcimus (Jakim) High Priest; massacre of the Assidæans.
161. Judas victorious at Adasa; his defeat and death at Eleasa.
160. Death of Alcimus.
158–142. Jonathan (successor of Judas).
153. Jonathan High Priest; occupation of Jerusalem.
146. Destruction of Carthage by the Romans.
142. Assassination of Jonathan; Simon succeeds.

B.C.

142–135. Simon Maccabæus.

135. Assassination of Simon ; his son, John Hyrcanus, succeeds.

135–105. John Hyrcanus.

135. The parties called Pharisees and Sadducees emerge for the first time.

132 ?. Wisdom of Ben-Sira translated into Greek.

109–108. Destruction of the Samaritan temple on Mount Gerizim by John Hyrcanus.

105–104. Aristobulus I. (assumes title of " king ").

104–78. Alexander Jannæus.

78–69. Salome Alexandra (widow of Alexander Jannæus) queen-regnant ; the Pharisaic reaction.

69 and following years. The brothers Hyrcanus II. and Aristobulus II. ; rise of Antipater, who attaches himself to Hyrcanus ; outbreak of civil war.

65. Intervention of the Roman general Scaurus.

64–63 Pompey arrives in Syria ; Hyrcanus and Aristobulus submit their claims to him.

63. Jerusalem surrenders to Pompey ; the Temple captured —Pompey enters the Holy of Holies.

63. Hyrcanus II. High Priest ; Judæa controlled by the Romans.

57. Reorganisation of Judæa by Gabinius.

48. Battle of Pharsalia ; death of Pompey.

63–48 ?. Composition of the *Psalms of Solomon*.

37–4. Herod the Great king of Judæa.

4 B.C.–6 A.D. Archelaus, ethnarch of Judæa, Samaria, and Idumea.

6 A.D. Deposition of Archelaus ; Judæa becomes a Roman province.

II.—*To the Destruction of Jerusalem and the Suppression of the Second Revolt* (A.D. 135).

4 B.C.–39 A.D. Herod Antipas ruler over Galilee and Peræa (Jesus' sovereign).

4 B.C.–34 A.D. Philip (son of Herod the Great) tetrarch of Iturea.

40 B.C.–20 A.D. Philo of Alexandria.

A.D.

6. Census of Quirinius ; revolt of Zealots under Judas.

6–9. Coponius Roman procurator of Judæa.

9–12. Marcus Ambivius procurator.

12–15. Annius Rufus procurator.

14–37. Tiberius Emperor.

A.D.
26–36. Pontius Pilate procurator.
29 ?. Crucifixion of Jesus.
30 (or 35). Conversion of St. Paul.
36–37. Marcellus procurator of Judæa.
37–41. Marullus procurator.
37–41. Caligula Emperor.
37. Birth of Josephus.
38. Jews persecuted in Alexandria.
41–54. Claudius Emperor.
41–44. Herod Agrippa I. king of Judæa.
44. Death of Herod (cf. Acts xii.).
44–46. Cuspius Fadus procurator of Judæa.
46–48. Tiberius Alexander procurator.
48–52. Cumanus procurator.
50–100. Herod Agrippa II. ruler of various districts in
    the north of Palestine (the last of the Herods).
52–58. Felix procurator.
54–68. Nero Emperor.
58 ?–61. Portius Festus procurator.
61–65. Albinus procurator.
64. Burning of Rome and persecution of Christians ;
    [? death of St. Paul and St. Peter by martyrdom.]
65–66. Gessius Florus procurator of Judæa.
66. Outbreak of the Jewish revolt in Palestine.
69–79. Vespasian Emperor.
70. Titus destroys Jerusalem and the Temple.
70. Jochanan ben Zakkai establishes a Rabbinical School
    at Jamnia.
76–79. Josephus completes his history of the Jewish War.
79–81. Titus Emperor.
81–96. Domitian Emperor.
93–94. Josephus completes his Antiquities.
96–98. Nerva Emperor.
98–117. Trajan Emperor.
100 ?. Synod of Jamnia ; O.T. Canon finally fixed.
117–118. Revolt of Jews in Palestine.
117–138. Hadrian Emperor.
132–135. Revolt of Bar-Cochba.
135 ?. Martyrdom of R. Aķiba.

III.—The Talmudic and Geonic Period.

A.D.
140–175. Revival of the Jewish Schools in Palestine.
C. 190. Official text of the Mishnah fixed by R. Judah
    ha-Nasi.

A.D.
219. Babylonian Schools founded at Sura and Nehardea
by Rab and Samuel respectively.
[Later a School at Pumbeditha founded by Judah
b. Ezekiel (220–299).]
220–500. Period of the Amoraim.
320–370. Decay of Palestinian Schools ; completion of the
Palestinian (Jerusalem) Talmud.
360. The Patriarch (Palestinian) Hillel II. fixes the Jewish
calendar (still in use).
499. Death of Rabina ; Babylonian Talmud completed.
589–1038. Period of the Geonim (heads of the Babylonian
Schools at Sura and Pumbeditha ; see pp. 209 f.).
711. Conquest of Spain by the Arabs.
[Eighth to thirteenth centuries Jews flourish in
Spain.]
729. Victory of Charles Martel over the Arabs at Tours.
761 and following years. Rise of the Ḳaraite sect (founded
by Anam).
892–942. Saadya (appointed Gaon of Sura in 928).
980–1037. Avicenna (Mohammedan philosopher).
998–1038. Hai, the last of the Geonim.

IV.—*The Mediæval Period.*

A.D.
1021–1058 (or 1070). Solomon ibn Gebirol.
1040–1105. Rashi (founder of French school of exegesis).
1096. Beginning of the Crusades (followed by persecution
of Jews).
1070–1139. Moses ibn Ezra (Spanish Jewish poet).
1085–1145. Judah ha-Levi.
1092 ?–1167. Abraham ibn Ezra (exegete).
1135–1204. Maimonides.
1160–1235. David Ḳimḥi.
1165–1173. Benjamin of Tudela (traveller).
1233. The writings of Maimonides burnt at Paris.
1242. Copies of the Talmud burnt at Paris.
1290. Expulsion of the Jews from England.
1310 ?. Publication of the Zohar.
1340. The law-code known as *Turim* completed by R.
Jacob b. Asher (*cf.* p. 137).
1437–1509. Don Isaac Abarbanel.
1453. Constantinople falls to the Turks.
1455–1522. Reuchlin.
1475. First Hebrew books printed.
1469–1589. Elias Levita.

A.D.

1492. The Arabs finally driven from Spain ; expulsion of the Jews from Spain.

1497. Expulsion of the Jews from Portugal.

1520–1523. First complete edition of the Babylonian Talmud (in twelve vols. folio) printed by David Bomberg at Venice.

1523–1524. First printed edition of the Jerusalem Talmud (in one volume) issued by Bomberg at Venice.

1591. Spanish Jews settle in Holland.

1604–1657. Manasseh ben Israel.

1626–1676. Sabbatai Levi (false Messiah).

1632–1677. Baruch Spinoza.

1729. Birth of Moses Mendelssohn.

1783. Mendelssohn's *Jerusalem* published.

APPENDIX

Short Titles of some Important Rabbinical Authorities.

MaHaRIL = R. Jacob b. Moses Molin ha-Levi of Mayence (1365–1427) ; a liturgical authority (see *JE* viii. 469).
RABaD (I.) = Abraham ibn Daud ha-Levi (1110–1180) ; *cf.* p. 262 above (Jewish philosopher).
RABaD (II.) = Abraham b. Isaac of Narbonne (1110–1179) ; Talmudist (see *JE* i. 111 *f.*).
RABaD (III.) = Abraham b. David of Posquières (1125–1198) ; French Talmudic commentator (see *JE f.* 103).
RaLBaG = R. Levi ben Gershon (" Gersonides ") (1288–1344) ; philosopher, exegete, etc. (*cf.* pp. 266 *f.* above).
RaM = R. Meir ben Samuel (1060–1136) ; French Tosaphist (*cf. JE* viii. 440).
RaMBaM = R. Moses b. Maimon (" Maimonides ") (1135–1204) ; see pp. 222 *ff.* above.
RaMBaN = R. Moses b. Nachman (" Nachmanides ") (1195–1270) ; exegete (see above, p. 232).
RaN = R. Nissim b. Reuben (*c.* 1340–1380) ; Talmudist and philosopher, teacher of Crescas (see *JE* ix. 317).
RaSHBa = R. Shelomoh b. Abraham Adret (1235–1310) ; famous Spanish Rabbi (see *JE* i. 212 *f.*).
RaSHBaM = R. Samuel ben Meir (son of RaM), Rashi's grandson (1100–1160) ; *cf.* pp. 220 *f.* above.
RaSHBaZ = R. Shimeon (Simon) b. Zemach Duran (1361–1444) ; see above, p. 269.
RaSHI = R. Shelomoh Yiṣḥaḳi (1040–1105) ; see above, p. 220.
ReDaḲ = R. David Ḳimḥi (1160–1235), youngest son of Joseph Ḳimḥi (RIḲaM) ; see above, pp. 225 *ff.*
ReMaḲ = R. Moses Ḳimḥi (died about 1190), elder brother of David Ḳimḥi.
RIBaM = R. Isaac b. Meir (brother of RaSHBaM and grandson of Rashi).

306 APPENDIX

RIBaSH = R. Isaac b. Sheshet, famous for his *responsa*,
contemporary of Crescas (1340–1410).
RiF = R. Isaac Alfasi (1013–1103) ; author of a compendium of the Talmud (see above, p. 136).
RIḴaM = R. Joseph b. Isaac Ḳimḥi (1105–1170) ; see
above, pp. 224 *f.*

ADDENDA.

P. 66. A German translation of the entire Midrash Rabbah (Pentateuch and Megilloth) was published in ten parts by Dr. A. Wünsche under the title *Bibliotheca Rabbinica* (Leipzig, 1880–85).

P. 68 (footnote) ;

P. 72 (Deuteronomy). Further Tannaitic Midrashic material which exists in a scattered form in the *Midrash ha-gadol* (see p. 80) has been collected and published by Dr. D. Hoffmann in the following : *Mechilta de-Rabbi Simon b. Jochai* (to Exodus) (1905), and *Midrasch Tannaim* (to Deuteronomy) (Heft I. [Berlin], 1908 ; Heft II., 1909)—all very important.

A valuable translation in German of the important Midrash *Mekilta* by Winter and Wünsche was published in Leipzig in 1909(*Mechilta : ein tannaitischer Midrasch zu Exodus*). It contains some important appendices and notes.

P. 70. The best edition of *Sifra* (on Leviticus) is that of I. H. Weiss (Hebrew text, with notes ; Vienna, 1862).

The best edition of *Sifre* (on Numbers V. to end and the whole of Deuteronomy) is that of M. Friedmann (Vienna, 1864). It contains the Hebrew text, with introduction and notes (in Hebrew).

A Latin translation of *Mekilta, Sifra,* and *Sifre* is given (with the Hebrew text) in Ugolini's *Thesaurus,* vols. xiv. and xv. (Vienna, 1752).

P. 72. A German translation of the Midrash on the Psalms by Dr. A. Wünsche was published in 2 vols. Trier (1892–93).

P. 78. *Midrash Tanchuma.* A critical edition of this Midrash, based upon several MSS. and edited by Buber, was published in 3 vols. at Wilna in 1885. No translation has yet appeared.

P. 79. The following parts of the *Yalḳut ha-Machiri* have been published. On the Psalms (ed. by Buber, 1899 [Berdychev]), on Isaiah (ed. by Spira ; Berlin, 1894), on Proverbs (ed. by Grünhut, 1902), on Hosea and Zechariah (ed. by Greenup, 1909 and 1910).

P. 79. *Yalḳut Shimeoni.* The *editio princeps* is that of Salonica (1526–27 ; 152a) ; a recent edition was published at Warsaw (1876–77). A translation of the *Yalḳut* on Zechariah by E. G. King was published at Cambridge in 1882.

P. 98. Add the following English translations which have recently appeared : Of *Pirḳe Aboth* (English translation and notes), by R. Travers Herford, in Charles's *Apocrypha and Pseudepigrapha*, vol. ii. ; and by W. O. E. Oesterley (S.P.C.K., 1919) ; of *Sanhedrin* (Mishnah and Tosephta) by H. Danby (S.P.C.K. 1919); and of *Berakoth* (Mishnah and Tosephta), by A. Lukyn Williams (S.P.C.K., 1920).

P. 114. To the literature on the Talmud the following may be added : *Berakoth* (text, German translation and notes), by E. M. Pinner (very helpful to students), 1 vol. folio (Berlin, 1842) ; and (to the lexicographical aids) G. Dalman, *Aramäische-Neuhebräisches Wörterbuch zum Targum, Talmud, und Midrasch* (Frankfort a/M., 1901) ; J. Levy, *Neuhebräisches und Chaldäisches Wörterbuch über die Talmudim und Midraschim,* 4 vols. (Leipzig, 1876–83) ; also by the same editor, *Chaldäisches Wörterbuch über die Targumim und einen grossen Theil des Rabbinischen Schriftthums,* 2 vols. (Leipzig, 1881).

P. 220. *Rashi's Pentateuch Commentary.* The best edition is that of Berliner (Berlin, 1866) ; a German translation with accompanying text of Scripture, by Jul. Dessauer, appeared in 1887.

P. 222. The commentary of Ibn Ezra on Isaiah has been edited (Heb. text, with glossary and notes) by M. Friedländer (1877), who published an English translation of the same work in 1873.

P. 270. A Hebrew (metrical) translation of *The Choice of Pearls* (*cf.* p. 259)—which is a collection of ethical maxims—made by Joseph Ḳimḥi and entitled *Sheḳel ha-Ḳōdesh* (" The Holy Shekel ") has recently been printed and published for the first time, with English translation and introduction (Dr. Hermann Gollancz ; Oxford Press, 1919). In the same volume is included an edition of the text (with English translation and notes) of the treatise *Yesod Hayirah* (" The Foundation of Religious Fear ").

P. 271. *Ethical wills.* A collection of these documents has been edited by Dr. Israel Abrahams, and is now in the press (1920 : Columbia University Press).

INDEX

INDEX

A

Aaron ben Elijah, 268
Aaron ben Samuel ha-Nasi, 240
'*Ab beth din*, 93
Ab, ninth of, 77, 274, 276, 285
Abarbanel, 229 *f.*, 234, 270
Abaye, 123 *f.*
Abba Arika, 119
—— Hoshaya, R., 66
—— Mari, 229
—— Shaul, 106
Abbahu, 120, 121
Abd al-Rachman, 30
Abinu Malkenu, 199
Abina, Rab, 126
Abitur, Joseph, 289
Aboab, Isaac, 270
'*Abodah*, 175, 277
——, hymn, 281
'*Aboth de Rabbi Nathan*, 97
Abraham, 67, 75
——, *Apocalypse of*, 237
—— bar Chiyya, 261
—— Bedaresi, 289
—— ben David, 242
—— ben Nathan ha-Jarchi, 150
—— Bihago, 269
—— de Porta Leone, 295
—— Farissol, 293
—— ibn Daud, 262, 279, 294
—— ibn Ezra, 218, 282
—— Judæus, 261

Abraham the patriarch, 257
—— Zachuto, 295
'Abtalyon, 93
Abn Harun Musa, 281
Abudraham, David, 150
Abulafia, Abraham, 246
Abulwalid, 218, 263
Abuya, Elisha ben, 95
——, the Faust of the Talmud, 95
Academies, Babylonian, 83
—— of Palestine, 23
Academy of Jabne, 20
Achai, 211
Acher, name for Abuya, 95
Acrostic, alphabetic, 273
Adam, the first, 71
'*Adon 'Olam*, 35, 155, 157, 194
Adra, 30
Adret, Solomon ben, 264
Ælia Capitolina, 21
Æsop-cycle, 291
Agapé, the, 142
'*Aggada*, 89
'*Aggadath Bereshith*, 68
—— *Chazitha*, 75
'*Ahabah*, 156, 163, 274
" Aims of Philosophers, The," 260
'*Akedah*, The, 156, 160, 273
'*Akedath Yitzhak*, 229
Akiba, R., 21, 66, 69, 70, 95, 111, 213
——, " Alphabet of R.," 240
—— and the Mishnah, 95
——, school of, 214

311

Y